Praise for *The Reactionary Mind*

"I think that the best model [of conservatism] is . . . the Corey Robin notion that it's about preserving hierarchy."

—Paul Krugman, *New York Times*

"*The Reactionary Mind* has emerged as one of the more influential political works of the last decade. . . .Robin . . . is a synthesizer and a brilliant and ruthless diviner of the hidden wellsprings of absolutely everything."

—*The Washington Monthly*

"When *The Reactionary Mind* first appeared in 2011, it met with a good deal of critical skepticism. . . . Six years later, Robin has been vindicated."

—*Bookforum*

"I confess to being one of those who likes to divide conservatives into their parts as opposed to treating them as a whole. Robin makes a vigorous case that I am wrong, and I am tempted by his analysis. . . .Robin is an engaging writer, and just the kind of broad-ranging public intellectual all too often missing in academic political science. . . .Robin's arguments deserve widespread attention."

—*The New Republic*

"*The Reactionary Mind* certainly cuts hard against the common view that the radical populist conservatism epitomized by Sarah Palin represents a sharp break with the cautious, reasonable, moderate, pragmatic conservatism inaugurated by the 18th-century British statesman Edmund Burke. . . .This counterrevolutionary spirit, Mr. Robin argues, animates every conservative, from the Southern slaveholders to Ayn Rand to Antonin Scalia, to name just a few of the figures he pulls into his often slashing analysis."

—*New York Times*

"... ground-breaking book ..."

—*Rolling Stone*

"The common opinion on the Left is that conservatives are fire-breathing idiots, who make up in heat what they lack in light. Robin's book is a welcome correction of this simplistic view and puts the debate where it ought to be: on the force and content of conservative ideas."

—*Dissent*

"'The Reactionary Mind' demands to be taken seriously by conservatives, and it helps that it's written with panache. The series of scholarly strikes Robin makes against conventional wisdom are often exhilarating."

—*The Daily*

"It is a thoughtful, even-tempered sort of book. The old maid tendency that dominates liberal polemic in the U.S.A.—the shrieking, clutching at skirts, and jumping up on kitchen chairs that one gets from a Joe Nocera, a Maureen Dowd, or a Keith Olbermann—is quite absent."

—*The American Conservative*

"This little book will continue to spark controversy, but that is not the reason to read it: it is a witty, erudite and opinionated account of one of the most significant movements of our times."

—*Times Higher Education*

"Robin, a New York-based political scientist and regular contributor to publications like *The Nation* and the *London Review of Books*, has written an original book with an armful of theses that shed revealing light on the whys and wherefores of right-wing politics in the United States and beyond."

—*The National*

"Stemming from a conversation he had with the late William F. Buckley, Robin's book provides clear, well-documented insight on how the right came to be what it now is."

—*Washington Times*

"Corey Robin's extraordinary collection, constantly fresh, continuously sharp, and always clear and eloquent, provides the only satisfactory philosophically coherent account of elite conservatism I have ever read. Then there's this bonus: his remarkably penetrating side inquiry into the notion of 'national security' as a taproot of America's contemporary abuse of democracy. It's all great, a model in the exercise of humane letters."

—Rick Perlstein, author of *Nixonland*

"This book is a fascinating exploration of a central idea: that conservatism is, at its heart, a reaction against democratic challenges, in public and private life, to hierarchies of power and status. Corey Robin leads us through a series of case studies over the last few centuries—from Hobbes to Ayn Rand, from Burke to Sarah Palin—showing the power of this idea by illuminating conservatives both sublime and ridiculous."

—Kwame Anthony Appiah, Professor of Philosophy, Princeton University

"Beautifully written, these essays deepen our understanding of why conservatism remains a powerful force in American politics."

—Joyce Appleby, Professor Emerita of History, University of California-Los Angeles, and past president of the American Historical Association

"*The Reactionary Mind* is a wonderfully good read. It combines up-to-the-minute relevance with an eye to the intellectual history of conservatism in all its protean forms, going back as far as Hobbes, and taking in not only restrained and sentimental defenders of tradition such as Burke, but his more violent, proto-fascist contemporary Joseph de Maistre. Some readers will enjoy Corey Robin's dismantling of different recent thinkers—Barry Goldwater, Antonin Scalia, Irving Kristol; others will enjoy his demolition of Ayn Rand's intellectual pretensions. Some will be uncomfortable when they discover that those who too lightly endorse state violence, and even officially sanctioned torture, include some of their friends. That is one of the things that makes this such a good book."

—Alan Ryan, Professor of Political Theory, Oxford University

THE REACTIONARY MIND

Conservatism from Edmund Burke to Donald Trump

SECOND EDITION

COREY ROBIN

OXFORD
UNIVERSITY PRESS

OXFORD

UNIVERSITY PRESS

Oxford University Press is a department of the University of Oxford. It furthers
the University's objective of excellence in research, scholarship, and education
by publishing worldwide. Oxford is a registered trade mark of Oxford University
Press in the UK and certain other countries.

Published in the United States of America by Oxford University Press
198 Madison Avenue, New York, NY 10016, United States of America.

Library of Congress Cataloging-in-Publication Data
Names: Robin, Corey, 1967– author.
Title: The reactionary mind : conservatism from Edmund Burke
to Donald Trump / Corey Robin.
Description: Second edition. | New York : Oxford University Press, [2018] |
Previous edition: 2011. | Includes bibliographical references and index.
Identifiers: LCCN 2017029793 | ISBN 9780190692001 (bc) |
ISBN 9780190842024 (bb) | ISBN 9780190692018 (updf) |
ISBN 9780190692025 (epub)
Subjects: LCSH: Conservatism—History.
Classification: LCC JC573 .R63 2018 | DDC 320.52—dc23
LC record available at https://lccn.loc.gov/2017029793

14

Printed in Canada on acid-free paper

For Laura

CONTENTS

Like most observers of American politics, I was shocked by Donald Trump's victory in the 2016 presidential election. Unlike most observers of American politics, I was not shocked by Trump's victory in the 2016 Republican Party primary. Somewhere between my surprise over Trump's election and non-surprise over his nomination lies the inspiration for this second edition of *The Reactionary Mind*.

The Reactionary Mind argued, among other things, that many of the characteristics we have come to associate with contemporary conservatism—racism, populism, violence, and a pervasive contempt for custom, convention, law, institutions, and established elites—are not recent or eccentric developments of the American right. They are instead constitutive elements of conservatism, dating back to its origins in the European reaction against the French Revolution. From its inception, conservatism has relied upon some mix of these elements to build a broad-based movement of elites and masses against the emancipation of the lower orders. As the most successful practitioner of the mass politics of privilege in contemporary America, Trump seemed to me entirely legible as both a conservative and a Republican.

In the original conclusion to *The Reactionary Mind*, however, I argued that conservatism—at least in its most recent incarnation as a reaction against international communism and social democracy, the New Deal and the liberation movements of the 1960s—was dying. Not because it was no longer popular, not because it had grown radical or extreme, but because it no longer had a compelling rationale. Rooted in its opposition to the Soviet Union, the labor movement, the welfare state, feminism, and civil rights, conservatism had achieved most of its basic goals as set by the benchmarks of the New Deal, the 1960s, and the Cold War. Its serial triumphs over communism, workers, African Americans, and to some degree women had divested the movement of its counterrevolutionary appeal, at least for a majority of the electorate. Its victory, in other words, would prove the source of its defeat. Something reactionary and insurgent—when the book first came out in 2011, that something was the Tea Party—might continue to awaken the right, causing the occasional spasm of activity, giving it a temporary hold on power. Long-term, the trajectory was downward. That is, unless and until the left inaugurated a new round of emancipatory politics, much as it had in 1789, in the nineteenth century's movements against slavery and on behalf of workers, in 1917, in the 1930s, and in the 1960s. Until that left insurgency arose in a profound and ongoing (rather than episodic) way, the prognosis for the right did not look good.

In the weeks since Trump's election and now several months into his presidency, his victory in November has come to seem less surprising to me. In retrospect, I don't think I underestimated or misunderstood Trump and the Republicans; I think I overestimated Hillary Clinton and the Democrats. Having watched Trump consistently accede to the party and the establishment he once threatened to remake—on trade, China, building a wall along the US-Mexico border, infrastructure, entitlements, and a host of other matters—and having seen the Republican Party, despite its control of all three elected branches of the federal government, consistently fail—at least thus far—to advance its agenda with regard to healthcare, taxes, and spending, I believe that my original claim about the weakness and incoherence of the conservative movement still holds.[1]

Even in office, even with its dominion over the federal government, the conservative cause is flailing. It is flailing because its predecessors, up through the administration of George W. Bush, were so successful in achieving the movement's defining goals, and because its traditional antagonists on the left are not yet fully present or potent enough to pose a real threat to the established distribution of power. Earlier reactionary movements parlayed their hostility to a thriving left into a comprehensive reconstruction of the old regime. The promise of those movements was that they could defend the regime against a progressive insurgency better than its more established voices could. From Goldwater through Reagan, that is how the conservative movement consolidated its power. Trump ran on a similar set of anti-establishment themes—he was not tied to the old regime; he had the populist touch; he would thumb his nose at the Republican pooh-bahs and liberal elites; he would vanquish the demons of political correctness; he would bust up the constraining norms of feminism and anti-racism. That old time religion was enough to get him and his party into power. It hasn't been enough to turn that power into rule. Trump's inability since the election to recast the Republican Party, his consistent reversion to the party's status quo, and his inability—outside executive actions that are not subject to or dependent upon the other branches of government—to act upon that status quo are signs of a movement that has no clear sense of power or purpose. Its failure to govern, to enact the most basic parts of its platform, at least thus far, is not a sign of incompetence but incoherence. (Asked in May 2017 what the Republican Party stands for, Nebraska GOP Senator Ben Sasse, replied, "I don't know." Asked to describe the Republican Party in one word,

Sasse, who has a doctorate in history from Yale, said, "Question mark." After Senate Republicans failed to deliver on their repeal of Obamacare before the Fourth of July recess in 2017, House Republican Steve Womack of Arkansas was equally blunt and unsparing: "We've been given this opportunity to govern and we are finding every reason in the world not to.")[2] Trump is not the source of that incoherence; he is its leading symptom, as I argue in chapter 11.

The purpose of this second edition, however, is not to make predictions about the future or to issue an assessment of Trump based on a mere few months of his presidency. I am not an empirical political scientist but rather a political theorist whose materials are texts and ideas and whose method is close reading and historical analysis. My goal in this new edition is to situate Trump's rise and rule within the long arc of the conservative tradition, which is by and large a tradition of enacted ideas. To understand his rise—how Trump speaks to the American people, the tropes and themes he mobilizes—we must pay attention to what he has said. To understand his rule, we must pay attention to what he has done. The bulk of my analysis focuses on Trump's rise and thus his words, though I try to point out where, as is often the case, his rule departs from his words. I argue that much of the Trump phenomenon that is most unsettling and upsetting—particularly the racism, lawlessness, and violence—is not new, but that there are elements of his rise and rule that are new. In order to get a handle on what is novel about Trump, in other words, I focus less on the rhetorical brutality for which he has been so justly reviled and universally condemned, and more on the unanticipated and often unnoticed innovations he has offered, particularly with respect to the right's attitudes about the state and the market. It is there, I think, that one can see clearly how Trump has broken with his predecessors.

Beyond Trump's election, I have two reasons for writing this new edition of *The Reactionary Mind*. First, I've long felt that the first edition suffered from an inattention to the economic ideas of the right. While some of the essays dealt with those ideas in passing, only one—on Ayn Rand—directly addressed them. Part of this neglect had to do with the genesis of my interest in conservatism and the moment in which many of the essays in this book were first conceived: the George W. Bush years, when neoconservatism was the right's dominant ideology and war making its dominant activity. That focus on war and violence naturally eclipsed some long-standing conservative themes about the market. In this edition, I have tried to remedy that. I've cut four of the chapters dealing with war and peace and have added three new chapters about the right's economic ideas: one on Burke and his theory of value; one on Nietzsche, Hayek, and the Austrian School of economics; and one on Trump. The result is a far more intensive account of the right's ideas about war and capitalism, demonstrating that a commitment to the free market is neither peculiar to American conservatism nor of recent vintage on the right. The tensions between the political and the economic, between an aristocratic conception of politics and the realities of modern capitalism, are a leitmotif of the conservative tradition, in Europe and the United States, and thus comprise a leitmotif of this book.

Second, of all the criticisms this book has generated, the one that hit closest to home was the one I heard from readers rather than reviewers. This criticism was less substantive than structural: the book, readers complained, opened with a strongly argued thesis but then slipped into a seemingly shapeless collection of essays. Over the years, I have taken this criticism to heart. While I had a clear structure in mind for the first edition, that structure was plainly not conveyed to my readers.

For the second edition, I have overhauled the book. It now opens with three theoretical essays that set out the building blocks of the right. I call this a "primer" on reaction. It examines what the right is reacting against (emancipatory movements of the left) and what it is seeking to protect (what I call "the private life of power"); how it makes its counterrevolutions through a reconfiguration of the old and a borrowing from the new, particularly a borrowing from the left; how it melds elitism and populism, making privilege popular; and the centrality of violence to its means and its ends.

The remainder of the book is organized chronologically and geographically. Part 2 takes us to ground zero of reactionary politics: Europe's old regimes from the seventeenth to the early twentieth centuries. Situated in three distinct moments of counterrevolutionary time—the English Civil War, the French Revolution, and the proto-socialist interregnum between the Paris Commune and the Bolshevik Revolution—it looks at how Hobbes, Burke, Nietzsche, and Hayek attempted to formulate a politics of privilege in and for a democratic age. The chapters on Burke, Nietzsche, and Hayek pay especially close attention to their attempts to forge, in the context of a capitalist economy, an aristocratic politics of war and an aristocratic politics of the market. Part 3 brings us to the reactionary apotheosis of US conservatism from the 1950s through today. Here I offer a close reading of five moments of the American reaction: Ayn Rand's midcentury capitalist utopia; the fusion of racial and gender anxiety in the Republican Party of Barry Goldwater and Richard Nixon; the drums of war in the neoconservative imagination; and the Darwinist visions of Antonin Scalia and Donald Trump.

The structure of this book is modeled on the "theme and variations" of classical music. Part 1 announces the theme. Parts 2 and 3 are the variations, with each chapter an amplification or modification of that original theme. The book is not a comprehensive history of the right; it is a collection of essays about the right. And while the sensibility that informs these essays is historicist, tracing change and continuity across time—showing how, for instance, Hayek and the Austrian School of economics reflect certain ideas contained in Burke's writing about the market, or how Trump's inconsistencies relate to earlier statements about contradiction in Burke and Bagehot—the structure of the whole is episodic rather than strictly historical. All of the chapters in Parts 2 and 3 can be read as instantiations of the theses in Part 1. But while the reader may not be persuaded of Part 1 if she does not read the remaining chapters, each of chapters can also be read as a stand-alone essay about a particular figure, theme, or moment.

With one exception: chapter 11. My case for what is new and what is old in the case of Donald Trump, which I set out in the concluding chapter of this book, follows from and depends upon my reading of the conservative tradition. However shocking and jarring Trump's speech acts have been, many of them are consistent with the speech acts of his antecedents. To make sense of my approach to Trump—what I emphasize and what I pass over—one must read the whole of this book. To avoid the risk of repetition, I have had to assume in the final chapter the reader's knowledge of the previous chapters. I recognize that this puts my argument at some risk of misinterpretation if not misrecognition; readers may feel that I have paid insufficient attention to those aspects of Trump that they find most troubling. But since I have revised this book with an eye toward the future—looking beyond the headlines of the moment in the hope that this edition might stand the test of time better than its predecessor—I have opted to rely upon the good faith of the reader of today and the historical distance of the reader of tomorrow.

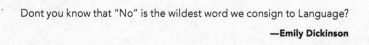

Dont you know that "No" is the wildest word we consign to Language?

—Emily Dickinson

The Reactionary Mind

PART 1 **Reaction**

A Primer

1

The Private Life of Power

A political party may find that it has had a history, before it is fully aware of or agreed upon its own permanent tenets; it may have arrived at its actual formation through a succession of metamorphoses and adaptations, during which some issues have been superannuated and new issues have arisen. What its fundamental tenets are, will probably be found only by careful examination of its behaviour throughout its history and by examination of what its more thoughtful and philosophical minds have said on its behalf; and only accurate historical knowledge and judicious analysis will be able to discriminate between the permanent and the transitory; between those doctrines and principles which it must ever, and in all circumstances, maintain, or manifest itself a fraud, and those called forth by special circumstances, which are only intelligible and justifiable in the light of those circumstances.

—**T. S. Eliot,** *"The Literature of Politics"*

Since the modern era began, men and women in subordinate positions have marched against their superiors in the state, church, workplace, and other hierarchical institutions. They have gathered under different banners—the labor movement, feminism, abolition, socialism—and shouted different slogans: freedom, equality, rights, democracy, revolution. In virtually every instance, their superiors have resisted them, violently and nonviolently, legally and illegally, overtly and covertly. That march and demarche of democracy is the story of modern politics, or at least one of its stories.

This book is about the second half of that story, the demarche, and the political ideas—variously called conservative, reactionary, revanchist, counterrevolutionary—that grow out of and give rise to it. These ideas, which occupy the right side of the political spectrum, are forged in battle. They always have been, at least since they first emerged as formal ideologies during the French Revolution, battles between social groups rather than nations; roughly speaking, between those with more power and those with less. To understand these ideas, we have to understand that story. For that is what conservatism is: a meditation on—and theoretical rendition of—the felt experience of having power, seeing it threatened, and trying to win it back.

Despite the very real differences between them, workers in a factory are like secretaries in an office, peasants on a manor; slaves on a plantation—even wives in a marriage—in that they live and labor in conditions of unequal power. They submit and obey, heeding the demands of their managers and masters, husbands and lords. They are disciplined and punished. They do much and receive little. Sometimes their lot is freely chosen—workers contract with their employers, wives with their husbands—but its entailments seldom are. What contract, after all, could ever itemize the ins and outs, the daily pains and ongoing sufferance, of a job or a marriage? Throughout American history, the contract often has served as a conduit to unforeseen coercion and constraint, particularly in institutions like the workplace and the family where men and women spend so much of their lives. Employment and marriage contracts have been interpreted by judges, themselves friendly to the interests of employers and husbands, to contain all sorts of unwritten and unwanted provisions of servitude to which wives and workers tacitly consent, even when they have no knowledge of such provisions or wish to stipulate otherwise.[1]

Until 1980, for example, it was legal in every state in the union for a husband to rape his wife.[2] The justification for this dates back to a 1736 treatise by English jurist Matthew Hale. When a woman marries, Hale argued, she implicitly agrees to give "up herself in this kind [sexually] unto her husband." Hers is a tacit, if unknowing, consent "which she cannot retract" for the duration of their union. Having once said yes, she can never say no. As late as 1957—during the era of the Warren Court—a standard legal treatise could state, "A man does not commit rape by having sexual intercourse with his lawful wife, even if he does so by force and against her will." If a woman (or man) tried to write into the marriage contract a requirement that express consent had to be given in order for sex to proceed, judges were bound by common law to ignore or override it. Implicit consent was a structural feature of the contract that neither party could alter. With the exit option of divorce not widely available until the second half of the twentieth century, the marriage contract doomed women to be the sexual servants of their husbands.[3] A similar dynamic was at work in the employment contract: workers consented to be hired by their employers, but until the twentieth century that consent was interpreted by judges to contain implicit and irrevocable provisions of servitude; meanwhile, the exit option of quitting was not nearly as available, legally or practically, as many might think.[4]

Every once in a while, however, the subordinates of this world contest their fates. They protest their conditions, write letters and petitions, join movements, and make demands. Their goals may be minimal and discrete—better safety guards on factory machines, an end to marital rape—but in voicing them, they raise the specter of a more fundamental change in power. They cease to be servants or supplicants and become agents, speaking and acting on their own behalf. More than the reforms themselves, it is this assertion of agency by the subject class—the appearance of an insistent and independent voice of demand—that vexes their superiors. Guatemala's Agrarian Reform of 1952 redistributed a million and a half acres of land to 100,000 peasant families. That was nothing, in the minds of the country's ruling classes, compared to the riot of political talk the bill seemed to unleash. Progressive reformers, Guatemala's archbishop complained, sent local peasants "gifted with facility with words" to the capital, where they were given opportunities "to speak in public." That was the great evil of the Agrarian Reform.[5]

In his last major address to the Senate, John C. Calhoun, former vice president and chief spokesman of the Southern cause, identified the decision by Congress in the mid-1830s to receive abolitionist petitions as the moment when the nation set itself on an irreversible course of confrontation over slavery. In a four-decade career that had seen such defeats to the slaveholder position as the Tariff of Abominations, the Nullification Crisis, and the Force Bill, the mere appearance of slave speech in the nation's capital stood out for the dying Calhoun as the sign that the revolution had begun.[6] And when, a half-century later, Calhoun's successors sought to put the abolitionist genie back into the bottle, it was this same assertion of black agency that they targeted. Explaining the proliferation across the South in the 1890s and 1900s of constitutional conventions restricting the franchise, a delegate to one such convention declared, "The great underlying principle of this Convention movement . . . was the elimination of the negro from the politics of this State."[7]

American labor history is filled with similar complaints from the employing classes and their allies in government: not that unionized workers are violent, disruptive, or unprofitable but that they are independent and self-organizing. Indeed, so potent is their self-organization that it threatens—in the eyes of their superiors—to render superfluous the employer and the state. During the Great Upheaval of 1877, striking railroad workers in St. Louis took to running the trains themselves. Fearful the public might conclude the workers were capable of managing the railroad, the owners tried to stop them—in effect, launching a strike of their own in order to prove it was the owners, and only the owners, who could make the trains run on time. During the Seattle general strike of 1919, workers went to great lengths to provide basic government services, including law and order. So successful were they that the mayor concluded it was the workers' independent capacity to limit violence and anarchy that posed the greatest threat.

> The so-called sympathetic Seattle strike was an attempted revolution. That there was no violence does not alter the fact. . . . True, there were no flashing guns, no bombs, no killings. Revolution, I repeat, doesn't need violence. The general strike, as practiced in Seattle, is of itself the weapon of revolution, all the more dangerous because quiet. . . . That is to say, it puts the government out of operation. And that is all there is to revolt—no matter how achieved.[8]

Into the twentieth century, judges regularly denounced unionized workers for formulating their own definitions of rights and compiling their own register of shop-floor rules. Workers like these, claimed one federal court, saw themselves as "exponents of some higher law than that . . . administered by courts." They were exercising "powers belonging only to Government," declared the Supreme Court, constituting themselves as a "self-appointed tribunal" of law and order.[9]

Conservatism is the theoretical voice of this animus against the agency of the subordinate classes. It provides the most consistent and profound argument as to why the lower orders should not be allowed to exercise their independent will, why they should not be allowed to govern themselves or the polity. Submission is their first duty, and agency the prerogative of the elite.

Though it is often claimed that the left stands for equality while the right stands for freedom, this notion misstates the actual disagreement between right and left. Historically, the conservative has favored liberty for the higher orders and constraint for the lower orders. What the conservative sees and dislikes in equality, in other words, is not a threat to freedom but its extension. For in that extension, he sees a loss of his own freedom. "We are all agreed as to our own liberty," declared Samuel Johnson. "But we are not agreed as to the liberty of others: for in proportion as we take, others must lose. I believe we hardly wish that the mob should have liberty to govern us."[10] Such was the threat Edmund Burke saw in the French Revolution: not merely an expropriation of property or explosion of violence but an inversion of the obligations of deference and command. "The levellers," he claimed, "only change and pervert the natural order of things."

> The occupation of an hair-dresser, or of a working tallow-chandler, cannot be a matter of honour to any person—to say nothing of a number of other more servile employments. Such descriptions of men ought not to suffer oppression from the state; but the state suffers oppression, if such as they, either individually or collectively, are permitted to rule.[11]

By virtue of membership in a polity, Burke allowed, men had a great many rights—to the fruits of their labor, their inheritance, education, and more. But the one right he refused to concede to all men was that "share of power, authority, and direction" they might think they ought to have "in the management of the state."[12]

Even when the left's demands shift to the economic realm, the threat of freedom's extension looms large. If women and workers are provided with the economic resources to make independent choices, they will be free not to obey their husbands and employers. That is why Lawrence Mead, one of the leading intellectual opponents of the welfare state in the 1980s and 1990s, declared that the welfare recipient "must be made *less* free in certain senses rather than more."[13] For the conservative, equality portends more than a redistribution of resources, opportunities, and outcomes—though he certainly dislikes these, too.[14] What equality ultimately means is a rotation in the seat of power.

The conservative is not wrong to construe the threat of the left in these terms. Before he died, G. A. Cohen, one of contemporary Marxism's most acute voices, made the case that much of the left's program of economic redistribution could be understood as entailing not a sacrifice of freedom for the sake of equality, but an extension of freedom from the few to the many.[15] And, indeed, the great modern movements of emancipation—from abolition to feminism to the struggle for workers' rights and civil rights—have always posited a nexus between freedom and equality. Marching out of the family, the factory, and the field, where unfreedom and inequality are the flip sides of the same coin, they have made freedom and equality the irreducible yet mutually reinforcing parts of a single whole. The link between freedom and equality has not made the argument for redistribution any more palatable to the right. As one conservative wag complained of John Dewey's vision of social democracy, "The definitions of liberty and of equality have been so juggled that both refer to approximately the same condition."[16] Far from being a sleight of the progressive hand, however, this synthesis of freedom and equality is a central postulate of the politics of emancipation. Whether the politics conforms to the postulate is, of course, another story. But for the conservative, the concern is less the betrayal of the postulate than its fulfillment.

One of the reasons the subordinate's exercise of agency so agitates the conservative imagination is that it takes place in an intimate setting. Every great political blast—the storming of the Bastille, the taking of the Winter Palace, the March on Washington—is set off by a private fuse: the contest for rights and standing in the family, the factory, and the field. Politicians and parties talk of constitution and amendment, natural rights and inherited privileges. But the real subject of their deliberations is the private life of power. "Here is the secret of the opposition to woman's equality in the state," Elizabeth Cady Stanton wrote. "Men are not ready to recognize it in the home."[17] Behind the riot in the street or debate in Parliament is the maid talking back to her mistress, the worker disobeying her boss. That is why our political arguments—not only about the family but also the welfare state, civil rights, and much else—can be so explosive: they touch upon the most personal relations of power. It is also why it has so often fallen to our novelists to explain to us our politics. At the height of the Civil Rights Movement, James Baldwin traveled to Tallahassee. There, in an imagined handshake, he found the hidden transcript of a constitutional crisis.[18]

I am the only Negro passenger at Tallahassee's shambles of an airport. It is an oppressively sunny day. A black chauffeur, leading a small dog on a leash, is meeting his white employer. He is attentive to the dog, covertly very aware of me and respectful of her in a curiously watchful, waiting way. She is middle-aged, beaming and powdery-faced, delighted to see both the beings who make her life agreeable. I am sure that it has never occurred to her that either of them has the ability to judge her or would judge her harshly. She might almost, as she goes toward her chauffeur, be greeting a friend. No friend could make her face brighter. If she were smiling at me that way I would expect to shake her hand. But if I should put out my hand, panic, bafflement, and horror would then overtake that face, the atmosphere would darken, and danger, even the threat of death, would immediately fill the air.

On such small signs and symbols does the southern cabala depend.[19]

The conflict over American slavery—the looming precedent to this set piece of Baldwin's imagination—offers an instructive example. One of the distinguishing characteristics of slavery in the United States is that unlike slaves in the Caribbean or serfs in Russia, many slaves in the South lived on smallholdings with their masters in residence. Masters knew their slaves' names; tracked their births, marriages, and deaths; and held parties to honor these dates. The personal interaction between master and slave was unparalleled, leading a visiting Frederick Law Olmsted to remark upon the "close cohabitation and association of black and white" in Virginia, the "familiarity and closeness of intimacy that would have been noticed with astonishment, if not with manifest displeasure, in almost any chance company at the North."[20] Only the "relations of husband and wife, parent and child, brother and sister," wrote the slavery apologist Thomas Dew, produced "a closer tie" than that of master and slave; the latter relationship, declared William Harper, another defender of slavery, was "one of the most intimate relations of society."[21] Conversely, after slavery was abolished, many whites lamented the chill in relations between the races. "I'm fond of the Negro," said one Mississippian in 1918, "but the bond between us is not as close as it was between my father and his slaves."[22]

Most of this talk was propaganda and self-delusion, of course, but in one respect it was not: the nearness of master to slave did make for an exceptionally personal mode of rule. Masters devised and enforced "unusually detailed" rules for their slaves, dictating when they had to get up, eat, work, sleep, garden, visit, and pray. Masters decided upon their slaves' mates and marriages. They named their children, and when the market dictated, separated those children from their parents. And while masters—as well as their sons and overseers—availed themselves of the bodies of their female slaves whenever they wished, they saw fit to patrol and punish any and all sexual congress between their slaves.[23] Living with their slaves, masters had direct means to control their behavior and a detailed map of all the behavior there was to control.

The consequences of this proximity were felt not just by the slave but by the master as well. Living every day with his mastery, he became entirely identified with it. So complete was this identification that any sign of the slave's disobedience—much less her emancipation—was seen as an intolerable assault upon his person. When Calhoun declared that slavery "has grown up with our society and institutions, and is so interwoven with them, that to destroy it would be to destroy us as a people," he wasn't just referring to society in the aggregate or abstract.[24] He was thinking of individual men absorbed in the day-to-day experience of ruling other men and women. Take that experience away, and you destroyed not only the master but also the man—and the many men who sought to become, or thought they already were like, the master.

Because the master put so little distance between himself and his mastery, he would go to unprecedented lengths to keep his holdings. Throughout the Americas slaveholders defended their privileges, but nowhere with the intensity or violence of the master class in the South. Outside the South, wrote C. Vann Woodward, the end of slavery was "the liquidation of an investment." Inside, it was "the death of a society."[25] And when, after the Civil War, the master class fought with equal ferocity to restore its privileges and power, it was the proximity of command—the nearness of rule—that was uppermost in its mind. As Henry McNeal Turner, a black Republican in Georgia, put it in 1871: "They do not care so much about Congress admitting Negroes to their halls . . . but they do not want the negroes over them at home." One hundred years later, a black sharecropper in Mississippi would still resort to the most domestic of idioms to describe relations between blacks and whites: "We had to mind them as our children mind us."[26]

When the conservative looks upon a democratic movement from below, this (and the exercise of agency) is what he sees: a terrible disturbance in the private life of power. Witnessing the election of Thomas Jefferson in 1800, Theodore Sedgwick lamented, "The aristocracy of virtue is destroyed; personal influence is at an end."[27] Sometimes the conservative is personally implicated in that life, sometimes not. Regardless, it is his apprehension of the private grievance behind the public commotion that lends his theory its tactile ingenuity and moral ferocity. "The real object" of the French Revolution, Burke told Parliament in 1790, is "to break all those connexions, natural and civil, that regulate and hold together the community by a chain of subordination; to raise soldiers against their officers; servants against their masters; tradesmen against their customers; artificers against their employers; tenants against their landlords; curates against their bishops; and children against their parents."[28] Personal insubordination rapidly became a regular and consistent theme of Burke's pronouncements on the unfolding events in France. A year later, he wrote in a letter that because of the Revolution, "no house is safe from its servants, and no Officer from his Soldiers, and no State or constitution from conspiracy and insurrection."[29] In another speech before Parliament in 1791, he declared that "a constitution founded on what was called the rights of man" opened "Pandora's box" throughout the world, including Haiti: "Blacks rose against whites, whites against blacks, and each against one another in murderous hostility; subordination was destroyed."[30] Nothing to the Jacobins, he declared at the end of his life, was worthy "of the name of the publick virtue, unless it indicates violence on the private."[31]

So powerful is that vision of private eruption that it can turn a man of reform into a man of reaction. Schooled in the Enlightenment, John Adams believed that "consent of the people" was "the only moral foundation of government."[32] But when his wife suggested that a muted version of these principles be extended to the family, he was not pleased. "And, by the way," Abigail wrote him, "in the new code of laws which I suppose it will be necessary for you to make, I desire you would remember the ladies and be more generous and favorable to them than your ancestors. Do not put such unlimited power into the hands of the husbands. Remember, all men would be tyrants if they could."[33] Her husband's response:

> We have been told that our struggle has loosened the bands of government everywhere; that children and apprentices were disobedient; that schools and colleges were grown turbulent; that Indians slighted their guardians, and Negroes grew insolent to their masters. But your letter was the first intimation that another tribe, more numerous and powerful than all of the rest, were grown discontented.

Though he leavened his response with playful banter—he prayed that George Washington would shield him from the "despotism of the petticoat"[34]—Adams was clearly rattled by this appearance of democracy in the private sphere. In a letter to James Sullivan, he worried that the Revolution would "confound and destroy all distinctions," unleashing throughout society a spirit of insubordination so intense that all order would be dissolved. "There will be no end of it."[35] No matter how democratic the state, it was imperative that society remain a federation of private dominions, where husbands ruled over wives, masters governed apprentices, and each "should know his place and be made to keep it."[36]

Historically, the conservative has sought to forestall the march of democracy in both the public and the private spheres, on the assumption that advances in the one necessarily spur advances in the other. "In order to keep the state out of the hands of the people," wrote the French monarchist Louis de Bonald, "it is necessary to keep the family out of the hands of women and children."[37] Even in the United States, this effort has periodically yielded fruit. Despite our Whiggish narrative of the steady rise of democracy, historian Alexander Keyssar has demonstrated that the struggle for the vote in the United States has been as much a story of retraction and contraction as one of progress and expansion, "with class tensions and apprehensions" on the part of political and economic elites constituting "the single most important obstacle to universal suffrage . . . from the late eighteenth century to the 1960s."[38]

Still, the more profound and prophetic stance on the right has been Adams's: cede the field of the public, if you must, but stand fast in the private. Allow men and women to become democratic citizens of the state; make sure they remain feudal subjects in the family, the factory, and the field. The priority of conservative political argument has been the maintenance of private regimes of power—even at the cost of the strength and integrity of the state. We see this political arithmetic at work in the ruling of a Federalist court in Massachusetts that a Loyalist woman who fled the Revolution was the adjutant of her husband, and thus should not be held responsible for fleeing and should not have her property confiscated by the state; in the refusal of Southern slaveholders to yield their slaves to the Confederate cause; and the more recent insistence of the Supreme Court that women could not be legally obliged to sit on juries because they are "still regarded as the center of home and family life" with their "own special responsibilities."[39]

Conservatism, then, is not a commitment to limited government and liberty—or a wariness of change, a belief in evolutionary reform, or a politics of virtue. These may be the byproducts of conservatism, one or more of its historically specific and ever-changing modes of expression. But they are not its animating purpose. Neither is conservatism a makeshift fusion of capitalists, Christians, and warriors, for that fusion is impelled by a more elemental force—the opposition to the liberation of men and women from the fetters of their superiors, particularly in the private sphere. Such a view might seem miles away from the libertarian defense of the free market, with its celebration of the atomistic and autonomous individual. But it is not. When the libertarian looks out upon society, he does not see isolated individuals; he sees private, often hierarchical, groups, where a father governs his family and an owner his employees.[40]

No simple defense of one's own place and privileges—the conservative, as I've said, may or may not be directly involved in or benefit from the practices of rule he defends; many, as we'll see, are not—the conservative position stems from a genuine conviction that a world thus emancipated will be ugly, brutish, base, and dull. It will lack the excellence of a world where the better man commands the worse. When Burke adds, in the letter quoted above, that the "great Object" of the Revolution is "to root out that thing called an *Aristocrat* or Nobleman and Gentleman," he is not simply referring to the power of the nobility; he is also referring to the distinction that power brings to the world.[41] If the power goes, the distinction goes with it. This vision of the connection between excellence and rule is what brings together in postwar America that unlikely alliance of the libertarian, with his vision of the employer's untrammeled power in the workplace; the traditionalist, with his vision of the father's rule at home; and the statist, with his vision of a heroic leader pressing his hand upon the face of the earth. Each in his way subscribes to this typical statement, from the nineteenth century, of the conservative creed: "To obey a real superior . . . is one of the most important of all virtues—a virtue absolutely essential to the attainment of anything great and lasting."[42]

The notion that conservative ideas are a mode of counterrevolutionary practice is likely to raise some eyebrows, even hackles, on the right and the left. It has long been an axiom on the left that the defense of power and privilege is an enterprise devoid of ideas. "Intellectual history," a recent study of American conservatism submits, "is never unwelcome," but it "is not the most direct approach to explaining the power of conservatism in America."[43] Liberal writers have always portrayed right-wing politics as an emotional swamp rather than a movement of considered opinion: Thomas Paine claimed counterrevolution entailed "an obliteration of knowledge"; Lionel Trilling described American conservatism as a mélange of "irritable mental gestures which seek to resemble ideas"; Robert Paxton called fascism an "affair of the gut," not "of the brain."[44] Conservatives, for their part, have tended to agree.[45] It was Palmerston, after all, when he was still a Tory, who first attached the epithet "stupid" to the Conservative Party. Playing the part of the dull-witted country squire, conservatives have embraced the position of F. J. C. Hearnshaw that "it is commonly sufficient for practical purposes if conservatives, without saying anything, just sit and think, or even if they merely sit."[46] While the aristocratic overtones of that discourse no longer resonate, the conservative still holds onto the label of the untutored and the unlettered; it's part of his populist charm and demotic appeal. As the conservative *Washington Times* observes, Republicans "often call themselves the 'stupid party.'"[47] Nothing, as we shall see, could be further from the truth. Conservatism is an idea-driven praxis, and no amount of preening from the right or polemic from the left can reduce or efface the catalog of mind one finds there.

Conservatives will likely be put off by this argument for a different reason: it threatens the purity and profundity of conservative ideas. For many, the word "reaction" connotes an unthinking, lowly grab for power.[48] But reaction is not reflex. It begins from a position of principle—that some are fit, and thus ought, to rule others—and then recalibrates that principle in light of a democratic challenge from below. This recalibration is no easy task, for such challenges tend by their very nature to disprove the principle. After all, if a ruling class is truly fit to rule, why and how has it allowed a challenge to its power to emerge? What does the emergence of the one say about the fitness of the other?[49] The conservative faces an additional hurdle: How to defend a principle of rule in a world where nothing is solid, all is in flux? From the moment conservatism came onto the scene, it has had to contend with the decline of ancient and medieval ideas of an orderly universe, in which permanent hierarchies of power reflected the eternal structure of the cosmos. The overthrow of the old regime reveals not only the weakness and incompetence of its leaders but also a larger truth about the lack of design in the world. (The idea that conservatism reflects the revelation that the world has no natural hierarchies might seem odd in our age of Intelligent Design. But as Kevin Mattson and others have pointed out, Intelligent Design is not based on the same kind of medieval assumption of a firm eternal structure to the universe, and there is more than a touch of relativism and skepticism to its arguments. Indeed, one of Intelligent Design's leading proponents has claimed that though he's "no postmodernist," he has "learned a lot" from postmodern-ism.[50]) Reconstructing the old regime in the face of a declining faith in permanent hierarchies has proven to be a difficult feat. Not surprisingly, it also has produced some of the most remarkable works of modern thought.

But there is another reason we should be wary of the effort to dismiss the reactionary thrust of conservatism, and that is the testimony of the tradition itself. Ever since Burke, it has been a point of pride among conservatives that theirs is a contingent mode of thought. Unlike their opponents on the left, they do not unfurl a blueprint in advance of events. They read situations and circumstances, not texts and tomes; their preferred mode is adaptation and intimation rather than assertion and declamation. There's a certain truth to this claim, as we will see: the conservative mind is extraordinarily supple, alert to changes in context and fortune long before others realize they are occurring. With his deep awareness of the passage of time, the conservative possesses a tactical virtuosity few can match. It's only logical that conservatism would be intimately bound up with, its antennae ever sensitive to, the movements and countermovements of power sketched above. These are, as I've said, the story of modern politics, and it would seem strange if a mind so attuned to the contingencies around it were not well versed in that story. Not just well versed, but awakened and aroused by it as by no other story.

Indeed, from Burke's claim that he and his ilk had been "alarmed into reflexion" by the French Revolution to Russell Kirk's admission that conservatism is a "system of ideas" that "has sustained men . . . in their resistance against radical theories and social transformation ever since the beginning of the French Revolution," the conservative has consistently affirmed that his is a knowledge produced in reaction to the left.[51] (Burke would go on to lay down as his "foundation" the notion that "never greater" an evil had "existed" than the French Revolution.)[52] Sometimes, that affirmation has been explicit. Three times prime minister of Britain, Salisbury wrote in 1859 that "hostility to Radicalism, incessant, implacable hostility, is the essential definition of Conservatism. The fear that the Radicals may triumph is the only final cause that the Conservative Party can plead for its own existence."[53] More than a half-century later, his son Hugh Cecil—among other things, best man at Winston Churchill's wedding and provost of Eton—reaffirmed the father's stance: "I think the government will find in the end that there is only one way of defeating revolutionary tactics and that is by presenting an organized body of thought which is non-revolutionary. That body of thought I call Conservatism."[54] Others, like Peel, have taken a more circuitous route to get to the same place:

> My object for some years past, that which I have most earnestly labored to accomplish, has been to lay the foundation of a great party, which, existing in the House of Commons, and deriving its strength from the popular will, should diminish the risk and deaden the shock of a collision between the two deliberative branches of the legislature—which should enable us to check the too importunate eagerness of well-intending men, for hasty and precipitate changes in the constitution and laws of the country, and by which we should be enabled to say, with a voice of authority, to the restless spirit of revolutionary change, "Here are thy bounds, and here shall thy vibrations cease."[55]

Lest we think such sentiments—and circumlocutions—are peculiarly English, consider how the court historian of the American right approached the matter in 1976. "What is conservatism?" George Nash asked in his now classic *The Conservative Intellectual Movement in America since 1945*. After a page of hesitation—conservatism resists definition, it should not be "confused with the Radical Right," it "varies enormously with time and place" (what political idea doesn't?)—Nash settled upon an answer that could have been given (indeed, was given) by Peel, Salisbury and son, Kirk, and most of the thinkers on the radical right. Conservatism, he said, is defined by "resistance to certain forces perceived to be leftist, revolutionary, and profoundly subversive of what conservatives at the time deemed worth cherishing, defending, and perhaps dying for."[56]

These are the explicit professions of the counterrevolutionary creed. More interesting are the implicit statements, where antipathy to radicalism and reform is embedded in the very syntax of the argument. Take Michael Oakeshott's famous definition in his essay "On Being Conservative": "To be conservative, then, is to prefer the familiar to the unknown, to prefer the tried to the untried, fact to mystery, the actual to the possible, the limited to the unbounded, the near to the distant, the sufficient to the superabundant, the convenient to the perfect, present laughter to utopian bliss." One cannot, it seems, enjoy fact *and* mystery, near *and* distant, laughter *and* bliss. One must choose. Far from affirming a simple hierarchy of preferences, Oakeshott's either/or signals that we are on existential ground, where the choice is not between something and its opposite but between something and its negation. The conservative would enjoy familiar things in the absence of forces seeking their destruction, Oakeshott concedes, but his enjoyment "will be strongest when" it "is combined with evident risk of loss." The conservative is a "man who is acutely aware of having something to lose which he has learned to care for." And while Oakeshott suggests that such losses can be engineered by a variety of forces, the most skilled engineers work on the left. (Marx and Engels are "the authors of the most stupendous of our political rationalisms," he writes elsewhere. "Nothing . . . can compare with" their abstract utopianism.) For that reason, "it is not at all inconsistent to be conservative in respect of government and radical in respect of almost every other activity."[57] Not at all inconsistent—or altogether necessary? Radicalism is the raison d'être of conservatism; if it goes, conservatism goes too.[58] Even when the conservative seeks to extricate himself from this dialogue with the left, he cannot, for his most lyrical motifs— organic change, tacit knowledge, ordered liberty, prudence, and precedent—are barely audible without the call and response of the left. As Disraeli discovered in his *Vindication of the English Constitution* (1835), it is only by contrast to a putative revolutionary rationalism that the invocation of ancient and tacit wisdom can have any purchase on the modern mind.

The formation of a free government on an extensive scale, while it is assuredly one of the most interesting problems of humanity, is certainly the greatest achievement of human wit. Perhaps I should rather term it a superhuman achievement; for it requires such refined prudence, such comprehensive knowledge, and such perspicacious sagacity, united with such almost illimitable powers of combination, that it is nearly in vain to hope for qualities so rare to be congregated in a solitary mind. Assuredly this *summum bonum* is not to be found ensconced behind a revolutionary barricade, or floating in the bloody gutters of an incendiary metropolis. It cannot be scribbled down—this great invention—in a morning on the envelope of a letter by some charter-concocting monarch, or sketched with ludicrous facility in the conceited commonplace book of a Utilitarian sage.[59]

There is more to this antagonistic structure of argument than the simple antinomies of partisan politics, the oppositional position taking that is a requirement of winning elections. As Karl Mannheim argued, what distinguishes conservatism from traditionalism—the universal "vegetative" tendency to remain attached to things as they are, which is manifested in nonpolitical behaviors such as a refusal to buy a new pair of pants until the current pair is shredded beyond repair—is that conservatism is a deliberate, conscious effort to preserve or recall "those forms of experience which can no longer be had in an authentic way." Conservatism "becomes conscious and reflective when other ways of life and thought appear on the scene, against which it is compelled to take up arms in the ideological struggle."[60] Where the traditionalist can take the objects of desire for granted—he can enjoy them as if they are at hand because they are at hand—the conservative cannot. He seeks to enjoy them precisely as they are being—or have been—taken away. If he hopes to enjoy them again, he must contest their divestment in the public realm. He must speak of them in a language that is politically serviceable and intelligible. But as soon as those objects enter the medium of political speech, they cease to be items of lived experience and become incidents of an ideology. They get wrapped in a narrative of loss—in which the revolutionary or reformist plays a necessary part—and presented in a program of recovery. What was tacit becomes articulate, what was fluid becomes formal, what was practice becomes polemic.[61] Even if the theory is a paean to practice—as conservatism often is—it cannot escape becoming a polemic. The fussiest conservative who would deign to enter the street is compelled by the left to pick up a paving stone and toss it at the barricades. As Lord Hailsham put it in his 1947 *Case for Conservatism*:

> Conservatives do not believe that political struggle is the most important thing in life. In this they differ from Communists, Socialists, Nazis, Fascists, Social Creditors and most members of the British Labour Party. The simplest among them prefer fox-hunting—the wisest religion. To the great majority of Conservatives, religion, art, study, family, country, friends, music, fun, duty, all the joy and riches of existence of which the poor no less than the rich are the indefeasible freeholders, all these are higher in the scale than their handmaiden, the political struggle. This makes them easy to defeat—at first. But, once defeated, they will hold to this belief with the fanaticism of a Crusader and the doggedness of an Englishman.[62]

Because there is so much confusion about conservatism's opposition to the left, it is important that we be clear about what the conservative is and is not opposing in the left. It is not change in the abstract. No conservative opposes change as such or defends order as such. The conservative defends particular orders—hierarchical, often private regimes of rule—on the assumption, in part, that hierarchy is order. "Order cannot be had," declared Johnson, "but by subordination."[63] For Burke, it was axiomatic that "when the multitude are not under this discipline" of "the wiser, the more expert, and the more opulent," "they can scarcely be said to be in civil society."[64]

In defending such orders, moreover, the conservative invariably launches himself on a program of reaction and counterrevolution, often requiring an overhaul of the very regime he is defending. "If we want things to stay as they are," in Lampedusa's classic formulation, "things will have to change."[65] To preserve the regime, the conservative must reconstruct the regime. This program entails far more than clichés about "preservation through renovation" would suggest: often, it can require the conservative to take the most radical measures on the regime's behalf.

Some of the stuffiest partisans of order on the right have been more than happy, when it has suited their purposes, to indulge in a little bit of mayhem and madness. Kirk, the self-styled Burkean, wished to "espouse conservatism with the vehemence of a radical. The thinking conservative, in truth, must take on some of the outward characteristics of the radical, today: he must poke about the roots of society, in the hope of restoring vigor to an old tree strangled in the rank undergrowth of modern passions." That was in 1954. Fifteen years later, at the height of the student movement, he wrote, "Having been for two decades a mordant critic of what is foolishly called the higher learning in America, I confess to relishing somewhat . . . the fulfillment of my predictions and the present plight of the educationist Establishment. I even own to a sneaking sympathy, after a fashion, with the campus revolutionaries." In *God and Man at Yale*, William F. Buckley declared conservatives "the new radicals." Upon reading the first few issues of *National Review*, Dwight Macdonald was inclined to agree: "Had [Buckley] been born a generation earlier, he would have been making the cafeterias of 14th Street ring with Marxian dialectics."[66] Burke himself wrote that "the madness of the wise" is "better than the sobriety of fools."[67]

There's a fairly simple reason for the embrace of radicalism on the right, and it has to do with the reactionary imperative that lies at the core of conservative doctrine. The conservative not only opposes the left; he also believes that the left has been in the driver's seat since, depending on who's counting, the French Revolution or the Reformation.[68] If he is to preserve what he values, the conservative must declare war against the culture as it is. Though the spirit of militant opposition pervades the entirety of conservative discourse, Dinesh D'Souza has put the case most clearly.

> Typically, the conservative attempts to conserve, to hold on to the values of the existing society. But . . . what if the existing society is inherently hostile to conservative beliefs? It is foolish for a conservative to attempt to conserve that culture. Rather, he must seek to undermine it, to thwart it, to destroy it at the root level. This means that the conservative must . . . be philosophically conservative but temperamentally radical.[69]

By now, it should also be clear that it is not the style or pace of change that the conservative opposes. The conservative theorist likes to draw a "manifest marked distinction" between evolutionary reform and radical change.[70] The first is slow, incremental, and adaptive; the second is fast, comprehensive, and by design. But that distinction, so dear to Burke and his followers, is often less clear in practice than the theorist allows.[71] Political theory is designed to be abstract, but what abstraction has impelled such diametrically opposed political programs as the preference for reform over radicalism, evolution over revolution? In the name of slow, organic, adaptive change, self-declared conservatives opposed the New Deal (Robert Nisbet, Kirk, and Whittaker Chambers) and endorsed the New Deal (Peter Viereck, Clinton Rossiter, and Whittaker Chambers).[72] A belief in evolutionary reform could lead one to adopt a Hayekian defense of the free market or the democratic socialism of Eduard Bernstein. "Even Fabian Socialists," Nash tartly observes, "who believed in 'the inevitability of gradualness' might be labeled conservatives."[73] Conversely, as Abraham Lincoln pointed out, it's just as easy for the left to claim the mantle of preservation as it is for the right. "You say you are conservative," he declared to the slaveholders.

Eminently conservative—while we are revolutionary, destructive, or something of the sort. What is conservatism? Is it not adherence to the old and tried, against the new and untried? We stick to, contend for, the identical old policy on the point in controversy which was adopted by "our fathers who framed the Government under which we live"; while you with one accord reject, and scout, and spit upon that old policy, and insist upon substituting something new. . . . Not one of all your various plans can show a precedent or an advocate in the century within which our Government originated. Consider, then, whether your claim of conservatism for yourself, and your charge of destructiveness against us, are based on the most clear and stable foundations.[74]

More often, however, the blurriness of the distinction has allowed the conservative to oppose reform on the grounds either that it will lead to revolution or that it is revolution. (Indeed, with the exception of Peel and Baldwin, no Tory leader has ever pursued a consistent program of preservation through reform, and even Peel could not persuade his party to follow him.[75]) Burke himself was not immune to the argument that reform leads to revolution. Even though he spent the better part of the decade preceding the American Revolution contesting that argument, he still wondered, "When you open" a constitution "to enquiry in one part," which would seem to be the definition of slow reform, "where will the enquiry stop?"[76] Other conservatives have argued that any demand from or on behalf of the lower orders, no matter how tepid or tardy, is too much, too soon, too fast. Reform is revolution, improvement insurrection. "It may be good or bad," a gloomy Lord Carnarvon wrote of the Second Reform Act of 1867—a bill twenty years in the making that tripled the size of the British electorate—"but it is a revolution." Minus the opening qualification, this was a repeat of what Wellington had said about the first Reform Act.[77] Across the Atlantic, Wellington's contemporary Nicholas Biddle was denouncing Andrew Jackson's veto of the Second Bank (that most constitutionally exercised of constitutional powers) in similar terms: "It has all the fury of a chained panther biting at the bars of his cage. It really is a manifesto of anarchy—such as Marat or Robespierre might have issued to the mob."[78]

Today's conservative may have made his peace with some emancipations past; others, like labor unions and reproductive freedom, he still contests. But that does not alter the fact that when those emancipations first arose as a question, whether in the context of revolution or reform, his predecessor was in all likelihood against them. Michael Gerson, former speechwriter for George W. Bush, is one of the few contemporary conservatives who acknowledge the history of conservative opposition to emancipation. Where other conservatives like to lay claim to the abolitionist or civil rights mantle, Gerson admits that "honesty requires the recognition that many conservatives, in other times, have been hostile to religiously motivated reform" and that "the conservative habit of mind once opposed most of these changes."[79] Indeed, as Samuel Huntington suggested a half-century ago, saying no to such movements in real time may be what makes someone a conservative throughout time.[80]

Most accounts of conservatism dwell on its internal differences and distinctions.* I treat the right as a unity, as a coherent

* In the last two decades, there has been a flurry of interest in the American right, resulting in a body of scholarship—much of it by younger historians, many of them on the left—that has dramatically transformed our understanding of

body of theory and practice that transcends the divisions so often emphasized by scholars and pundits.[94] I use the words conservative, reactionary, and counterrevolutionary interchangeably: not all counterrevolutionaries are conservative—Walt Rostow immediately comes to mind—but all conservatives are, in one way or another, counterrevolutionary. I seat philosophers, statesmen, slaveholders, scribblers, Catholics, fascists, evangelicals, businessmen, racists, and hacks at the same table: Hobbes is next to Hayek, Burke across from Donald Trump, Nietzsche in between Ayn Rand and Antonin Scalia, with Adams, Calhoun, Oakeshott, Ronald Reagan, Tocqueville, Theodore Roosevelt, Margaret Thatcher, Ernst Jünger, Carl Schmitt, Winston Churchill, Phyllis Schlafly, Richard Nixon, Irving Kristol, Francis Fukuyama, and George W. Bush interspersed throughout.

This is not to say that there is no change in conservatism across time or space. If conservatism is a specific reaction to a specific movement of emancipation, it stands to reason that each reaction will bear the traces of the movement it opposes. As I argue in subsequent chapters, not only has the right reacted against the left, but

conservatism in the United States.[81] Much of my own reading of conservative thought has been informed by this literature—its emphasis on the lived realities of race, class, and gender as they have manifested themselves in the partisan struggles of the last half-century; the syncretism between high politics and mass culture; and the creative tension between elites and activists, businessmen and intellectuals, suburbs and Southerners, movement and media. Believing with T. S. Eliot that conservatism is best understood by "careful examination of its behavior throughout its history and by examination of what its more thoughtful and philosophical minds have said on its behalf,"[82] I have read the theory in light of the practice (and the practice in light of the theory). With the help of this scholarship, I have listened for the "metaphysical pathos" of conservative thought—the hum and buzz of its implications, the assumptions it invokes and associations it evokes, the inner life of the movement it describes.[83] The felt in the course of conducting its reaction, it also has consistently bor-rowed from the left. As the movements of the left change—from the French Revolution to abolition to the right to vote to the right to organize to the Bolshevik Revolution to the struggles for black free-dom and women's liberation—so too do the reactions of the right.

Beyond these contingent changes, we can also trace a longer structural change in the imagination of the right: namely, the gradual acceptance of the entrance of the masses onto the political stage. From Hobbes to the slaveholders to the neoconservatives, the right has grown increasingly aware that any successful defense of the old regime must incorporate the lower orders in some capacity other than as underlings or starstruck fans. The masses must either be able to locate themselves symbolically in the rul-ing class or be provided with real opportunities to become faux aristocrats in the family, the factory, and the field. The former path makes for an upside-down populism, in which the lowest of the low see themselves projected in the highest of the high; the latter makes for a democratic feudalism, in which the husband or super-visor or white man plays the part of a lord. The former path was

presence of this scholarship is what distinguishes, I hope, my interpretation of conservative thought from other interpretations, which tend to read the theory in seclusion from the practice or in relation to a highly stylized account of that practice.[84]

As sophisticated as the recent literature about conservatism is, however, it suffers from three weaknesses. The first is a lack of comparative perspective. Scholars of the American right rarely examine the movement in relation to its European counterpart. Indeed, among many writers, it seems to be an article of faith that, like all things American, conservatism in the United States is excep-tional. "There is a distinctly *American* feel to Bush and his intellectual defenders," writes Kevin Mattson. "A conservatism that draws on Edmund Burke, a conserv-atism of wisdom and tradition deeply rooted in a European context" is "the sort of conservatism that has never taken hold in America."[85] The commitment to pioneered by Hobbes and Maistre, and the latter by Southern slave-holders, European imperialists, and Gilded Age apologists. (And neo–Gilded Age apologists: "There is no single elite in America," writes David Brooks. "Everyone can be an aristocrat within his own Olympus."[95]) Occasionally, as in the writing of Werner Sombart, the two paths converge: ordinary people get to see them-selves in the ruling class by virtue of belonging to a great nation among nations, and they also get to govern lesser beings through the exercise of imperial rule.

We Germans, too, should go through the world of our time in the same way, proud heads held high, in the secure feeling of being God's people. Just as the German bird, the eagle, soars high over all animals on this earth, so the German must feel himself above all other peoples that surround him and that he sees in boundless depth below him.

But aristocracy has its obligations, and this is true here, too. The idea that we are chosen people places formidable duties—and only duties—on us. We must above all maintain ourselves as a strong nation in the world.[96]

laissez-faire capitalism on this side of the Atlantic is supposed to differentiate American conservatism from the traditionalism of a Burke or Disraeli; a native pragmatism renders American conservatism inhospitable to the pessimism and fanaticism of a Bonald; democracy and populism make untenable the aristo-cratic biases of a Tocqueville. But this assumption is premised on misapprehen-sions about the European right: not even Burke was as traditional as writers have made him out to be, while Maistre and Burke held views on the economy that were—like so much else in their revanchist writings—surprisingly modern.[86] There are deep points of contact—particularly over questions of race and vio-lence—between the radical right in Europe and American figures like Calhoun, Teddy Roosevelt, Barry Goldwater, and the neoconservatives. In the postwar era, many of conservatism's leading lights self-consciously turned to Europe in

While these historical differences on the right are real, there is an underlying affinity that draws these differences together. One cannot perceive this affinity by focusing on disagreements of policy or contingent statements of practice (states' rights, federalism, and so on); one must look to the underlying arguments, the idioms and metaphors, the deep visions and metaphysical pathos evoked in each disagreement and statement. Some conservatives criticize the free market, others defend it; some oppose the state, others embrace it; some believe in God, others are atheists. Some are localists, others nationalists, and still others internationalists. Some, like Burke, are all three at the same time. But these are historical improvisations—tactical and substantive—on a theme. Only by juxtaposing these voices—across time and space—can we make out the theme amid the improvisation.

Forged in response to challenges from below, conservatism has none of the calm or composure that attends an enduring inheritance of power. One will look in vain throughout the canon of the right for steady assurances of a Great Chain of Being. Conservative

search of guidance and instruction, a service European émigrés—most notably, Hayek, Ludwig von Mises, and Leo Strauss—were only too happy to provide.[87] Indeed, for all the focus on the Frankfurt School and Hannah Arendt, it seems that the only political movements in postwar America that truly felt the impress of the European mind were on the right.

The second weakness of recent literature on conservatism is a lack of historical perspective. No matter how far back writers and scholars push the origins of contemporary conservatism (the latest move argues for a long conservative movement that connects the Tea Party to the 1920s),[88] they cling to the assumption that contemporary conservatism is fundamentally different from earlier iterations. At some point, the argument goes, American conservatism broke with its predecessors—it became populist, ideological, and so on—and it is this break, depending upon one's perspective, that either saved or doomed statements of organic unity, such as they are, either have an air of quiet—and not so quiet—desperation about them or, as in the case of Kirk, lack the texture, the knowing feel, of a longstanding witness to power. Even Maistre's professions of divine providence cannot conceal or contain the turbulent democracy that generated them. Made and mobilized to counter the claims of emancipation, such statements do not disclose a dense ecology of deference; they open out onto a rapidly thinning forest. Conservatism is about power besieged and power protected. It is an activist doctrine for an activist time. It waxes in response to movements from below and wanes in response to their disappearance, as Hayek and other conservatives admit.[97]

Far from compromising the vision of excellence set out above—in which the prerogatives of rule are supposed to bring an element of grandeur to an otherwise drab and desultory world— the activist imperative only strengthens it. "Light and perfection," Matthew Arnold wrote, "consist, not in resting and being, but in growing and becoming, in a perpetual advance in beauty and wisdom."[98] To the conservative, power in repose is power in

it.[89] But this argument ignores the continuities between figures like Adams and Calhoun and more recent voices on the American right. Far from an innovation of the last decades, the populism of the Tea Party and the futurism of a Reagan or Gingrich can be found in the earliest voices of conservatism, on both sides of the Atlantic. Likewise the adventurism, racism, and penchant for ideological thinking.

The third weakness derives from the second. The further back analysts trace the origins of contemporary conservatism, the less inclined they are to believe that it is a politics of reaction or backlash. If the commitments of the contemporary conservative can be situated in the writings of Albert Jay Nock or John Adams, these scholars argue, conservatism must reflect ideas and commitments more transcendent than mere opposition to the Great Society would suggest.[90] But a recognition of the long history of the right need not undermine decline. The "mere husbanding of already existing resources," wrote Joseph Schumpeter, "no matter how painstaking, is always characteristic of a declining position."[99] If power is to achieve the distinction the conservative associates with it, it must be exercised, and there is no better way to exercise power than to defend it against an enemy from below.[100] Counterrevolution, in other words, is one of the ways in which the conservative makes feudalism fresh and medievalism modern.

But it is not the only way. Conservatism also offers a defense of rule, independent of its counterrevolutionary imperative, that is agonistic and dynamic and also dispenses with the staid traditionalism and harmonic registers of hierarchies past. And here we come to the conservative's deepest intimations of the good life, of that reactionary utopia he hopes one day to bring into being. Unlike the feudal past, where power was presumed and privilege inherited, the conservative future envisions a world where power is demonstrated and privilege earned: not in the antiseptic and anodyne halls of the meritocracy, where admission is readily secured—"the road to eminence and power, from obscure condition, ought not to be made too easy, nor a thing too much

the claim that contemporary conservatism is a backlash politics. Instead, the long view should help us to understand better the nature and dynamics, as well as the idiosyncrasies and contingencies, of that backlash. Indeed, only by setting the contemporary right against the backdrop of its predecessors can we understand its specificity and particularity.

For many, the notion of a unity on the right is a contentious claim. Even though we continue to use the term "conservative" in our everyday discourse (indeed, political discussion would be inconceivable without it); even though conservatism in both Europe and the United States has managed, for more than a century, to attract and hold together a coalition of traditionalists, warriors, and capitalists; even though the opposition between left and right has proven to be an enduring "political distinction" of the modern era (despite the attempt, every generation or so, to deny or overcome this opposition via a "third way"),[91] of course"[101]—but in the arduous struggle for supremacy. In that struggle, nothing matters: not inheritance, social connections, or economic resources, but rather one's native intelligence and innate strength. Genuine excellence is revealed and rewarded; true nobility is secured. "*Nitor in adversum*' [I strive against adversity] is the motto for a man like me," declares Burke, after dismissing a to-the-manor-born politician who was "swaddled, and rocked, and dandled into a legislator."[102] Even the most biologically inclined and deterministic racist believes that the members of the superior race must personally wrest their entitlement to rule through the subjugation or elimination of the inferior races.

The recognition that race is the substratum of all civilization must not, however, lead any one to feel that membership in a superior race is a sort of comfortable couch on which he can go to sleep. . . . the biological heritage of the mind is no more imperishable than the biological heritage of the body. If we continue to squander that biological mental heritage as we have been squandering it during the last few decades, it will not be many generations before we cease to be the superiors

many continue to believe the differences on the right are so great that it is impossible to say anything about the right.[92] But if it is impossible to say anything about the right—to define, describe, explain, analyze, and interpret the right as a distinctive formation—how can we say that it even exists?

Hoping to avoid that radical skepticism, which would render unintelligible much of what goes on in our politics, some scholars have retreated to a nominalist position: conservatives are people who call themselves conservative or, more elaborately, conservatives are people who people who call themselves conservative call conservative.[93] This only begs the question: What do these people who call themselves conservative—or who others who call themselves conservative call conservative—mean by "conservative"? Why do they opt for that self-description as opposed to liberal, socialist, or aardvark? Unless these people think they are referring to idiosyncratic identities—in which case we're of the Mongols. Our ethnological studies must lead us, not to arrogance, but to action.[103]

The battlefield is the natural proving ground of superiority; there, it is only the soldier, with his wits and weapon, who determines his standing in the world. With time, however, the conservative would find another proving ground in the marketplace. Though most early conservatives were ambivalent about capitalism,[104] their successors would come to believe that warriors of a different kind can prove their mettle in the manufacture and trade of commodities. Such men wrestle the earth's resources to and from the ground, taking for themselves what they want and thereby establishing their superiority over others. The great men of money are not born with privilege or right; they seize it for themselves, without let or permission.[105] "Liberty is a conquest," wrote William Graham Sumner.[106] The primal act of transgression—requiring daring, vision, and an aptitude for violence and violation[107]—is what makes the capitalist a warrior, entitling him not only to great wealth but also, ultimately, to command. For that is what the capitalist is: not a Midas of riches but a ruler of men. A title to property is a license to dispose, and if a man has the title to another's labor, he has a license to dispose of it—to dispose, that is, of the body in motion—as he sees fit.

back to the skeptical position—we need to understand what the term means, independent of its use. How else can we understand why individuals from different times and places, adopting different positions on different issues, would call themselves and their kindred spirits conservative? Not every reader need or will accept my claim about what unites the right. But it does seem a necessary condition of intelligent discussion that we agree that there is something called the right and that it has some set of common features that make it right. That, at any rate, is the assumption of this book, the validity of which will be tested in the following chapters.

Such have been called "captains of industry." The analogy with military leaders suggested by this name is not misleading. The great leaders in the development of the industrial organization need those talents of executive and administrative skill, power to command, courage, and fortitude, which were formerly called for in military affairs and scarcely anywhere else. The industrial army is also as dependent on its captains as a military body is on its generals. . . . Under the circumstances there has been a great demand for men having the requisite ability for this function. . . . The possession of the requisite ability is a natural monopoly.[108]

The warrior and the businessman will become twin icons of an age in which, as Burke foresaw, membership in the ruling classes must be earned, often through the most painful and humiliating of struggles. "At every step of my progress in life (for in every step was I traversed and opposed), and at every turnpike I met, I was obliged to shew my passport, and again and again to prove my sole title to the honour of being useful to my Country. . . . Otherwise, no rank, no toleration even, for me."[109]

Even though war and the market are the modern agones of power—with Nietzsche the theoretician of the first and Hayek of the second—the embrace of capitalism on the right has never been unqualified. To this day, conservatives remain leery of the shabbiness and shallowness of making money, of the political obtuseness the market seems to induce in the governing classes, and of the foolishness and frivolity of consumer culture. For this wing of the movement, war will always remain the only activity where the best man can truly prove his right to rule. It's a bloody business, to be sure, but how else to be an aristocrat when all that's solid melts into air?

2

On Counterrevolution

Ever since Edmund Burke invented conservatism as an idea, the conservative has styled himself a man of prudence and moderation, his cause a sober—and sobering—recognition of limits. "To be conservative," we heard Michael Oakeshott declare in the previous chapter, "is to prefer the familiar to the unknown . . . the tried to the untried, fact to mystery, the actual to the possible, the limited to the unbounded, the near to the distant."[1] Yet the political efforts that have roused the conservative to his most profound reflections—the reactions against the French and Bolshevik revolutions; the defense of slavery and Jim Crow; the attack on social democracy and the welfare state; and the serial backlashes against the New Deal, the Great Society, civil rights, feminism, and gay rights—have been anything but that. Whether in Europe or the United States, in this century or previous ones, conservatism has been a forward movement of restless and relentless change, partial to risk taking and ideological adventurism, militant in its posture and populist in its bearings, friendly to upstarts and insurgents, outsiders and newcomers alike. While the conservative theorist claims for his tradition the mantle of prudence and moderation, there is a not-so-subterranean and counterintuitive strain of imprudence and immoderation running through that tradition.

A consideration of this deeper strain of conservatism gives us a clearer sense of what conservatism is about. While conservatism is an ideology of reaction—originally against the French Revolution, more recently against the liberation movements of the sixties and seventies—that reaction has not been well understood. Far from yielding a knee-jerk defense of an unchanging old regime or a thoughtful traditionalism, the reactionary imperative presses conservatism in two rather different directions: first, to a critique and reconfiguration of the old regime; and second, to an absorption of the ideas and tactics of the very revolution or reform it opposes. What conservatism seeks to accomplish through that reconfiguration of the old and absorption of the new is to make privilege popular, to transform a tottering old regime into a dynamic, ideologically coherent movement of the masses. A new old regime, one could say, which brings the energy and dynamism of the street to the antique inequalities of a dilapidated estate.

Over the last two decades, various writers and journalists have claimed that conservatism went into decline when Trump, or Palin, or Bush, or Reagan, or Goldwater, or Buckley, or someone took it off the rails. Originally, the argument goes, conservatism was a responsible discipline of the governing classes, but somewhere between Joseph de Maistre and Joe the Plumber, it got carried away with itself. It became adventurous, fanatical, populist, ideological. What this story of decline overlooks—whether it emanates from the right or the left—is that all of these supposed vices of contemporary conservatism were present at the beginning, in the writings of Burke and Maistre, only they weren't viewed as vices. They were seen as virtues. Conservatism has always been a wilder and more extravagant movement than many realize—and it is precisely this wildness and extravagance that has been one of the sources of its continuing appeal.

It is hardly provocative to say that conservatism arose in reaction to the French Revolution. Most historically minded conservatives would agree.[2] But if we look more carefully at two emblematic voices of that reaction—Burke and Maistre—we find several surprising and seldom-noticed elements. The first is an antipathy, bordering on contempt, for the old regime they claim as their cause. The opening chapters of Maistre's *Considerations on France* are an unrelenting assault on the three pillars of the ancien régime: the aristocracy, the church, and the monarchy. Maistre divides the nobility into two categories: the treasonous and the clueless. The clergy is corrupt, weakened by its wealth and lax morals. The monarchy is soft and lacks the will to punish. Maistre dismisses all three with a line from Racine: "Now see the sad fruits your faults produced,/Feel the blows you have yourselves induced."[3]

In Burke's case, the criticism is subtler but runs deeper (though by the end of his life, he was speaking in the same unmodulated tones as Maistre).[4] It comes during his account in *Reflections on the Revolution in France* of the storming of the palace at Versailles and the capture of the royal family. There, Burke describes Marie Antoinette as a "delightful vision . . . glittering like the morning star, full of life, and splendor, and joy." Burke takes her beauty as a symbol of the loveliness of the old regime, where feudal manners and mores "made power gentle" and "by a bland assimilation, incorporated into politics the sentiments which beautify and soften private society."[5]

Ever since he wrote those lines, Burke has been mocked for his sentimentality. But readers of Burke's earlier work on aesthetics, *A Philosophical Enquiry into the Origins of Our Ideas of the Sublime and the Beautiful*, will know that beauty, for Burke, is never a sign of power's vitality; it is always a sign of decadence. Beauty arouses pleasure, which gives way to indifference or leads to a total dissolution of the self. "Beauty acts," Burke writes, "by relaxing the solids of the whole system."[6] It is this relaxation and dissolution of bodies—physical, social, political bodies—that makes beauty such a potent symbol and agent of degeneration and death. "Our most salutary and most beautiful institutions yield nothing but dust and smut."[7]

What these two opening statements of the conservative persuasion suggest is that the greatest enemy of the old regime is neither the revolutionary nor the reformer; instead, it is the old regime itself or, to be more precise, the defenders of the old regime.[8] They simply lack the ideological wherewithal to press the cause of the old regime with the requisite vigor, clarity, and purpose. As Burke declared of George Grenville, in the very different context of Britain's relationship with its American colonies:

> But it may be truly said, that men too much conversant in office, are rarely minds of remarkable enlargement. . . . persons who are nurtured in office do admirably well as long as things go on in their common order; but when the high roads are broken up, and the waters out, when a new and troubled scene is opened, and the file affords no precedent, then it is that a greater knowledge of mankind, and a far more extensive comprehension of things, is requisite, than ever office gave, or than office can ever give.[9]

Later conservatives will make this claim in various ways. Sometimes they'll accuse the defenders of the old regime of having been cowed by the revolutionary or reformist challenge. According to Thomas Dew, one of the earliest and most aggressive apologists for American slavery, the Nat Turner rebellion destroyed "all feeling of security and confidence" among the master class. So frightened were they that "reason was almost banished from the mind." It wasn't just the slaves' violence that frightened them. It was also the moral indictment leveled by the slaves and the abolitionists, which had somehow insinuated itself into the slaveholders' minds and made them unsure of their own position. "We ourselves," wrote William Harper, another defender of slavery, "have in some measure pleaded guilty to the impeachment."[10]

More than a century later, Barry Goldwater would take up the same theme. The very first paragraph of *The Conscience of a Conservative* directs its fire not at liberals or Democrats or even the welfare state; it is aimed at the moral timidity of what will later be called the "Republican Establishment."

I have been much concerned that so many people today with Conservative instincts feel compelled to apologize for them. Or if not to apologize directly, to qualify their commitment in a way that amounts to breast beating. "Republican candidates," Vice President Nixon has said, "should be economic conservatives, but conservatives with a heart." President Eisenhower announced during his first term, "I am conservative when it comes to economic problems but liberal when it comes to human problems." . . . These formulations are tantamount to an admission that Conservatism is a narrow, mechanistic economic theory that may work very well as a bookkeeper's guide, but cannot be relied upon as a comprehensive political philosophy.[11]

More often, conservatives have argued that the defender of the old regime is simply obtuse. He has grown lazy, fat, and complacent, so roundly enjoying the privileges of his position that he cannot see the coming catastrophe. Or, if he can see it, he can't do anything to fend it off, his political muscles having atrophied long ago. John C. Calhoun was one such conservative, and throughout the 1830s, when the abolitionists began pressing their cause, he drove himself into a rage over the easy living and willful cluelessness of his comrades on the plantation. His fury reached a peak in 1837. "All we want is concert," he pleaded with his fellow Southerners, to "unite with zeal and energy in repelling approaching dangers." But, he went on, "I dare not hope that any thing I can say will arouse the South to a due sense of danger. I fear it is beyond the power of the mortal voice to awaken it in time from the fatal security into which it has fallen."[12]

In his influential essay, Oakeshott argued that conservatism "is not a creed or a doctrine, but a disposition." Specifically, he thought, it is a disposition to enjoy the present. Not because the present is better than the alternatives or even because it is good on its own terms. That would imply a level of conscious reflection and ideological choice that Oakeshott believes is alien to the conservative. No, the reason the conservative enjoys the present is simply and merely because it is familiar, because it is there, because it is at hand.[13]

Oakeshott's view of the conservative—and this view is widely shared on both the left and the right—is not an insight; it is a conceit. It overlooks the fact that conservatism invariably arises in response to a threat to the old regime or after the old regime has been destroyed. (Oakeshott openly admits that loss or threatened loss makes us value the present, as I argued in chapter 1, but he does not allow that insight to penetrate or dislodge his overall understanding of conservatism.) Oakeshott is describing the old regime in an easy chair, when its mortality is a distant notion and time is a warming medium rather than an acrid solvent. This is the old regime of Charles Loyseau, who wrote nearly two centuries before the French Revolution that the nobility has no "beginning" and thus no end. It "exists time out of mind," without consciousness or awareness of the passage of history.[14]

Conservatism appears on the scene precisely when—and precisely because—such statements can no longer be made. Walter Berns, one of the many future neoconservatives at Cornell who were traumatized in 1969 by the black students' takeover of Willard Straight Hall, stated in his farewell speech when he resigned from the university: "We had too good a world; it couldn't last."[15] Nothing so disturbs the idyll of inheritance as the sudden and often brutal replacement of one world with another. Having witnessed the death of what was supposed to live forever, the conservative can no longer look upon time as the natural ally or habitat of power. Time is now the enemy. Change, not permanence, is the universal governor, with change signifying neither progress nor improvement but death, and an early, unnatural death at that. "The decree of violent death," says Maistre, is "written on the very frontiers of life."[16] The problem with the defender of the old regime, says the conservative, is that he doesn't know this truth or, if he does, he lacks the will to do anything about it.

The second element we find in these early voices of reaction is a surprising admiration for the very revolution they are writing against. Maistre's most rapturous comments are reserved for the Jacobins, whose brutal will and penchant for violence—their "black magic"—he plainly envies. The revolutionaries have faith, in their cause and themselves, which transforms a movement of mediocrities into the most implacable force Europe has ever seen. Thanks to their efforts, France has been purified and restored to its rightful pride of place among the family of nations. "The revolutionary government," Maistre concludes, "hardened the soul of France by tempering it in blood."[17]

Burke, again, is more subtle but cuts more deeply. Great power, he suggests in *The Sublime and the Beautiful,* should never aspire to be—and can never actually be—beautiful. What great power needs is sublimity. The sublime is the sensation we experience in the face of extreme pain, danger, or terror. It is something like awe but tinged with fear and dread. Burke calls it "delightful horror." Great power should aspire to sublimity rather than beauty because sublimity produces "the strongest emotion which the mind is capable of feeling." It is an arresting yet invigorating emotion, which has the simultaneous but contradictory effect of diminishing and magnifying us. We feel annihilated by great power; at the same time, our sense of self "swell[s]" when "we are conversant with terrible objects." Great power achieves sublimity when it is, among other things, obscure and mysterious, and when it is extreme. "In all things," writes Burke, the sublime "abhors mediocrity."[18]

In the *Reflections*, Burke suggests that the problem in France is that the old regime is beautiful while the revolution is sublime. The landed interest, the cornerstone of the old regime, is "sluggish, inert, and timid." It cannot defend itself "from the invasions of ability," with ability standing in here for the new men of power that the revolution brings forth. Elsewhere in the *Reflections*, Burke says that the moneyed interest, which is allied with the revolution, is stronger than the aristocratic interest because it is "more ready for any adventure" and "more disposed to new enterprises of any kind." The old regime, in other words, is beautiful, static, and weak; the revolution is ugly, dynamic, and strong. And in the horrors that the revolution perpetrates—the rabble rushing into the bedchamber of the queen, dragging her half-naked into the street, and marching her and her family to Paris—the revolution achieves a kind of sublimity: "We are alarmed into reflexion," writes Burke of the revolutionaries' actions. "Our minds . . . are purified by terror and pity; our weak unthinking pride is humbled, under the dispensations of a mysterious wisdom."[19]

Beyond these simple professions of envy or admiration, the conservative actually copies and learns from the revolution he opposes. "To destroy that enemy," Burke wrote of the Jacobins, "by some means or other, the force opposed to it should be made to bear some analogy and resemblance to the force and spirit which that system exerts."[20] This is one of the most interesting and least understood aspects of conservative ideology. While conservatives are hostile to the goals of the left, particularly the empowerment of society's lower castes and classes, they often are the left's best students. Sometimes, their studies are self-conscious and strategic, as they look to the left for ways to bend new vernaculars, or new media, to their suddenly delegitimated aims. Fearful that the philosophes had taken control of popular opinion in France, reactionary theologians in the middle of the eighteenth century looked to the example of their enemies. They stopped writing abstruse disquisitions for each other and began to produce Catholic agitprop, which would be distributed through the very networks that brought enlightenment to the French people. They spent vast sums funding essay contests, like those in which Rousseau made his name, to reward writers who wrote accessible and popular defenses of religion. Previous treatises of faith, declared Charles-Louis Richard, were "useless to the multitude who, without arms and without defenses, succumbs rapidly to *Philosophie*." His work, by contrast, was written "with the design of putting in the hands of all those who know how to read a victorious weapon against the assaults of this turbulent *Philosophie*."[21]

Pioneers of the Southern Strategy in the Nixon administration, to cite a more recent example, understood that after the rights revolutions of the sixties they could no longer make simple appeals to white racism. From now on, they would have to speak in code, preferably one palatable to the new dispensation of color blindness. As White House chief of staff H. R. Haldeman noted in his diary, Nixon "emphasized that you have to face the fact that the whole problem is really the blacks. The key is to devise a system that recognized this while not appearing to."[22] Looking back on this strategy in 1981, Republican strategist Lee Atwater spelled out its elements more clearly:

> You start out in 1954 by saying, "Nigger, nigger, nigger." By 1968 you can't say "nigger"—that hurts you. Backfires. So you say stuff like forced busing, states' rights and all that stuff. You're getting so abstract now you're talking about cutting taxes, and all these things you're talking about are totally economic things and a by-product of them is blacks get hurt worse than whites. And subconsciously maybe that is part of it.[23]

More recently still, David Horowitz has encouraged conservative students "to use the language that the left has deployed so effectively in behalf of its own agendas. Radical professors have created a 'hostile learning environment' for conservative students. There is a lack of 'intellectual diversity' on college faculties and in academic classrooms. The conservative viewpoint is 'underrepresented' in the curriculum and on its reading lists. The university should be an 'inclusive' and intellectually 'diverse' community."[24]

At other times, the education of the conservative is unknowing, happening, as it were, behind his back. By resisting and thus engaging with the progressive argument day after day, he comes to be influenced, often in spite of himself, by the very movement he opposes. Setting out to bend a vernacular to his will, he finds his will bent by the vernacular. Atwater claims this is precisely what occurred within the Republican Party. After suggesting "subconsciously maybe that is part of it," he adds:

> I'm not saying that. But I'm saying that if it is getting that abstract, and that coded, that we are doing away with the racial problem one way or the other. You follow me—because obviously sitting around saying, "We want to cut this," is much more abstract than even the busing thing, and a hell of a lot more abstract than "Nigger, nigger."[25]

interesting

Republicans have learned to disguise their intentions so well, in other words, that the disguise has seeped into and transformed the intention.

Even without directly engaging the progressive argument, conservatives may absorb, by some elusive osmosis, the deeper categories and idioms of the left, even when those idioms run directly counter to their official stance. After years of opposing the women's movement, for example, Phyllis Schlafly seemed genuinely incapable of conjuring the prefeminist view of women as deferential wives and mothers. Instead, she celebrated the activist "power of the positive woman." And then, as if borrowing a page from *The Feminine Mystique*, she railed against the meaninglessness and lack of fulfillment among American women; the difference was that she blamed these ills on feminism rather than on sexism.[26] When she spoke out against the Equal Rights Amendment (ERA), she didn't claim that it introduced a radical new language of rights. Her argument was the opposite. The ERA, she told the *Washington Star*, "is a takeaway of women's rights." It will "take away the right of the wife in an ongoing marriage, the wife in the home."[27] Schlafly was obviously using the language of rights in a way that was opposed to the aims of the feminist movement; she was using rights talk to put women back into the home, to keep them as wives and mothers. But that is the point: conservatism adapts and adopts, often unconsciously, the language of democratic reform to the cause of hierarchy.

One also can detect a certain sexual frankness—even feminist concern—in the early conversations of the Christian Right that would have been unthinkable prior to the women's movement. In 1976, Beverly and Tim LaHaye wrote a book, *The Act of Marriage*, which Susan Faludi has rightly called "the evangelical equivalent of *The Joy of Sex*." There, the LaHayes claimed that "women are much too passive in lovemaking." God, the LaHayes told their female readers, "placed [your clitoris] there for your enjoyment." They also complained that "some husbands are carryovers from the Dark Ages, like the one who told his frustrated wife, 'Nice girls aren't supposed to climax.' Today's wife knows better."[28]

What the conservative ultimately learns from his opponents, wittingly or unwittingly, is the power of political agency and the potency of the mass. From the trauma of revolution, conservatives learn that men and women, whether through willed acts of force or some other exercise of human agency, can order social relationships and political time. In every social movement or revolutionary moment, reformers and radicals have to invent—or rediscover—the idea that inequality and social hierarchy are not natural phenomena but human creations. If hierarchy can be created by men and women, it can be uncreated by men and women, and that is what a social movement or revolution sets out to do. From these efforts, conservatives learn a version of the same lesson. Where their predecessors in the old regime thought of inequality as a naturally occurring phenomenon, an inheritance passed on from generation to generation, the conservatives' encounter with revolution teaches them that the revolutionaries were right after all: inequality is a human creation. And if it can be uncreated by men and women, it can be recreated by men and women.

"Citizens!" exclaims Maistre at the end of *Considerations on France*. "This is how counterrevolutions are made."[29] Under the old regime, monarchy—like patriarchy or Jim Crow—isn't made. It just is. It would be difficult to imagine a Loyseau or Bossuet declaring, "Men"—much less citizens—"this is how a monarchy is made." But once the old regime is threatened or toppled, the conservative is forced to realize that it is human agency, the willed imposition of intellect and imagination upon the world, that generates and maintains inequality across time. Coming out of this confrontation with revolution, the conservative voices the kind of affirmation of political agency one finds in this 1957 editorial from William F. Buckley's *National Review*: "The central question that emerges" from the Civil Rights Movement "is whether the White community in the South is entitled to take such measures as are necessary to prevail, politically and culturally, in areas in which it does not predominate numerically? The sobering answer is Yes— the White community is so entitled because, for the time being, it is the advanced race."[30]

The revolutionary declares the Year I, and in response the conservative declares the Year Negative I. From the revolution, the conservative develops a particular attitude toward political time, a belief in the power of men and women to shape history, to propel it forward or backward; and by virtue of that belief, he comes to adopt the future as his preferred tense. Ronald Reagan offered the perfect distillation of this phenomenon when he invoked, repeatedly, Thomas Paine's dictum that "we have it in our power to begin the world over again."[31] Even when the conservative claims to be preserving a present that's threatened or recovering a past that's been lost, he is impelled by his own activism and agency to confess that he's making a new beginning and creating the future.

Burke was especially attuned to this problem and was often at pains to remind his comrades in the battle against the Revolution that whatever was rebuilt in France after the restoration would inevitably, as he put it in a letter to an émigré, "be in some measure a new thing."[32] Other conservatives have been less ambivalent, happily affirming the virtues of political creativity and moral originality. Alexander Stephens, vice president of the U.S. Confederacy, proudly declared that "our new government is the first, in the history of the world," to be founded upon the "great physical, philosophical, and moral truth" that "the negro is not equal to the white man; that slavery—subordination to the superior race—is his natural and normal condition."[33] Barry Goldwater said simply, "Our future, like our past, will be what we make it."[34]

From revolutions, conservatives also develop a taste and talent for the masses, mobilizing the street for spectacular displays of power while making certain power is never truly shared or redistributed. That is the task of right-wing populism: to appeal to the mass without disrupting the power of elites or, more precisely, to harness the energy of the mass in order to reinforce or restore the power of elites. Far from being a recent innovation of the Christian Right, the Tea Party movement, or Trump, reactionary populism runs like a red thread throughout conservative discourse from the very beginning.

Maistre was a pioneer in the theater of mass power, imagining scenes and staging dramas in which the lowest of the low could see themselves reflected in the highest of the high. "Monarchy," he writes, "is without contradiction, the form of government that gives the most distinction to the greatest number of persons." Ordinary people "share" in its "brilliance" and glow, though not, Maistre is careful to add, in its decisions and deliberations: "man is honored not as an agent but as a portion of sovereignty."[35] Archmonarchist that he was, Maistre understood that the king could never return to power if he did not have a touch of the plebeian about him. So when Maistre imagines the triumph of the counterrevolution, he takes care to emphasize the populist credentials of the returning monarch. The people should identify with this new king, says Maistre, because like them he has attended the "terrible school of misfortune" and suffered in the "hard school of adversity." He is "human," with humanness here connoting an almost pedestrian, and reassuring, capacity for error. He will be like them. Unlike his predecessors, he will know it, which "is a great deal."[36]

But to appreciate fully the inventiveness of right-wing populism, we have to turn to the master class of the Old South. The slaveholder created a quintessential form of democratic feudalism, turning the white majority into a lordly class, sharing in the privileges and prerogatives of governing the slave class. Though the members of this ruling class knew that they were not equal to each other, they were compensated by the illusion of superiority—and the reality of rule—over the black population beneath them.

One school of thought—call it the equal opportunity school— located the democratic promise of slavery in the fact that it put the possibility of personal mastery within the reach of every white man. The genius of the slaveholders, wrote Daniel Hundley in his *Social Relations in Our Southern States*, is that they are "not an exclusive aristocracy. Every free white man in the whole Union has just as much right to become an Oligarch." This was not just propaganda: by 1860, there were 400,000 slaveholders in the South, making the American master class one of the most democratic in the world. The slaveholders repeatedly attempted to pass laws encouraging whites to own at least one slave and even considered granting tax breaks to facilitate such ownership. Their thinking, in the words of one Tennessee farmer, was that "the minute you put it out of the power of common farmers to purchase a Negro man or woman . . . . you make him an abolitionist at once."[37]

That school of thought contended with a second, arguably more influential, school. American slavery was not democratic, according to this line of thinking, because it offered the opportunity for personal mastery to white men. Instead, American slavery was democratic because it made every white man, slaveholder or not, a member of the ruling class by virtue of the color of his skin. In the words of Calhoun: "With us the two great divisions of society are not the rich and poor, but white and black; and all the former, the poor as well as the rich, belong to the upper class, and are respected and treated as equals."[38] Or as his junior colleague James Henry Hammond put it, "In a slave country every freeman is an aristocrat."[39] Even without slaves or the material prerequisites for freedom, a poor white man could style himself a member of the nobility and thus be relied upon to take the necessary measures in its defense.

Whether one subscribed to the first or second school of thought, the master class believed that democratic feudalism was a potent counter to the egalitarian movements then roiling Europe and Jacksonian America. European radicals, declared Dew, "wish all mankind to be brought to one common level. We believe slavery, in the United States, has accomplished this." By freeing whites from "menial and low offices," slavery had eliminated "the greatest cause of distinction and separation of the ranks of society."[40] As the nineteenth-century ruling classes contended with challenge after challenge to their power, the master class offered up racial domination as a way of harnessing the energy of the white masses, in support of, rather than in opposition to, the privileges and powers of established elites. This program would find its ultimate fulfillment a century later and a continent away.

These populist currents can help us make sense of a final element of conservatism. From the beginning, conservatism has appealed to and relied upon outsiders. Maistre was from Savoy, Burke from Ireland. Alexander Hamilton was born out of wedlock in Nevis and rumored to be part black. Disraeli was a Jew, as are many of the neoconservatives who helped transform the Republican Party from a cocktail party in Darien into the party of Scalia, D'Souza, Gonzalez, and Yoo. (It was Irving Kristol who first identified "the historical task and political purpose of neoconservatism" as the conversion of "the Republican Party, and American conservatism in general, against their respective wills, into a new kind of conservative politics suitable to governing a modern democracy.")[41] Allan Bloom was a Jew and a homosexual. And as she never tired of reminding us during the 2008 campaign, Sarah Palin is a woman in a world of men, an Alaskan who said no to Washington (though she really didn't), a maverick who rode shotgun to another maverick.

Conservatism has not only depended upon outsiders; it also has seen itself as the voice of the outsider. From Burke's cry that "the gallery is in the place of the house" to Buckley's complaint that the modern conservative is "out of place," the conservative has served as a tribune for the displaced, his movement a conveyance of their grievances.[42] Far from being an invention of the politically correct, victimhood has been a talking point of the right ever since Burke decried the mob's treatment of Marie Antoinette. The conservative, to be sure, speaks for a special type of victim: one who has lost something of value, as opposed to the wretched of the earth, whose chief complaint is that they never had anything to lose. His constituency is the contingently dispossessed—William Graham Sumner's "forgotten man"—rather than the preternaturally oppressed. Far from diminishing his appeal, this brand of victimhood endows the conservative complaint with a more universal significance. It connects his disinheritance to an experience we all share—namely, loss—and threads the strands of that experience into an ideology promising that that loss, or at least some portion of it, can be made whole.

People who aren't conservative often fail to realize this, but conservatism really does speak to and for people who have lost something. It may be a landed estate or the privileges of white skin, the unquestioned authority of a husband or the untrammeled rights of a factory owner. The loss may be as material as money or as ethereal as a sense of standing. It may be a loss of something that was never legitimately owned in the first place; it may, when compared with what the conservative retains, be small. Even so, it is a loss, and nothing is ever so cherished as that which we no longer possess. It used to be one of the great virtues of the left that it alone understood the often zero-sum nature of politics, where the gains of one class necessarily entail the losses of another. But as that sense of conflict diminishes on the left, it has fallen to the right to remind voters that there really are losers in politics and that it is they—and only they—who speak for them. "All conservatism begins with loss," Andrew Sullivan rightly notes, which makes conservatism not the Party of Order, as Mill and others have claimed, but the party of the loser.[43]

The chief aim of the loser is not—and indeed cannot be—preservation or protection. It is recovery and restoration. That is one of the secrets of conservatism's success. For all of its demotic frisson and ideological grandiosity, for all of its insistence upon triumph and will, movement and mobilization, conservatism can be an ultimately pedestrian affair. Because his losses are recent—the right agitates against reform in real time, not millennia after the fact—the conservative can credibly claim to his constituency, indeed to the polity at large, that his goals are practical and achievable. He merely seeks to regain what is his, and the fact that he once had it—indeed, probably had it for some time—suggests that he is capable of possessing it again. "It is not an old structure," as Burke declared of Jacobin France, but "a recent wrong" that the conservative addresses himself to.[44] Where the left's program of redistribution raises the question of whether its beneficiaries are truly prepared to wield the powers they seek, the conservative project of restoration suffers from no such challenge. Unlike the reformer or the revolutionary, who faces the nearly impossible task of empowering the powerless—that is, of turning people from what they are into what they are not—the conservative merely asks his followers to do more of what they always have done (albeit, better and differently). As a result, his counterrevolution will not require the same disruption that the revolution has visited upon the country. "Four or five persons, perhaps," writes Maistre, "will give France a king."[45]

For some, perhaps many, in the conservative movement, this knowledge comes as a source of relief: their sacrifice will be small, their reward great. For others, it is a source of bitter disappointment. To this subset of activists and militants, the battle is all. To learn that it soon will be over and will not require so much from them is enough to prompt a complex of despair: disgust over the shabbiness of their effort, grief over the disappearance of their foe, anxiety over the early retirement into which they have been forced. As Irving Kristol complained after the end of the Cold War, the defeat of the Soviet Union and the left more generally "deprived" conservatives like himself "of an enemy," and "in politics, being deprived of an enemy is a very serious matter. You tend to get relaxed and dispirited. Turn inward."[46] Depression haunts conservatism as surely as does great wealth. But again, far from diminishing the appeal of conservatism, this darker dimension only enhances it. Onstage, the conservative waxes Byronic, moodily surveying the sum of his losses before an audience of the lovelorn and the starstruck. Offstage, and out of sight, his managers quietly compile the sum of their gains.

3

The Soul of Violence

I enjoy wars. Any adventure's better than sitting in an office.
—Harold Macmillan

Despite the support among self-identified conservative voters and politicians for the death penalty, torture, and war, intellectuals on the right often deny any affinity between conservatism and violence.[1] "Conservatives," writes Andrew Sullivan, "hate war."

> Their domestic politics is rooted in a loathing of civil wars and violence, and they know that freedom is always the first casualty of international warfare. When countries go to war, their governments invariably get bigger and stronger, individual liberties are whittled away, and societies which once enjoyed the pluralist cacophony of freedom have to be marshaled into a single, collective note to face down an external foe. A state of permanent warfare—as George Orwell saw—is a virtual invitation to domestic tyranny.[2]

Channeling a tradition of skepticism from Oakeshott to Hume, the conservative identifies limited government as the extent of his faith, the rule of law his one requirement for the pursuit of happiness. Pragmatic and adaptive, disposed rather than committed, such a sensibility—and it is a sensibility, the conservative insists, not an ideology—is not interested in violence. His endorsements of war, such as they are, are the weariest of concessions to reality. Unlike his friends on the left—conservative that he is, he values friendship more than agreement—he knows we live and love in the midst of great evil. This evil must be resisted, sometimes by violent means. All things being equal, he would like to see a world without violence. But all things are not equal, and he is not in the business of seeing the world as he'd like it to be.

The historical record of conservatism—not only as a political practice, which is not my primary concern here, but as a theoretical tradition—suggests otherwise. Far from being saddened, burdened, or vexed by violence, the conservative has been enlivened by it. I don't mean in a personal sense, though many a conservative, like Harold Macmillan quoted above or Winston Churchill quoted below, has expressed an unanticipated enthusiasm for violence. My concern is with ideas and argument rather than character or psychology. Violence, the conservative intellectual has maintained, is one of the experiences in life that makes us feel the most alive, and violence is an activity that makes life, well, lively.[3] Such arguments can be made nimbly—"Only the dead have seen the end of war," as Douglas MacArthur once put it[4]—or laboriously, as in the case of Treitschke:

> To the historian who lives in the world of will it is immediately clear that the demand for a perpetual peace is thoroughly reactionary; he sees that with war all movement, all growth, must be struck out of history. It has always been the tired, unintelligent, and enervated periods that have played with the dream of perpetual peace.[5]

Pithy or prolix, the case boils down to this: war is life, peace is death.

This belief can be traced back to Edmund Burke's *A Philosophical Enquiry into the Origin of Our Ideas of the Sublime and the Beautiful.* There Burke develops a view of the self desperately in need of negative stimuli of the sort provided by pain and danger, which Burke associates with the sublime. The sublime is most readily found in two political forms: hierarchy and violence. But for reasons that shall become clear, the conservative—again, consistent with Burke's arguments—often favors the latter over the former. Rule may be sublime, but violence is more sublime. Most sublime of all is when the two are fused, when violence is performed for the sake of creating, defending, or recovering a regime of domination and rule. But as Burke warned, it's always best to enjoy pain and danger at a remove. Distance and obscurity enhance sublimity; nearness and illumination diminish it. Counterrevolutionary violence may be the Everest of conservative experience, but one should view it from afar. Get too close to the mountaintop, and the air becomes thin, the view clouded. At the end of every conservative discourse on violence, then, lies a waiting disappointment.

The Sublime and the Beautiful begins on a high note, with a discussion of curiosity, which Burke identifies as "the first and simplest emotion." The curious roam "from place to place to hunt out something new." Their sights are fixed, their attention rapt. Then the world turns gray. They begin to stumble across the same things, "with less and less of any agreeable effect." Novelty diminishes: how much, really, is there new in the world? Curiosity "exhausts" itself. Enthusiasm and engagement give way to "loathing and weariness."[6] Burke moves on to pleasure and pain, which are supposed to transform the quest for novelty into experiences more sustaining and profound. But rather than a genuine additive to curiosity, pleasure offers more of the same: a moment's enthusiasm, followed by dull malaise. "When it has run its career," Burke says, pleasure "sets us down very nearly where it found us." Any kind of pleasure "quickly satisfies; and when it is over, we relapse into indifference."[7] Quieter enjoyments, less intense than pleasure, are equally soporific. They generate complacency; we "give ourselves over to indolence and inaction."[8] Burke turns to imitation as yet another force of outward propulsion. Through imitation, we learn manners and mores, develop opinions, and are civilized. We bring ourselves to the world, and the world is brought to us. But imitation contains its own narcotic. Imitate others too much and we cease to better ourselves. We follow the person in front of us "and so on in an eternal circle." In a world of imitators, "there never could be any improvement." Such "men must remain as brutes do, the same at the end that they are at this day, and that they were in the beginning of the world."[9]

Curiosity leads to weariness, pleasure to indifference, enjoyment to torpor, and imitation to stagnation. So many doors of the psyche open onto this space of inertial gloom we might well conclude that it lurks not at the edge but at the center of the human condition. Here, in this dark courtyard of the self, all action ceases, creating an ideal environment for "melancholy, dejection, despair, and self-murder."[10] Even love, the most outward of raptures, carries the self back to a state of internal dissolution.[11] Suicide, it seems, is the inevitable fate awaiting anyone who takes pleasure in the world as it is.

For a certain type of conservative theorist, passages like these pose something of a challenge. Here is the inventor of the conservative tradition articulating a vision of the self dramatically at odds with the idealized self of conservative thought. The conservative self, as we have seen, claims to prefer "the familiar to the unknown . . . the tried to the untried, fact to mystery, the actual to the possible, the limited to the unbounded, the near to the distant, the sufficient to the superabundant, the convenient to the perfect, present laughter to utopian bliss."[12] He is partial to things as they are not because he finds things just or good, but because he finds them familiar. He knows them and is attached to them. He wishes neither to lose them nor to have them taken away. Enjoying what he has, rather than acquiring something better, is his highest good. But should the self of *The Sublime and the Beautiful* be assured of his attachments and familiars, he would quickly find himself confronting the specter of his own extinction, more than likely at his own hand.

Perhaps it is this lethal ennui, lurking just beneath the surface of conservative discourse, that explains the failure of the conservative politician to follow the lead of the conservative theorist. Far from embracing the cause of quiet enjoyments and secure attachments, the conservative politician has consistently opted for an activism of the not-yet and the will-be. Ronald Reagan's first inaugural address was a paean to the power of dreams: not small dreams but big, heroic dreams, of progress and betterment, and not dreams for their own sake, but dreams as a necessary and vital prod to action. Three months later, in an address before Congress, Reagan drove the point home with a quote from Carl Sandburg: "Nothing happens unless first a dream." And nothing happening, or too few things happening, or things not happening quickly enough, is what the conservative in politics dislikes. Reagan could scarcely contain his impatience with the dithering of politicians: "The old and comfortable way is to shave a little here and add a little there. Well, that's not acceptable anymore." Old and comfortable was the indictment, no "half-measures" the verdict.[13]

Reagan was hardly the first conservative to act for the sake of the invisible and the ideal as against the material and the real. In his acceptance speech to the 1964 Republican National Convention,

Barry Goldwater could find no more potent charge to level at the welfare state than that it had made a great nation "becalmed." Thanks to the New Deal, the United States had lost its "brisk pace" and was now "plodding along." Calm, slow, and plodding are usually welcomed by the conservative theorist as signs of present bliss. But to the conservative politician, they are evils. He must declare war, rallying his armies against the listless and the languid with talk of "causes," "struggle," "enthusiasm," and "devotion."[14]

[margin note: interesting]

That crusading zeal is not peculiar to American conservatism. It is found in Europe as well, even in England, the land that made moderation the moniker of conservatism. "Whoever won a battle," scoffed Margaret Thatcher, "under the banner 'I stand for Consensus'?"[15] And then there is Winston Churchill, traveling to Cuba in 1895 to report on the Spanish war against Cuban independence.[16] Ruminating on the disappointments of his generation—latecomers to the Empire, they were deprived of the opportunity for imperial conquest (as opposed to imperial administration)—he arrived in Havana. This is what he had to say (looking back on the experience in 1930):

[margin note: What would he say about Trump?]

> The minds of this generation, exhausted, brutalized, mutilated and bored by War, may not understand the delicious yet tremulous sensations with which a young British Officer bred in the long peace approached for the first time an actual theatre of operations. When first in the dim light of early morning I saw the shores of Cuba rise and define themselves from dark-blue horizons, I felt as if I sailed with Long John Silver and first gazed on Treasure Island. Here was a place where real things were going on. Here was a scene of vital action. Here was a place where anything might happen. Here was a place where something would certainly happen. Here I might leave my bones.[17]

Whatever the relationship between theory and practice in the conservative tradition, it is clear from *The Sublime and the Beautiful* that if the self is to survive and flourish it must be aroused by an experience more vital and bracing than pleasure or enjoyment. Pleasure and enjoyment act like beauty, as we saw in chapter 2, "relaxing the solids of the whole system."[18] That system, however, must be made taut and tense. The mind must be quickened, the body exerted. Otherwise, the system will soften and atrophy, and ultimately die.

What most arouses this heightened state of being is the confrontation with non-being. Life and health are pleasurable and enjoyable, and that is what is wrong with them: "they make no such impression" on the self because "we were not made to acquiesce in life and health." Pain and danger, by contrast, are "emissaries" of death, the "king of terrors." They are sources of the sublime, "the strongest"—most powerful, most affecting—"emotion which the mind is capable of feeling."[19] Pain and danger, in other words, are generative experiences of the self.

That is so because pain and danger have the contradictory effect of minimizing and maximizing our sense of self. When sensing pain or danger, our mind "is so entirely filled with its object, that it cannot entertain any other." The "motions" of our soul "are suspended," as harm and the fears it arouses "rush in upon the mind." In the face of these fears, "the mind is hurried out of itself." When we experience the sublime, we feel ourselves evacuated, overwhelmed by an external object of tremendous power and threat. Everything that gave us a sense of internal being and vitality ceases to exist. The external is all, we are nothing. God is a good example, and the ultimate expression, of the sublime: As Burke wrote, "Whilst we contemplate so vast an object, under the arm, as it were, of almighty power, and invested upon every side with omnipresence, we shrink into the minuteness of our own nature, and are, in a manner, annihilated before him."[20]

Paradoxically, we also feel our existence to an extent we never have felt it before. Seized by terror, our "attention" is roused and our "faculties" are "driven forward, as it were, on their guard." We are pulled out of ourselves. We are cognizant of the immediate terrain and our presence upon it. Before, we barely noticed ourselves or our surroundings. Now we spill out of ourselves, inhabiting not only our bodies and minds but also the space around us. We feel "a sort of swelling"—a sense that we are greater, our perimeter extends further—that "is extremely grateful to the human mind." But this "swelling," Burke reminds us, "is never more perceived, nor operates with more force, than when without danger we are conversant with terrible objects."[21]

In the face of the sublime, the self is annihilated, occupied, crushed, overwhelmed; in the face of the sublime, the self is heightened, aggrandized, magnified. Whether the self can truly occupy such opposing, almost irreconcilable, poles of experience at the same time—it is this contradiction, the oscillation between wild extremes that generates a strong and strenuous sense of self. As Burke writes, intense light resembles intense darkness not only because it blinds the eye and thus approximates darkness, but also because both are extremes. And extremes, particularly opposing extremes, are sublime because sublimity "in all things abhors mediocrity."[22] The extremity of opposing sensations, the savage swing from being to nothingness, makes for the most intense experience of selfhood.*

---

* This fraught account of human nature also sheds light on Burke's view of the relationship of history to the self. Readers of Burke often assimilate his theory of the relationship between history and the self to a vaguely communitarian position, which holds that history, culture, and inheritance make us who we are. We might call this a root theory of identity, in which the past is the soil and seed of our personhood, the condition of our agency without which we

The question for us, which Burke neither poses nor answers, is: What kind of political form entails this simultaneity of—or oscillation between—self-aggrandizement and self-annihilation? One possibility would be hierarchy, with its twin requirements of submission and domination; the other is violence, particularly warfare, with its rigid injunction to kill or be killed. Not coincidentally, both are of great significance to conservatism as a theoretical tradition and a historical practice.

Rousseau and John Adams are not usually thought of as ideological bedfellows, but on one point they agreed: social hierarchies persist because they ensure that everyone, save those at the very bottom and the very top, enjoys the opportunity to rule and be ruled in turn. Not, to be sure, in the Aristotelian sense of self-governance, but in the feudal sense of reciprocal governance: each person dominates someone below him in exchange for submitting to someone above him. "Citizens only allow themselves to be oppressed to the degree that they are carried away by blind ambition," writes Rousseau. "Since they pay more attention to what is

would be stumbling in the dark, unable to find our way. But this interpretation misses what's most interesting in Burke's account of our historical being. Far from situating an integrated self in the warm and loamy soil of a nurturing history, Burke's moral psychology demonstrates that, for him, history is a more disruptive presence. This is how he describes things in *Reflections on the Revolution in France*:

> Our political system is placed in a just correspondence and symmetry with the order of the world, and with the mode of existence decreed to a permanent body composed of transitory parts; wherein, by the disposition of a stupendous wisdom, moulding together the great mysterious incorporation of the human race, the whole, at one time, is never old, or middle-aged, or young, but in a condition of unchangeable constancy, moves on through the varied tenour of perpetual decay, fall, renovation, and progression. Thus, by preserving the method of nature in the conduct of the state, in

below them than to what is above, domination becomes dearer to them than independence, and they consent to wear chains so that they may in turn give them to others. It is very difficult to reduce to obedience anyone who does not seek to command."[23] The aspirant and the authoritarian are not opposing types: the will to rise precedes the will to bow. More than thirty years later, Adams would write that every man longs "to be observed, considered, esteemed, praised, beloved, and admired."[24] To be praised, one must be seen, and the best way to be seen is to elevate oneself above one's circle. Even the American democrat, Adams reasoned, would rather rule over an inferior than dispossess a superior. His passion is for supremacy, not equality, and so long as he is assured an audience of lessers, he will be content with his lowly status:

> Not only the poorest mechanic, but the man who lives upon common charity, nay the common beggars in the streets . . . court a set of admirers, and plume themselves on that superiority which they have, or fancy they have, over some others. . . . When a wretch could no longer attract the

what we improve we are never wholly new; in what we retain, we are never wholly obsolete.

At each and every moment, writes Burke, the polity we are a part of inhabits three modes of time: past, present, and future. That polity, and the self that comprises a part of it, is not comfortably situated in time; it is distended by time. Temporal multiplicity and fragmentation—not integration and rootedness—are the essence of our experience. Flux and fluidity haunt the Burkean polity and the Burkean self, making for the kind of sublimity that Burke believes is necessary to sustain the self in the face of its ever present and irrepressible drive toward death. History, in short, is not the root of our identity, making us who we are; it is the contradictory poles of our experience, forever pushing and pulling us in opposite directions. History makes it possible for us to feel, however fleetingly, the potential density and perimeter of our being.

notice of a man, woman or child, he must be respectable in the eyes of his dog. "Who will love me then?" was the pathetic reply of one, who starved himself to feed his mastiff, to a charitable passenger who advised him to kill or sell the animal.[25]

One can see in these descriptions of social hierarchy lineaments of the sublime: annihilated from above, aggrandized from below, the self is magnified and miniaturized by its involvement in the practice of rule. But here's the catch: once we actually are assured of our power over another being, says Burke, our inferior loses her capacity to harm or threaten us. She loses her sublimity. "Strip" a creature "of its ability to hurt," and "you spoil it of every thing sublime."[26] Lions, tigers, panthers, and rhinoceroses are sublime not because they are magnificent specimens of strength but because they can and will kill us. Oxen, horses, and dogs are also strong but lack the instinct to kill or have had that instinct suppressed. They can be made to serve us and in the case of dogs even love us. Because such creatures, however strong, cannot threaten or harm us, they are incapable of sublimity. They are objects of

Burke also sees in the past a great weight. But far from intimating some kind of plodding traditionalism or conventionalism, that weight is also suggestive of the sublime:

Always acting as if in the presence of canonized forefathers, the spirit of freedom, leading in itself to misrule and excess, is tempered with an awful gravity. The idea of a liberal descent inspires us with a sense of habitual native dignity, which prevents that upstart insolence almost inevitably adhering to and disgracing those who are first acquirers of any distinction. By this means our liberty becomes a noble freedom. It carries an imposing and majestic aspect. It has a pedigree, and illustrating ancestors. It has its bearings, and its ensigns armorial. It has its gallery of portraits; its monumental inscriptions; its records, evidences, and titles.

This is not a simple theory of history's constraints. For Burke, history does not limit our freedom; its constraints enlarge and magnify our freedom. They contempt, contempt being "the attendant on a strength that is subservient and innoxious."[27]

We have continually about us animals of a strength that is considerable, but not pernicious. Amongst these we never look for the sublime: it comes upon us in the gloomy forest, and in the howling wilderness. . . . Whenever strength is only useful, and employed for our benefit or our pleasure, then it is never sublime; for nothing can act agreeably to us, that does not act in conformity to our will; but to act agreeably to our will, it must be subject to us; and therefore can never be the cause of a grand and commanding conception.[28]

At least one-half, then, of the experience of social hierarchy— not the experience of being ruled, which carries the possibility of being destroyed, humiliated, threatened, or harmed by one's superior, but the experience of easily ruling another—is incompatible with, and indeed weakens, the sublime. Confirmed of our power, we are lulled into the same ease and comfort, undergo the same inward melting, we experience while in the throes of pleasure. The assurance of rule is as debilitating as the passion of love.

give our freedom depth, majesty, grandeur, awe—"an awful gravity." The weight of the past does not weigh down on the present; it gives weight to a present that might otherwise be weightless. Through that weight, the present—and the small selves of that present—acquires largeness, profundity, extent.

Rather than securing for us an identity, without which we would be at sea, history is the source of sublimity, of dissonant experience and agonistic passion, without which we would be dead. Not because history is the secure ground of everyday experience but because it subverts the secure ground of everyday experience. The real threat lurking beneath the revolutionary assault on history, to Burke's mind, is not anarchy or disorder; it's weightlessness. (Burke, *Reflections on the Revolution in France*, ed. J.C.D. Clark [Stanford, Calif.: Stanford University Press, 2001], 184–185.)

Burke's intimations about the perils of long-established rule reflect a surprising strain within conservatism: a persistent, if unacknowledged, discomfort with power that has ripened and matured, authority that has grown comfortable and secure. Beginning with Burke himself, conservatives have expressed a deep unease about ruling classes so assured of their place in the sun that they lose their capacity to rule: their will to power dissipates; the muscles and intelligence of their command attenuate.

Joseph de Maistre was less tactful than Burke in his condemnations of the Old Regime, perhaps because he took its failings more personally. Long before the Revolution, he claims, the leadership of the Old Regime had been confused and bewildered. Naturally, the ruling classes were unable to comprehend, much less resist, the onslaught unleashed against them. Impotence, physical and cognitive, was—and remains—the Old Regime's great sin. The aristocracy cannot understand; it cannot act. Some portion of the nobility may be well meaning, but they cannot see their projects through. They are foppish and foolish. They have virtue but not *virtú*. The aristocracy "fails ridiculously in everything it undertakes." The clergy has been corrupted by wealth and luxury. The monarchy consistently has shown that it lacks the will "to punish" that is the hallmark of every real sovereign.[29] Faced with such decadence, the inevitable outgrowth of centuries in power, Maistre concludes it is a good thing the counterrevolution has not yet triumphed (he is writing in 1797). The Old Regime needs several more years in the wilderness if it is to shed the corrupting influences of its once beautiful life:

The restoration of the throne would mean a sudden relaxation of the driving force of the state. The black magic working at the moment would disappear like mist before the sun. Kindness, clemency, justice, all the gentle and peaceful virtues, would suddenly reappear and would bring with them a general meekness of character, a certain cheerfulness entirely opposed to the rigours of the revolutionary regime.[30]

A century later, a similar case would be made by Georges Sorel against the *belle époque*. Sorel is not usually seen as an emblematic figure of the right—then again, even Burke's conservatism remains a subject of dispute[31]—and, indeed, his greatest work, *Reflections on Violence*, is often thought of as a contribution, albeit minor, to the Marxist tradition. Yet Sorel's beginnings are conservative and his endings proto-fascist, and even in his Marxist phase his primary worry is decadence and vitality rather than exploitation and justice. The criticisms he lodges against the French ruling classes at the end of the nineteenth century are not dissimilar to those made by Burke and Maistre at the end of the eighteenth. He even makes the comparison explicit: the French bourgeoisie, Sorel writes, "has become almost as stupid as the nobility of the eighteenth century." They are "an ultra-civilized aristocracy that demands to be left in peace." Once, the bourgeoisie was a race of warriors. "Bold captains," they were "creators of new industries" and "discovers of unknown lands." They "directed gigantic enterprises," inspired by that "conquering, insatiable and pitiless spirit" that laid railroads, subdued continents, and made a world economy. Today, they are timid and cowardly, refusing to take the most elemental steps to defend their own interests against unions, socialists, and the left. Rather than unleash violence against striking workers, they surrender to the workers' threat of violence. They lack the ardor, the fire in the belly, of their ancestors. It is difficult not to conclude that "the bourgeoisie is condemned to death and that its disappearance is only a matter of time."[32]

Carl Schmitt formalized Sorel's contempt for the weaknesses of the ruling classes into an entire theory of politics. According to Schmitt, the bourgeois was as he was—risk-averse, selfish, uninterested in bravery or violent death, desirous of peace and security—because capitalism was his calling and liberalism his faith. Neither provided him with a good reason to die for the state. In fact, both gave him good reasons, indeed an entire vocabulary, not to die for the state. Interest, freedom, profit, rights, property, individualism, and other such words had created one of the most self-absorbed ruling classes in history, a class that enjoyed privilege but did not feel itself obliged to defend that privilege. After all, the premise of liberal democracy was the separation of politics from economics and culture. One could pursue profit, at someone else's expense, and think freely, no matter how subversive the thoughts, without disrupting the balance of power. The bourgeoisie, however, were confronting an enemy that very much understood the connections between ideas, money, and power, that economic arrangements and intellectual arguments were the stuff of political combat. Marxists got the friend-enemy distinction, which is constitutive of politics; the bourgeoisie did not.[33] The spirit of Hegel used to reside in Berlin; it has long since "wandered to Moscow."[34]

Sorel identified one exception to this rule of capitalist decadence: the robber barons of the United States. In the Carnegies and the Goulds of American industry, Sorel thought he saw "the indomitable energy, the audacity based on an accurate appreciation of strength, the cold calculation of interests, which are the qualities of great generals and great capitalists." Unlike the pampered bourgeoisie of France and Britain, the millionaires of Pittsburgh and Pittston "lead to the end of their lives a galley-slave existence without ever thinking of leading a nobleman's life, as the Rothschilds do."[35]

Sorel's spiritual counterpart across the Atlantic, Teddy Roosevelt, was not so sanguine about American industrialists and financiers. The capitalist, Roosevelt declared, sees his country as a "till," always weighing the "the honor of the nation and the glory of the flag" against a "temporary interruption of money-making." He is not "willing to lay down his life for little things" like the defense of the nation. He cares "only whether shares rise or fall in value."[36] He shows no interest in great affairs of state, domestic or international, unless they impinge upon his own. It was no accident, Roosevelt claimed, perhaps with a nod to Carnegie, that such men opposed the great imperial expedition that was the Spanish-American War.[37] Complacent and comfortable, assured of their riches by the success of the labor wars of previous decades and the election of 1896, these were not men who could be counted upon to defend the nation or even themselves. "We may some day have bitter cause," Roosevelt declared, "to realize that a rich nation which is slothful, timid, or unwieldy is an easy prey" for other, more martial peoples. The danger facing a ruling class, and a ruling nation, that has grown "skilled in commerce and finance" is that it "loses the hard fighting virtues."[38]

Roosevelt was hardly the last American conservative to worry about ruling classes gone soft and hierarchies overripe with power. Nor was he the first. Throughout the 1830s, we have seen, as the abolitionists began pressing their cause, John C. Calhoun complained that his fellow slaveholders had lost the will to rule.[39] Barry Goldwater likewise expressed contempt for the Republican Establishment.[40] And throughout the 1990s—to jump ahead by another three decades— one could hear Roosevelt's heirs on the right direct the same venom against the American capitalist at the masters of the universe on Wall Street and the geeky entrepreneurs of Silicon Valley.[41]

If the ruling class is to be vigorous and robust, the conservative has concluded, its members must be tested, exercised, and challenged. Not just their bodies, but also their minds, even their souls. Echoing Milton—"I cannot praise a fugitive and cloistered virtue, unexercised and unbreathed, that never sallies out and sees her adversary, but slinks out of the race. . . . That which purifies us is trial, and trial is by what is contrary"[42]—Burke believes that adversity and difficulty, the confrontation with affliction and suffering, make for stronger, more virtuous beings.

> The great virtues turn principally on dangers, punishments, and troubles, and are exercised rather in preventing mischiefs, than in dispensing favours; and are therefore not lovely, though highly venerable. The subordinate turn on reliefs, gratifications, and indulgences; and are therefore more lovely, though inferior in dignity. Those persons who creep into the hearts of most people, who are chosen as the companions of their softer hours, and their reliefs from care and anxiety, are never persons of shining qualities, nor strong virtues.[43]

But where Milton and other like-minded republicans believe that impurity and corruption await the complacent and the comfortable, Burke espies the more terrifying specter of dissipation, degeneration, and death. If the powerful are to continue to be powerful, if they are to remain alive at all, their power, indeed the credibility of their own existence, must be continuously challenged, threatened, and defended.

One of the more arresting—though I hope by now intelligible—features of conservative discourse is the fascination, indeed appreciation, one finds there for the conservative's enemies on the left, particularly for their use of violence against the conservative and his allies. From the perspective of the Burkean sublime, however, the conservative's argument—at least in the hands of a theorist like Maistre—only goes so far. The Revolution rejuvenates the Old Regime by forcing it from power and purifying the people through violence. It delivers a clarifying shock to the system. But Maistre never imagines, never specifically discusses, the revivifying effect that wresting power back from the Revolution might have on the leaders of the Old Regime. And indeed, once he gets around to describing how he thinks the counterrevolution will occur, the final battle turns out to be an anticlimax, with scarcely a shot fired at all. "How Will the Counter-Revolution Happen if it Comes?" Maistre asks, as we saw in the previous chapter. "Four or five persons, perhaps, will give France a king." Not exactly the stuff of a virile, transformed ruling class, battling its way back to power.[44]

Maistre never contemplated the restorative possibilities of hand-to-hand combat between the Old Regime and the Revolution; for this one must turn to Sorel. And while Sorel's allegiances in the war between the rulers and the ruled of the late nineteenth century are more ambiguous than Maistre's, his account of the effect of the violence of the ruled upon the rulers is not. The French bourgeoisie has lost its fighting spirit, Sorel claims, but that spirit is alive and well among the workers. Their battlefield is the workplace, their weapon is the general strike, and their aim is the overthrow of the state. It is the last that most impresses Sorel, for the desire to overthrow the state signals just how unconcerned the workers are about "the material profits of conquest." Not only do they not seek higher wages and other improvements in their well-being; instead they have set their sights on the most improbable of goals—overthrowing the state by a general strike. It is that improbability, the distance between means and ends, that makes the violence of the proletariat so glorious. The proletarians are like Homeric warriors, absorbed in the grandeur of the battle and indifferent to the aims of the war: Who really has ever overthrown a state by a general strike? Theirs is a violence for its own sake, without concern for costs, benefits, and the calculations in between.[45] As Ernst Jünger wrote a generation later, it "is not what we fight for but how we fight."[46]

But what grips Sorel is not the proletariat but the rejuvenating effects their violence might have on the bourgeoisie. Can the violence of the general strike "give back to the bourgeoisie an ardour which is extinguished?" Certainly the vigor of the proletariat might reawaken the bourgeoisie to its own interests and the threats its withdrawal from politics has posed to those interests. More tantalizing to Sorel, however, is the possibility that the violence of workers will "restore to [the bourgeoisie] the warlike qualities it formerly possessed," forcing the "capitalist class to remain ardent in the industrial struggle." Through the struggle against the proletariat, in other words, the bourgeoisie may recover its ferocity and ardor. And ardor is everything. From ardor alone, from that splendid indifference to reason and self-interest, an entire civilization, drowning in materialism and complacency, will be reawakened. A ruling class, threatened by violence from the ruled, roused to its own taste for violence—that is the promise of the civil war in France.[47]

For the conservative, no matter how modulated or moderate, a rejuvenation of the ruling class has always been the promise of civil war. For between the easy cases of a Catholic reactionary like Maistre and a proto-fascist like Sorel stands the more difficult but ultimately more revealing example of Alexis de Tocqueville. His drift from the moderation of the July Monarchy to the revanchism of 1848 demonstrates how easily and inexorably the Burkean conservative will swing from the beautiful to the sublime, how the music of prudence and moderation gives way to the march of violence and vitriol.[48]

Publicly presenting himself as the consummate realist, discriminating and judicious, with little patience for enthusiasm of any sort, Tocqueville was actually a closet romantic. He confessed to his brother that he shared their father's "devouring impatience," his "need for lively and recurring sensations." Reason, he said, "has always been for me like a cage," behind which he would "gnash [his] teeth." He longed for "the sight of combat." Looking back on the French Revolution, which he missed (he was born in 1805), he lamented the end of the Terror, claiming that "men thus crushed can not only no longer attain great virtues, but they seem to have become almost incapable of great crimes." Even Napoleon, scourge of conservatives, moderates, and liberals everywhere, earned Tocqueville's admiration as the "most extraordinary being who has appeared in the world for many centuries." Who, by contrast, could find inspiration in the parliamentary politics of the July Monarchy, that "little democratic and bourgeois pot of soup"?

Yet once he set upon a career in politics, it was into that little bourgeois pot of soup that Tocqueville jumped. Predictably, it was not to his taste. Tocqueville may have mouthed the words of moderation, compromise, and the rule of law, but they did not move him. Without the threat of revolutionary violence, politics was simply not the grand drama he imagined it had been between 1789 and 1815. "Our fathers observed such extraordinary things that compared with them all of our works seem commonplace." The politics of moderation and compromise produced moderation and compromise; it did not produce politics, at least not as Tocqueville understood the term. During the 1830s and 1840s, "what was most wanting . . . was political life itself." There was "no battlefield for contending parties to meet upon." Politics had been "deprived" of "all originality, of all reality, and therefore of all genuine passions."

Then came 1848. Tocqueville didn't support the Revolution in France. Indeed, he was among its most vociferous opponents. He voted for the full suspension of civil liberties, which he happily announced was done "with even more energy than had been done under the Monarchy." He welcomed talk of a dictatorship— to protect the very regime he had spent the better part of two decades disparaging. And he loved it all: the violence, the counter-violence, the battle. Defending moderation against radicalism, Tocqueville was given a chance to use radical means for moderate ends, and it is not entirely clear which of the two most stirred him.

> Let me say, then, that when I came to search carefully into the depths of my own heart, I discovered, with some surprise, a certain sense of relief, a sort of gladness mingled with all the griefs and fears to which the Revolution had given rise. I suffered from this terrible event for my country, but clearly not for myself; on the contrary, I seemed to breathe more freely than before the catastrophe. I had always felt myself stifled in the atmosphere of the parliamentary world which had just been destroyed: I had found it full of disappointments, both where others and where I myself was concerned.

A self-styled poet of the tentative, the subtle, and the complex, Tocqueville burned with enthusiasm upon waking up to a world divided into two camps. Timid parliaments sowed a gray confusion; civil war forced upon the nation a bracing clarity of black and white. "There was no field left for uncertainty of mind: on this side lay the salvation of the country; on that, its destruction. . . . The road seemed dangerous, it is true, but my mind is so constructed that it is less afraid of danger than of doubt." For this member of the ruling class, sublimity welling up from the violence of the lower orders offered an opportunity to escape the stifling beauty of life on the bourgeois Parnassus.

Francis Fukuyama is perhaps the most thoughtful of recent writers to pursue this conservative line of argument about violence. Unlike Maistre, however, or Tocqueville and Sorel—all of whom wrote in the midst of battle, when the outcome was unclear—Fukuyama writes in *The End of History and the Last Man* from the vantage of victory. It is 1992, and the capitalist classes have beaten their socialist opponents in the long civil war of the short twentieth century. It is not a pretty sight, at least not for Fukuyama. For the revolutionary was one of the few thymotic men of the twentieth century. Thymotic man is like Sorel's worker: he who risks his life for the sake of an improbable principle, who is unconcerned with his own material interests and cares only for honor, glory, and the values for which he fights. After a strange but brief homage to the Bloods and the Crips as thymotic men, Fukuyama looks back fondly to men of purpose and power like Lenin, Trotsky, and Stalin, "striving for something purer and higher" and possessed of "greater than usual hardness, vision, ruthlessness, and intelligence." By virtue of their refusal to accommodate themselves to the reality of their times, they were the "most free and therefore the most human of beings." But somehow or other, these men and their successors lost the civil war of the twentieth century, almost inexplicably, to the forces of "Economic Man." For Economic Man is "the true *bourgeois*." Such a man would never be "willing to walk in front of a tank or confront a line of soldiers" for any cause, even his own. Yet Economic Man is the victor, and far from rejuvenating or restoring him to his primal powers, the war seems only to have made him more bourgeois. Conservative that he is, Fukuyama can only chafe at the triumph of Economic Man and "the life of rational consumption" he has brought about, a life that is "in the end, *boring*."[49]

Far from being exceptional, Fukuyama's disappointment is emblematic. "The aims of battle and the fruits of conquest are never the same," E. M. Forster observed in *A Passage to India*. "The latter have their value and only the saint rejects them, but their hint of immortality vanishes as soon as they are held in the hand."[50] Deep within the conservative discourse on violence lurks an element of anticlimax that cannot be contained. While the conservative turns to violence as a way of liberating himself, or the ruling classes, from the deadening ennui and softening atrophy that comes with power, virtually every encounter with actual violence entails disillusion and deflation.

Recall Teddy Roosevelt, brooding on the materialism and weakness of America's capitalist classes. Where, he wondered, could one find an example of the "strenuous life"—the thrill of difficulty and danger, the strife that made for progress—in contemporary America? Perhaps in the foreign wars and conquests America had undertaken at the end of the century. Yet even here Roosevelt encountered frustration. Though his reports from the Spanish-American War were filled with bravery and bravado, a careful reading of his adventures in Cuba suggests that his exploits there were a fiasco. Each of the famous charges Roosevelt led up or down a hill was bathetic. The first culminated with him seeing exactly two Spanish soldiers felled by his men: "These were the only Spaniards I actually saw fall to aimed shots by any one of my men," he wrote, "with the exception of two guerillas in trees." The second found him leading an army that neither heard nor followed him. So it was with a grim appreciation that he recited the dyspeptic comments of one of the army's leaders in Cuba, a certain General Wheeler, who "had been through too much heavy fighting in the Civil War to regard the present fight as very serious."[51]

In the bloody occupations that followed the Spanish-American War, however, Roosevelt thought he saw the true bliss it was in that dawn to be alive. Roosevelt was sure that America's occupations of the Philippines and elsewhere were as close to a replay of the Civil War—that noble crusade of unsullied virtue—as he and his countrymen were ever likely to see. "We of this generation do not have to face a task such as that our fathers faced," he declared in 1899, "and woe to us if we fail to perform them! . . . We cannot avoid the responsibilities that confront us in Hawaii, Cuba,

Porto [*sic*] Rico, and the Philippines." Here—in the islands of the Caribbean and the Pacific—was the confluence of blood and purpose he had been searching for his entire life. The task of imperial uplift, of educating the natives in "the cause of civilization," was arduous and violent, imposing a mission upon America that would take years, God willing, to fulfill. If the imperial mission succeeded—and even if it failed—it would create a genuine ruling class in America, hardened and made strenuous by battle, nobler and less grubby-minded than Carnegie's minions.[52]

It was a beautiful dream. But it too could not bear the weight of reality. Though Roosevelt hoped the men who ruled the Philippines would be "chosen for signal capacity and integrity," running "the provinces on behalf of the entire nation from which they come, and for the sake of the entire people to which they go," he worried that America's colonial occupiers would come from the same class of selfish financiers and industrialists that had driven him abroad in the first place. And so his paeans to imperialism ended on a sour note of warning, even doom. "If we permit our public service in the Philippines to become the prey of the spoils politicians, if we fail to keep it up to the highest standard, we shall be guilty of an act, not only of wickedness, but of weak and short-sighted folly, and we shall have begun to tread the path which was trod by Spain to her own bitter humiliation."[53]

But if his dream ended badly, Roosevelt at least had the advantage of being able to say that he always suspected it would. The same could not be said of the Fascists of Italy, whose self-deception about the wresting of power from the left persisted for decades, testifying to an inability on the right to confront its own disappointment. For years, the Fascists celebrated the 1922 March on Rome as the violent and glorious triumph of will over adversity. October 28, the day of the Blackshirts' arrival in Rome, became a national holiday; it was declared the first day of the Fascist New

Year upon the introduction of the new calendar in 1927. The story of Mussolini's arrival in particular—wearing the proverbial black shirt—was repeated with awe. "Sire," he supposedly said to King Victor Emmanuel III, "forgive my attire. I come from the battlefields." In actual fact, Mussolini traveled by train overnight from Milan, where he had been conspicuously attending the theater, snoozing comfortably in the sleeping car. The only reason he even made it into Rome was that a timid establishment, led by the king, telephoned him in Milan with a request that he form a government. Barely a shot was fired, on either side.[54] Maistre could not have written it better.

We can see a similar phenomenon at play in the American war on terror. Though many have viewed the Bush administration and neoconservatism as departures from proper conservatism—the most recent statement of this thesis being Sam Tanenhaus's *The Death of Conservatism*[55]—the neocon project of imperial adventurism traces the Burkean arc of violence from beginning to end. As we shall see in chapter 9, the neoconservatives saw 9/11 and the war on terror as a chance to escape from the decadent and deadening peace and prosperity of the Clinton years, which they believed had weakened American society. Oozing in comfort, Americans—and more important their leaders—had supposedly lost the will, the desire, and ability, to govern the world. Then 9/11 happened, and suddenly it seemed as if they could.

That dream, of course, now lies in tatters, but one of its more idiosyncratic aspects is worth noting, for it presents a wrinkle in the long saga of conservative violence. According to many conservatives, one of the recent sources of American decadence, traceable to the Warren Court and the rights revolutions of the 1960s, is the liberal obsession with the rule of law. This obsession, in the eyes of the conservative, takes many forms: the insistence on due process in criminal procedure; a partiality to litigation over legislation; an emphasis on diplomacy and international law over war; attempts to restrain executive power through judicial and legislative oversight. However unrelated these symptoms may seem, conservatives see in them a single disease: a culture of rules and laws slowly disabling and devitalizing the blond beast of prey that is American power. These are signs of a Nietzschean unhealthiness, and 9/11 was the inevitable result.

If another 9/11 is to be prevented, that culture of rights and rules must be repudiated and reversed. As the reporting of Seymour Hersh and Jane Mayer made clear, however, the war on terror—with its push for torture, for overturning the Geneva Conventions, for illegal surveillance, for refusing the restrictions of international law, and for seeing terrorism through the lens of war rather than of crime and punishment—reflects as much, if not more, these conservative sensibilities and sensitivities as it does the actual facts of 9/11 and the need to prevent another attack.[56] "She's soft—too soft," says now-retired Lieutenant General Jerry Boykin about the United States, pre- and post-9/11. The way to make her hard is not merely to undertake difficult and strenuous military action but also to violate the rules—and the culture of rules—that made her soft in the first place. The United States must learn how to "live on the edge," says former NSA director Michael Hayden. "There's nothing we won't do, nothing we won't try," former CIA director George Tenet helpfully adds.[57]

The great irony of the war on terror is that far from emancipating the blond beast of prey, the war has made law, and lawyers, far more critical than one might imagine. As Mayer reports, the push for torture, unbridled executive power, the overthrow of the Geneva Conventions, and so on came not from the CIA or the military; the driving forces were lawyers in the White House and the Justice Department like David Addington and John Yoo. Far from Machiavellian virtuosos of transgressive violence, Addington and Yoo are fanatics about the law and insist on justifying their violence through the law. Lawyers, moreover, consistently oversee the actual practice of torture. As Tenet wrote in his memoir, "Despite what Hollywood might have you believe, in situations like this [the capture, interrogation, and torture of Al Qaeda logistics chief Abu Zubayda] you don't call in the tough guys; you call in the lawyers." Every slap on the face, every punch in the gut, every shake of the body—and much, much worse—must first be approved by higher-ups in the various intelligence agencies, inevitably in consultation with attorneys. Mayer compares the practice of torture to a game of "Mother, May I?" As one interrogator states, "Before you could lay a hand on him [the torture victim], you had to send a cable saying, 'He's uncooperative. Request permission to do X.' And permission would come, saying 'You're allowed to slap him one time in the belly with an open hand.' "[58]

Rather than free the blond beast to roam and prey as he wishes, the removal of the ban on torture and the suspension of the Geneva Conventions have made him, or at least the lawyers who hold his leash, more anxious. How far can he go? What can he do? Every act of violence, as this exchange between two Pentagon lawyers reveals, becomes a law school seminar:

What did "deprivation of light and auditory stimuli" mean? Could a prisoner be locked in a completely dark cell? If so, could he be kept there for a month? Longer? Until he went blind? What, precisely, did the authority to exploit phobias permit? Could a detainee be held in a coffin? What about using dogs? Rats? How far could an interrogator push this? Until a man went insane?[59]

Then there is the question of combining approved techniques of torture. May an interrogator withhold food from the prisoner and turn down the temperature of his cell at the same time? Does the multiplying effect of pains doubled and tripled cross a never-defined line?[60] As Orwell taught, the possibilities for cruelty and violence are as limitless as the imagination that dreams them up. But the armies and agencies of today's violence are vast bureaucracies, and vast bureaucracies need rules. Eliminating the rules does not Prometheus unbind; it just makes for more billable hours.

"No yielding. No equivocation. No lawyering this thing to death." That was George W. Bush's vow after 9/11 and his description of how the war on terror would be conducted. Like so many of Bush's other declarations, it turned out to be an empty promise. This thing was lawyered to death. But, and this is the critical point, far from minimizing state violence—which was the great fear of the neocons—lawyering has proven to be perfectly compatible with violence. In a war already swollen with disappointment and disillusion, the realization that inevitably follows—the rule of law can, in fact, authorize the greatest adventures of violence and death, thereby draining them of sublimity—must be, for the conservative, the greatest disillusion of all.

Had they been closer readers of Burke, the neoconservatives—like Fukuyama, Roosevelt, Sorel, Schmitt, Tocqueville, Maistre, Treitschke, and so many more on the American and European right—could have seen this disillusion coming. Burke certainly did. Even as he wrote of the sublime effects of pain and danger, he was careful to insist that should those pains and dangers "press too nearly" or "too close"—that is, should they become realities rather than fantasies, should they become "conversant about the present destruction of the person"—their sublimity would disappear. They would cease to be "delightful" and restorative and become simply terrible.[61] Burke's point was not merely that no one, in the end, really wants to die or that no one enjoys unwelcome, excruciating pain. It was that sublimity of whatever kind and source depends upon murkiness: get too close to anything, whether an object or experience, see and feel its full extent, and it loses its mystery and aura. It becomes familiar. A "great clearness" of the sort that comes from direct experience "is in some sort an enemy to all enthusiasms whatsoever."[62] "It is our ignorance of things that causes all our admiration, and chiefly excites our passions. Knowledge and acquaintance make the most striking causes affect but little."[63] "A clear idea," Burke concludes, "is therefore another name for a little idea."[64] Get to know anything, including violence, too well, and it loses whatever attribute—rejuvenation, transgression, excitement, awe— you ascribed to it when it was just an idea.

Earlier than most, Burke understood that if violence were to retain its sublimity, it had to remain a possibility, an object of fantasy—a horror movie, a video game, an essay on war. For the actuality (as opposed to the representation) of violence was at odds with the requirements of sublimity. Real, as opposed to imagined, violence entailed objects getting too close, bodies pressing too near, flesh upon flesh. Violence stripped the body of its veils; violence made its antagonists familiar to each other in a way they had never been before. Violence dispelled illusion and mystery, making things drab and dreary. That is why, in his discussion in the *Reflections* of the revolutionaries' abduction of Marie Antoinette, Burke takes such pains to emphasize her "almost naked" body and turns so effortlessly to the language of clothing—"the decent drapery of life," the "wardrobe of the moral imagination," "antiquated fashion," and so on—to describe the event.[65] The disaster of the revolutionaries' violence, for Burke, was not its cruelty; it was the unsought enlightenment.

Since 9/11, many have complained, and rightly so, about the failure of conservatives—or their sons and daughters—to fight the war on terror themselves. For those on the left, that failure is symptomatic of the class injustice of contemporary America. But there is an additional element to the story. So long as the war on terror remains an idea—a hot topic on the blogs, a provocative op-ed, an episode of 24—it is sublime. As soon as the war on terror becomes a reality, it can be as cheerless as a discussion of the tax code, as tedious as a trip to the DMV.

PART 2 Europe's Old Regimes

4

The First Counterrevolutionary

Revolution sent Thomas Hobbes into exile; counterrevolution sent him back. In 1640, parliamentary opponents of Charles I were denouncing anyone "preaching for absolute monarchy that the king may do what he list." Hobbes had recently finished writing *The Elements of Law*, which did just that. After the king's top adviser and a theologian arguing for unlimited royal power were both arrested, Hobbes decided it was time to go. Not waiting for his bags to be packed, he fled England for France.[1]

Eleven years and a civil war later, Hobbes fled France for England. This time, he was running from the royalists. As before, Hobbes had just finished a book. *Leviathan,* he would later explain, "fights on behalf of all kings and all those who under whatever name bear the rights of kings."[2] It was the second half of this claim, with its seeming indifference about the identity of the sovereign, that was now getting him into trouble. *Leviathan* justified, no, demanded, that men submit to any person or persons capable of protecting them from foreign attack and civil unrest. With the monarchy abolished and Oliver Cromwell's forces in control of England and providing for the people's safety, *Leviathan* seemed to suggest that everyone, including the defeated royalists, profess their allegiance to the Commonwealth. Versions of that argument had already gotten Anthony Ascham, ambassador for the Commonwealth, assassinated by royalist exiles in Spain. So when Hobbes learned that clergymen in France were trying to arrest him—*Leviathan* was also vehemently anti-Catholic, which offended the Queen Mother—he slipped out of Paris and made his way back to London.[3]

It's no accident that Hobbes fled his enemies and then his friends, for he was fashioning a political theory that shredded longstanding alliances. Rather than reject the revolutionary argument, he absorbed and transformed it. From its deepest categories and idioms he derived an uncompromising defense of the most hidebound form of rule. He sensed the centrifugal forces of early modern Europe—the priesthood of all believers; the democratic armies massing under the banner of ancient republican ideals; science and skepticism—and sought to channel them to a single center: a sovereign so terrible and benign as to make any challenge to such authority seem immoral and irrational. Not unlike the Italian Futurists, Hobbes put dissolution in the service of resolution. He was the first and, along with Nietzsche, the greatest philosopher of counterrevolution, a blender *avant la lettre* of cultural modernism and political reaction who understood that to defeat a revolution, you must become the revolution.

And how has he been treated by the right? Not well. T. S. Eliot (an adroit blender himself) called Hobbes "one of those extraordinary little upstarts whom the chaotic motions of the Renaissance tossed into an eminence which they hardly deserved."[4] Of the four twentieth-century political theorists identified by Perry Anderson as "The Intransigent Right"[5]—Leo Strauss, Carl Schmitt, Michael Oakeshott, and Friedrich Hayek—only Oakeshott saw in Hobbes a kindred spirit.[6] The rest viewed him as the source of a malignant liberalism, Jacobinism, or even Bolshevism.[7]

Orthodox custodians of the old regime often mistake the counterrevolutionary for the opposition. They can't grasp the alchemy of his argument. All they sense is what's there—a newfangled way of thinking that sounds dangerously like the revolutionary's— and what's not there: the traditional justification for authority. To the orthodox, the counterrevolutionary looks like a revolutionary. In their eyes that makes the counterrevolutionary a suspect, not a comrade. In this they are not entirely wrong. Neither left nor, conventionally speaking, right—one of Hayek's most famous pieces of writing is called "Why I Am Not a Conservative"[8]—the counterrevolutionary is a pastiche of incongruities, high and low, old and new, irony and faith. The counterrevolutionary attempts nothing less than to square the circle, making prerogative popular and remaking a regime that claims never to have been made in the first place (the old regime was, is, and will be; it is not made). These are tasks no other political movement must undertake. It's not that the counterrevolutionary is disposed to paradox; he's simply forced to straddle historical contradictions, for power's sake.

But why even bring Hobbes before the bar of conservatism, the right, and counterrevolution? After all, none of these terms came into circulation until the French Revolution or later, and most historians no longer believe the English Civil War was a revolution. The forces that overthrew the monarchy may have been looking for the Roman Republic or the ancient constitution. They may have wanted a reformation of religious manners or limitations on royal power. But a revolution lay nowhere in their sights. How could Hobbes have been a counterrevolutionary if there was no revolution for him to oppose?

Hobbes, for one, thought otherwise. In *Behemoth*, his most considered treatment of the issue, he firmly declared the English Civil War a revolution.[9] And though he meant by that term something like what the ancients meant—a cyclical process of regime change, more akin to the orbit of the planets than a great leap forward—Hobbes saw in the overthrow of the monarchy a zealous (and, to his mind, toxic) yearning for democracy, a firm desire to redistribute power to a greater number of men. That, for Hobbes, was the essence of the revolutionary challenge; and so it has remained ever since—whether in Russia in 1917, Flint in 1937, or Selma in 1965. That this democratic expansion was inspired by visions of the past rather than the future need not detain us any more than it did Hobbes—or Benjamin Constant or Karl Marx, for that matter, both of whom saw how easy it was for the French to make their revolution while (or even by) looking backward.[10]

Hobbes clearly opposed the "democraticals," as he called the parliamentary forces and their followers.[11] A considerable sum of his philosophical energy was expended in this opposition, and his greatest innovations derived from it.[12] His ultimate target was the democraticals' conception of liberty, their republican notion that individual freedom entailed men collectively governing themselves. Hobbes sought to unfasten the republican link between personal freedom and the possession of political power. He set out to argue that men could be free in an absolute monarchy—or at least no less free than they were in a republic or a democracy. It was "an epoch-making moment in the history of Anglophone political thought," says Quentin Skinner. The result was a novel account of liberty to which we remain indebted to this day.[13]

Every counterrevolutionary faces the same question: how to defend an old regime that has been or is being destroyed? The first impulse—to reiterate the regime's ancient truths—is usually the worst, for it is often those truths that got the regime into trouble in the first place. Either the world has so changed that these truths no longer command assent, or they have grown so pliable that they mutate into arguments for revolution. Either way, the counterrevolutionary must look elsewhere for materials from which to fashion his defense of the old regime. This need can put him at odds, as Hobbes came to realize, not only with the revolution, but also with the very regime he claims as his cause.

The monarchy's defenders in the first half of the seventeenth century offered two types of arguments, neither of which Hobbes could endorse. The first was the divine right of kings. A recent innovation—James I, Charles's father, was the major exponent in Britain—the doctrine held that the king was God's agent on earth (indeed, was rather like God on earth), that he was accountable only to God, and that he alone was authorized to govern and should not be restrained by the law, institutions, or the people. As Charles's adviser allegedly put it, "the king's little finger should be thicker than the loins of the law."[14]

While such absolutism appealed to Hobbes, the foundation of the theory was shaky. Most divine right theorists presumed what Hobbes and his contemporaries, particularly on the continent, believed no longer to exist: a teleology of human ends that mirrored the natural hierarchy of the universe and produced unassailable definitions of good and evil, just and unjust. After a century of bloodshed over the meaning of those terms and skepticism about the existence of a natural order or our ability to know it, defenses of divine right seemed neither credible nor reliable. With their dubious premises, they were just as likely to spark conflict as to settle it.

Arguably more troubling was that the theory depicted a political theater in which there were only two actors of any consequence—God and king—each performing for the other. Though Hobbes believed the sovereign should never share the stage with anyone, he was too attuned to the democratic distemper of his times not to notice that the theory neglected a third actor: the people. That was all well and good when the people were quiet and deferential, but during the 1640s a closet drama between God and the king was no longer viable. The people were onstage, demanding a leading role; they could not be ignored or given a bit part.

Changes in England, in short, had rendered divine right untenable. The challenge Hobbes faced was intricate: how to preserve the thrust of the theory (unquestioning submission to absolute, undivided power) while ditching its anachronistic premises. With his theory of consent, in which individuals contract with one another to create a sovereign with absolute power over them, and his theory of representation, in which the people are impersonated by the sovereign without his being obliged to them, Hobbes found his solution.

The theory of consent made no assumptions about the definition of good and evil, nor did it rely upon a natural hierarchy inherent in the universe, whose meaning must be apparent to all. To the contrary, the theory of consent presumed that men disagreed about such things; indeed, that they disagreed so violently that the only way they could pursue their conflicting goals and survive was to cede all of their power to the state and submit to it without protest or challenge. Protecting men from one another, the state guaranteed them the space and security to get on with their lives. When combined with Hobbes's account of representation, the theory of consent had an added advantage: though it gave all power to the sovereign, the people could still imagine themselves in his body, in every swing of his sword. The people created him; he represented them; to all intents and purposes, they were him. Except that they weren't: the people may have been the authors of Leviathan—Hobbes's infamous name for the sovereign, derived from the Book of Job—but like any author they had no control over their creation. It was an inspired move, characteristic of all great counterrevolutionary theories, in which the people become actors without roles, an audience that believes it is onstage.

The second argument offered in favor of the monarchy, the constitutional royalist position, had deeper roots in English thought and was therefore more difficult to counter. It held that England was a free society because royal power was limited by the common law or shared with Parliament. That combination of the rule of law and shared sovereignty, claimed Sir Walter Raleigh, was what distinguished the free subjects of the king from the benighted slaves of despots in the East.[15] It was this argument and its radical offshoots that quickened Hobbes's most profound and daring reflections about liberty.[16]

Beneath the constitutionalist conception of political liberty lay a distinction between acting for the sake of reason and acting at the behest of passion. The first is a free act; the second is not. "To act out of passion," writes Skinner in his account of the argument Hobbes arrayed himself against, "is not to act as a free man, or even distinctively as a man at all; such actions are not an expression of true liberty but of mere licence or animal brutishness." Freedom entails acting upon what we have willed, but will should not be confused with appetite or aversion. As Bishop Bramhall, Hobbes's great antagonist, put it: "A free act is only that which proceeds from the free election of the rational will." And "where there is no consideration nor use of reason, there is no liberty at all."[17] Being free entails acting in accordance with reason or, in political terms, living under laws as opposed to arbitrary power.

Like the divine right of kings, the constitutional argument had been rendered anachronistic by recent developments, most notably the fact that no English monarch in the first half of the seventeenth century claimed to believe it. Intent on turning England into a modern state, James and Charles were compelled to advance far more absolutist claims about the nature of their power than the constitutional argument allowed.

More troubling for the regime, however, was how easily the constitutional argument could be turned into a republican one and used against the king. Common lawyers and parliamentary supplicants argued that by flouting the common law and Parliament, Charles was threatening to turn England into a tyranny; radicals insisted that anything short of a republic or democracy, where men lived under laws to which they had consented, constituted a tyranny. All monarchy, in the eyes of the radicals, was despotism.

Hobbes thought that the latter argument derived from the "Histories, and Philosophy of the Antient Greeks, and Romans," which were so influential among educated opponents of the king.[18] That ancient heritage was given new life by Machiavelli's *Discorsi*, translated into English in 1636, which may have been Hobbes's ultimate target in his admonition against popular government. But as Skinner points out, the underlying premise of the republican argument—that what distinguishes a free man from a slave is that the former is subject to his own will while the latter is subject to the will of another—could also be found in English common law, in a "word-for-word" reproduction of "the *Digest* of Roman law," as early as the thirteenth century. Likewise, the distinction between will and appetite, liberty and license, was "deeply embedded" in both the scholastic traditions of the Middle Ages and the humanist culture of the Renaissance. This philosophy of will thus found expression not only in the royalist positions of Bramhall and his ilk, but also among the radicals and regicides who overthrew the king. Beneath the chasm separating royalist and republican lay a deep and volatile bedrock of shared assumption about the nature of liberty.[19] Hobbes's genius was to recognize that assumption; his ambition was to crush it.

While the notion that freedom entails living under laws lent support to the constitutional royalists (who made much of the distinction between lawful monarchs and despotic tyrants) it did not necessarily lead to the conclusion that a free regime had to be a republic or a democracy. To advance that argument, the radicals had to make two additional claims: first, to equate arbitrariness or lawlessness with a will that is not one's own, a will that is external or alien, like the passions; and second, to equate the decisions of a popular government with a will that is one's own, like reason. To be subject to a will that is mine—the laws of a republic or democracy—is to be free; to be subject to a will that is not mine— the edicts of a king or foreign country—is to be a slave.

In making these claims, the radicals were aided by a peculiar, though popular, understanding of slavery. What made someone a slave, in the eyes of many, was not that he was in chains or that his owner impeded or compelled his movements. It was that he lived and moved under a net, the ever-changing, arbitrary will of his master, which might fall upon him at any moment. Even if that net never fell—the master never told him what to do or never punished him for not doing it, or he never desired to do something different from what the master told him—the slave was still enslaved. The fact that he "lived in total dependence" on the will of another, that he was under the master's jurisdiction, "was sufficient in itself to guarantee the servility" that the master "expected and despised."[20]

> The mere presence of relations of domination and dependence . . . is held to reduce us from the status of . . ."free-men" to that of slaves. It is not sufficient, in other words, to enjoy our civic rights and liberties as a matter of fact; if we are to count as free-men, it is necessary to enjoy them in a particular way. We must never hold them merely by the grace or goodwill of

anyone else; we must always hold them independently of any-one's arbitrary power to take them away from us.[21]

At the individual level, freedom means being one's own master; at the political level, it requires a republic or democracy. Only a full share in public power will ensure we enjoy our freedom in the "particular way" freedom requires; without full political participation, freedom will be fatally abridged. It is this double movement between the personal and the political that is arguably the most radical element of the theory of popular government and, from Hobbes's view, the most dangerous.

Hobbes sets about destroying the argument from the ground up. Breaking with traditional understandings, he argues for a materialist account of the will. The will, he says, is not a decision resulting from our reasoned deliberation about our desires and aversions; it is simply the last appetite or aversion we feel before we act, which then prompts the act. Deliberation is like the oscillating rod of a metronome—back and forth our inclinations go, alternating between appetite and aversion—but less steady. Wherever the rod comes to rest, thereby producing an action or, conversely, no action at all, turns out to be our will. If this conception seems arbitrary and mechanistic, it should: the will does not stand freely and autonomously above our appetites and aversions, judging and choosing between them; the will is our "last Appetite, or Aversion, immediately adhaering to the action, or to the omission thereof."[22]

Imagine a man with the keenest appetite for wine, racing into a building on fire in order to rescue a case of it; now imagine a man with the fiercest aversion to dogs, racing into that same building to escape a pack of them. Hobbes's opponents would see in these examples the force of irrational compulsion; Hobbes sees the will in action. These may not be the wisest or sanest acts, Hobbes allows, but wisdom and sanity need not play any part in volition. Both acts may be compelled, but so are the actions of a man on a listing vessel who throws his bags overboard in order to lighten the load and save himself. Hard choices, actions taken under duress—these are as much expressions of my will as the decisions I make in the calm of my study. Extending the analogy, Hobbes would argue that the surrender of my wallet to someone holding a gun to my head is also a willed act: I have chosen my life over my wallet.

Against his opponents, Hobbes suggests that there can be no such thing as voluntarily acting against one's will; all voluntary action is an expression of the will. External constraints like being locked in a room can prevent me from acting upon my will; being on a chain gang can force me to act in ways I have not willed (when my neighbor takes a step forward or lifts his tool, I must follow him, unless I have sufficient physical force to resist him and the fellow behind me). But I cannot act voluntarily against my will. In the case of the mugger, Hobbes would say that his gun changed my will: I went from wanting to safeguard the money in my wallet to wanting to protect my life.

If I can't act voluntarily against my will, I can't act voluntarily in accordance with a will that is not my own. If I obey a king because I fear that he will kill or imprison me, that does not signify the absence, forfeiture, betrayal, or subjection of my will; it is my will. I could have willed otherwise—hundreds of thousands during Hobbes's lifetime did—but my survival or liberty was more important to me than whatever it was that may have called for my disobedience.

Hobbes's definition of freedom follows from his understanding of the will. Liberty, he says, is "the absence of . . . externall Impediments of motion," and a free man "*is he, that in those things, which by his strength and wit he is able to do, is not hindred to doe what he has a will to.*"²³ I can be rendered un-free, Hobbes insists, only by external obstacles to my movement. Chains and walls are such obstacles; laws and obligations are another, albeit a more meta-phorical, sort. If the obstacle lies within me—I don't have the abil-ity to do something; I am too afraid to do it—I lack power or will, not freedom. Hobbes, in a letter to the earl of Newcastle, attri-butes these deficiencies to "the nature and intrinsical quality of the agent," not the conditions of the agent's political environment.²⁴

And that is the purpose of Hobbes's effort: to separate the sta-tus of our personal liberty from the state of public affairs. Freedom is dependent on the presence of government but not on the form government takes; whether we live under a king, a republic, or a democracy does not change the quantity or quality of the free-dom we enjoy. The separation between personal and political lib-erty had the dramatic effect of making freedom seem both less present and more present under a king than Hobbes's republican and royalist antagonists had allowed.

On the one hand, Hobbes insists that there is no way to be free and subject at the same time. Submission to government entails an absolute loss of liberty: wherever I am bound by law, I am not free to move. Hobbes claims that when republicans argue that cit-izens are free because they make the laws, they are confusing sov-ereignty with liberty: what the citizen has is political power, not freedom. He is just as obliged (perhaps more obliged, Rousseau will later suggest) to submit to the law, and thus just as un-free, as he would be under a monarchy. And when the constitutional roy-alists argue that the king's subjects are free because the law limits the king's power, Hobbes claims that they are just confused.

On the other hand, Hobbes thinks that if freedom is unim-peded motion, it stands to reason that we are a lot freer under a monarch, even an absolute monarch, than the royalist and the republican realize or care to admit.[25] First and most simply, even when we act out of fear, we are acting freely. "Feare, and Liberty are consistent," says Hobbes, because fear expresses our negative inclinations; these inclinations may be negative, but that does not negate the fact that they are *our* inclinations. So long as we are not impeded from acting upon them, we are free. Even when we are most terrified of the King's punishments, we are free: "all actions which men doe in Common-wealths, for *feare* of the law, are actions, which the doers had *liberty* to omit."[26]

More important, wherever the law is silent, neither commanding nor prohibiting, we are free. One need only contemplate all the "ways a man may move himself," Hobbes says in *De Cive*, to see all the ways he can be free in a monarchy. These freedoms, Hobbes explains in *Leviathan*, include "the Liberty to buy, and sell, and otherwise contract with one another; to choose their own aboad, their own diet, their own trade of life, and institute their children as they themselves think fit; & the like."[27] To whatever degree the sovereign can guarantee the freedom of movement, the ability to go about our business without the hindrance of other men, we are free. Submission to his power, in other words, augments our freedom. The more absolute our submission, the more powerful he is and the freer we are. Subjugation is emancipation.

5

Burke's Market Value

On May 1, 1796, the reformer and writer Arthur Young traveled to Edmund Burke's estate at Beaconsfield, hoping to secure from the retired statesman his opinions on the regulation of wages. A minimum wage for agricultural laborers had been proposed in Parliament in December, and Burke had prepared a critical response. Young came away from his visit empty-handed: Burke had written something on the regulation of wages, but it would not be until 1800, three years after his death, that the public would see it.

Young wasn't bothered much by his failure to obtain the document; he was more concerned about the state of Burke's mind. Burke was nearing the end of his life (he would die a year later); his son and brother had died not long before, and his ambitions for a concert of Whigs against revolutionary France lay in ruins. "His conversation was remarkably desultory," Young wrote, "a broken mixture of agricultural observations, French madness, price of provisions, the death of his son, the absurdity of regulating labour, the mischief of our Poor-laws, and the difficulty of cottagers keeping cows."[1] The lion in winter was babbling like Lear on the heath.

Yet a reconsideration of three of Burke's late writings—*A Letter to a Noble Lord, Letters on a Regicide Peace,* and *Thoughts on Scarcity*—suggests there was more design than despair in his rant. Not only are French madness, his son's death, the regulation of labor, and the poor laws all addressed in these texts, but they are also brought together on behalf of a remarkable unity of vision about the nature and determinants of value. In the last years of his life, Burke repeatedly returned to the problem of value—primarily, though not exclusively, in the economic sphere. In his effort to make sense of a world in which some labors fetched a price while other sorts remained priceless, in which value was measurable yet unpredictable and variable, he laid the foundations for a vision of the market that was simultaneously commercial and chivalrous, ultra-modern and ultramontane.

Scholars have long noted the tension in Burke between his embrace of capitalist markets and his aristocratic traditionalism.[2] While these tensions in Burke's writing may be overplayed, moments of pressure in the texts cannot be ignored.[3] Burke's critique of the abstract ideal of equality, for example, where each person is shorn of her social identity and is treated as if she were no different from any other individual, sits uncomfortably with his endorsement of the capitalist abstraction of labor. In his *Reflections on the Revolution in France*, Burke refuses to indulge "any thing which relates to human actions, and human concerns, in all the nakedness and solitude of metaphysical abstraction." Against the revolutionaries in control of France, attempting "to confound all sorts of citizens . . . into one homogenous mass," Burke holds up the "coarse husbandman" who has "enough of common sense not to abstract and equalize" his sheep, horses, and oxen "into animals, without providing for each kind an appropriate food, care, and employment."[4] Yet five years later, writing about the labor market in his *Thoughts on Scarcity*, Burke proves more solicitous of abstraction, recommending that laborers quite different in their talents and temperament nevertheless be treated as if they were one mass:

> Unquestionably, there is a good deal of difference between the value of one man's labour and that of another, from strength, dexterity, and honest application. But I am quite sure, from my best observation, that any given five men will, in their total, afford a proportion of labour equal to any other five within the periods of life I have stated; that is, that among such five men there will be one possessing all the qualifications of a good workman, one bad, and the other three middling, and approximating to the first and the last. So that in so small a platoon as that of even five, you will find the full complement of all that five men *can* earn. Taking five and five through the kingdom, they are equal.[5]

Likewise, Burke's lament over the social contract's liquidation of history in the *Reflections* cannot be easily reconciled with his indifference to the economic contract's erasure of history in his *Thoughts on Scarcity*. Nor does his counsel in the earlier text to heed the slow wisdom of the past jibe with his readiness in the later text to toss away two centuries of English Poor Law and tradition.[6]

Yet it was in this crucible of value, heated to the highest degrees by the French Revolution, that Burke found a potential if uneasy settlement between the market—including, critically, an unregulated market of wage labor designed to serve the cause of capital accumulation—and the aristocratic order. In the meeting ground of the market, where personal identities were opaque but roles transparent, where the preferences of the buyer were as whimsical and weighty as the judgments of a king, Burke found an analog to the costume drama of the ancien régime. Burke knew the days of that regime were numbered. Not just in revolutionary France, where even a restoration of the monarchy would "be in some measure a new thing," but also in Britain, where the "antient divisions" of old Whigs and Tories were "nearly extinct."[7] But with the help of his new vision of value, Burke laid the foundation, in these last years of his life, for a system of rule in which the market might replicate the manor.

That he could not, in the end, fully envision the edifice that would be erected upon that foundation—and to the extent that he could, would shield his eyes from it—matters less than we might think. In the centuries that followed, others—most notably the conservative economists of the so-called Austrian School emerging out of fin-de-siècle Vienna, whose writings I examine in the next chapter—would take up his cause, creating an understanding of the economy in which the demiurges of capital would step forth as the modern equivalent of the feudal aristocracy. As Joseph Schumpeter was to write of these men of capital, "What may be attained by industrial and commercial success is still the nearest approach to medieval lordship possible to modern man."[8] That vision was first mooted in these late works of Burke.

Despite their proximity in time, the various circumstances that occasioned Burke's three late statements on value were different. Until recently, *Thoughts on Scarcity* was thought to be a response to the Speenhamland system,[9] a mode of poor relief described by Karl Polanyi as the last gasp of "reactionary paternalism" which helped forestall the emergence of a national market of wage labor in Britain.[10] In the mid-1790s, a rise in grain prices, brought about by two years of bad harvests and wartime limitations on imports from the Continent, provoked a wave of food riots in Britain of the sort that had preceded the French Revolution and propelled it on its ever-wilder course. Britain's ruling elites were mindful of the parallels to the French Revolution, which were reinforced by popular cartoons of the day. As Young would comment a few years later, "the relief which formerly was and still ought to be petitioned for as a favour, is now frequently demanded as a right." In May 1795, the magistrates of Berkshire, a county in southeastern England adjacent to Burke's Buckinghamshire, met at an inn in Speenhamland to address the problem. They determined that agricultural workers were entitled to a living wage, which would vary in relation to the size of their families and the price of bread. If work failed to supply the requisite income, the local government would make up the shortfall.[11]

In recent years, Burke scholars have deemphasized Speenhamland, linking *Thoughts on Scarcity* instead to a more complicated set of negotiations in Parliament over how to respond to the food crisis. Sometime in the fall of 1795, Pitt canvassed Burke and other trusted allies for their opinion on whether and how the government should intervene in the grain markets, perhaps by creating public granaries. In a memorandum to Pitt, Burke took sharp issue with any mode of government intervention. By December, the debate in Parliament had shifted to Whitbread's bill, which would have authorized local magistrates to set a minimum wage for agricultural workers (as the Berkshire magistrates had done in Speenhamland). Hovering in the background now was Charles Fox, with whom Burke had broken publicly over the French Revolution. Fox supported Whitbread, reinforcing Burke's sense that there was a connection between economic regulation at home and revolution abroad. Burke drafted a second statement on the regulation of wages. He never finished it, but in 1800 his literary executors cobbled parts of it together with his memorandum to Pitt, and published the result as *Thoughts on Scarcity*.[12]

Burke's *Letters on a Regicide Peace* was composed in fits and starts over the last two years of his life. He began one of the letters—there would ultimately be four—in the last months of 1795 and was still at work on another when he died in July 1797. The prod to these exertions was Pitt's effort to negotiate an end to the war with France and Burke's fear that Britain's counterrevolutionary ardor was diminishing. Pitt and his allies—careful, cautious, conservative—took Thermidor and the Directory as signals that the Revolution was winding down and the French were ready for business. Burke would have none of it. He called for a renewed war against Jacobinism, with restoration of the Old Regime as the final aim. (This should put to rest Marx's calumny that Burke was a "sycophant. . . in the pay of the English oligarchy."[13] To the end of his life, Burke was out in front of the counterrevolutionary crusade, struggling to pull his putative allies along.) He called for a fresh division of the political field: the days of Whig and Tory were over; a new distinction was called for. From now on, one would have to identify as either a Jacobin or a partisan of the "ancient order of things." In this new era of revolutionary and counterrevolutionary struggle, there would be no room for "creatures of the desk" and "creatures of favour" like Pitt and his associates. Only men of unyielding conviction, ideologues with a touch of that "generous wildness of Quixotism," could win the war against Jacobinism.[14]

It was amid these statements that Burke undertook—deep into the third letter, which he composed in December 1796—a lengthy excursus on the question of value. The immediate provocation was the growing sense among pamphleteers and parliamentarians that Britain could no longer afford its war with France and popular criticism of the government for relying on the infamous "loyalty" loan—with its generous terms to financiers—to wage it.[15] Not only did Burke defend the terms of the loan; he also seized upon the criticisms as an opportunity to reflect on the nature of markets and value, on the relationship between men of money and the state, and on the "puling jargon" of the phrase "laboring poor."[16]

The context for the other major work of his final years, *A Letter to a Noble Lord*, was more personal. Throughout his career, Burke was plagued by debts, which were estimated in 1794 to have been about £30,000. Lacking the means to sustain the life of a gentleman—which included two estates, a house in London, an expensive education for his son, and a retinue of servants and other employees—Burke relied to a great extent upon loans from his patron, Lord Rockingham, all of which were forgiven after Rockingham's death by a provision of his will. But Burke's creditors were relentless. Toward the end of his life he grew fearful that he would die in debtor's prison. He fantasized about fleeing to "America, Portugal, or elsewhere." He even remarked to one visitor that he might learn Italian in order to "end his days with tollerable Ease in Italy."[17]

Beginning in 1793, there was talk in ministerial circles of securing Burke a peerage and a pension. The topic was sensitive. Earlier in his career, Burke had led the effort to prevent the Crown from using positions and pensions as sources of patronage; an act he sponsored in 1782 capped Civil List pensions at £1200. Once he came out against the French Revolution in 1790, the charge was made repeatedly—most famously by Paine and Wollstonecraft— that he had turned his back on reform for the sake of a pension. Burke warmly denied this. Thanks to his friends, however, he was able to secure a Civil List pension of £1200 and two annuities. Between the three sources of government income, as well as rent from his estates, he was able to clear most of his debts and live out the remainder of his life unharried by creditors.[18]

Almost immediately, the pension came under attack. The Duke of Bedford fired the opening salvo in November 1795, calling Burke a hypocrite for taking a kind of payment from the Crown he had previously denounced. Bedford further insinuated that there was a connection between Burke's hypocrisy, the war against France, and the expense Britain had incurred in waging it. Bedford's charges were echoed by the Earl of Lauderdale. Both men were Whigs who sympathized with the French Revolution, affecting its clothes and hairstyle in the House of Lords. In responding to their attacks, Burke not only defended his contribution to the Crown and the compensation he had received for it, he also compared the value of his contribution and compensation to Bedford's. He staged a classic confrontation between the leisured aristocrat and resourceful bourgeois in which the criminal past of the landed gentry was arrayed against the present utility of the man of talents. The script could have been written by Robespierre or Desmoulins; it was even compared to the writings of Paine and Rousseau.[19]

There is a reason that Burke found himself, despite these differences of context and circumstance, repeatedly driven back to the question of value. Looming over all the particular controversies and arguments was the specter of revolution and destruction of the old regime. Not only had the French Revolution toppled the Old Regime but it also pried open, as Burke predicted it would, a great many other regimes to scrutiny. "The real object" of the Revolution, he warned Parliament in February 1790, is

> to break all those connexions, natural and civil, that regulate and hold together the community by a chain of subordination; to raise soldiers against their officers; servants against their masters; tradesmen against their customers; artificers against their employers; tenants against their landlords; curates against their bishops; and children against parents.[20]

With so many traditional orders of rule under siege, it's not surprising that the systems of value that undergirded them would be subject to the most ruthless criticism as well. As Nietzsche would later argue, all systems of value are predicated upon a hierarchy of judgment and status, taste and place.[21] Rank entails reward—offices, privileges, wealth—and reward must be worthy of rank. It was simply impossible to threaten so many orders of society without raising the question of their ranks and rewards, and the schemes of value that underlay them. At a moment of free fall like the mid-1790s, when the usual justifications for rule had been taken away or called into question, how could questions of value be resolved without interrogating the contributions of the persons who composed these ranks and received these rewards? What had any of these men done to merit his position? What contributions ought to merit rank or reward? Even those most resistant to raising these questions, like Burke, found themselves dragged into discussions of value—whether it was the wage of the laborer, the rate of the financier, or the rank and reward of the statesman.

The crisis of value that the French Revolution inaugurated found a corollary in the economic sphere with the imposition of price controls, grain requisitions, bread rations, and other market regulations. The latter were hardly new, but since the 1770s they had been implemented against a backdrop of growing unease about the conflict between equality and laissez-faire.[22] With the arrival of the French Revolution, that conflict intensified. Every economic choice was now refracted through the vocabulary of morals and politics; every economic development seemed a portent of a larger renovation of the human estate. Robespierre and the Convention had made it their top priority to keep Paris pacified with bread, at times nearly starving the provinces with requisitions for the capital. When the Directory began to loosen those controls and the bread lines started growing, Paris remembered.

As one policy spy explained in March 1795, "There is talk of the regime of before 9 Thermidor, when goods were not as dear and money and assignats [the paper money of the Revolution] were worth the same."[23]

The fact that value was now up for debate in so many realms meant that whatever systems of value came out of that debate—and whatever ranks and rewards were determined to coincide with these systems—would forever carry the taint of their having been debated. It would be difficult to forget that these values had once been argued over and chosen. Where theological notions of chosenness—Moses receiving the tablets at Sinai—endow the chosen and their values with an aura of the holy, secular chosenness does not generate the same glow. Values that are chosen in secular (as opposed to sacred) time are stained by their originating moment: they were chosen, but they might not have been chosen. Any chosen system of value, and the social distributions (of rights, resources, powers, and privileges) that follow from it, will seem contingent, even arbitrary. More important than its content is the fact that it has been ordained by real men and women at a not so distant moment in the past. Having been made in time, it must bear the weight of its contingency, the possibility of its non-being, throughout time. A sense of the accidental and the arbitrary will continue to haunt it.

The fact that values were now understood to have been made, rather than given, focused men and women on the activity of making more generally, on the act of bringing things into the world. While there are many ways of conceiving that activity of introduction and inauguration, no model at that moment seemed as pertinent as the production of commodities and the creation of wealth. Still in its infancy in the eighteenth century, the discourse of political economy captured this sense of creating something from nothing, of generating more from less. Labor epitomized that activity, as even Burke acknowledged when he associates the commandment to labor with God's "creation wrought by mere will out of nothing."[24] So labor—with its concomitant theory of value—was put at the center of political economy. *The Wealth of Nations* does not open with the landlord or the merchant or the market; it opens with workers in a pin factory, figuring out ways to economize their actions, increase the pace of production, and thereby create the conditions for the creation of value.[25]

It is thus not surprising that Burke should have returned to questions of value in the last years of his life. The French Revolution had unsettled the distribution of ranks and rewards throughout all of Europe. Whether the topic was the price of bread, the wage of the worker, the fees of the men of money, or the rank of the man of state, the question of value could not be avoided. Nor could its contingency or the labor that went into its making.

In *Thoughts on Scarcity* Burke argues that there is no value to a commodity apart from its price at market. That price is the product of a mutual agreement between buyer and seller. Each has the greatest interest in and knowledge of the matters upon which he is contracting, so both should be free to strike whatever bargain they make. Value is price; price is market; market is the communion between desire and capacity.

> The balance between consumption and production makes price. The market settles, and alone can settle, that price. Market is the meeting and conference of the *consumer* and *producer*, when they mutually discover each other's wants. Nobody, I believe, has observed with any reflection what market is, without being astonished at the truth, the correctness, the celerity, the general equity, with which the balance of wants is settled.[26]

One of the reasons the market is such an effective determinant of value is that it performs an alchemy whereby our conflicting interests are tossed into a mixer and transformed into a harmonious blend of identical interests.

> I deny that it is in this case, as in any other of necessary implication, that contracting parties should originally have had different interests. By accident it may be so undoubtedly at the outset; but then the contract is of the nature of a compromise, and compromise is founded on circumstances that suppose it in the interest of the parties to be reconciled in some medium. The principle of compromise adopted, of consequence the interests cease to be different.[27]

You and I may set different values on my labor before we enter the market, but once we enter the market, those differences will even out with our agreement on a price. Indeed, it is only when those different estimations materialize as price—that is, as a mutually agreed-upon charge for services—that we can say a value exists. It is only at the moment of sale that we can know that the value I put on my labor constitutes more than idle wish or private whimsy, that the value I put on my labor is capable of commanding the assent of a buyer, that a mere idea can materialize as a real price. The market doesn't just settle value; it makes it: "The value of money must be judged, *like every thing else*, from it's rate at market."[28]

Burke here anticipates a celebration of the market that historian Daniel Rodgers has argued is more characteristic of social thought since the 1970s than it is of the classical economics of Smith and Ricardo. More than producers or consumers, it is the impersonal market that grounds and drives the argument. More than individuals pursuing their self-interest, it is the market that does the work of creating harmony out of dissonance, settlement from conflict.[29]

Deeper into the argument, however, Burke moves away from the market as the settler or maker of value. We hear less of two estimates materializing as one price and more of the man of money as the decider, the diviner, of value. In the same way that Marx, in moving from the market to the workshop, speaks of a change "in the physiognomy of our *dramatis personae*" ("the money owner now strides out in front as a capitalist; the possessor of labour-power follows as his worker. The one smirks self-importantly and is intent on business; the other is timid and holds back, like someone who has brought his own hide to market and now has nothing else to expect but—a tanning") so does Burke effect a change in his dramatis personae.[30] It is no longer the market settling price but the man of capital determining value, whether he's buying or selling, whether the commodity is labor or money.

In *Letters on a Regicide Peace*, Burke writes, "Monied men ought to be allowed to set a value on their money."[31] In *Thoughts on Scarcity*, he insists that "labour is a commodity like every other, and rises or falls according to the demand" of the buyer of labor. The worker's wage need not provide for the worker's sustenance; it must, however, afford a profit to his employer: "There is an implied contract, much stronger than any instrument or article of agreement, between the labourer in any occupation and his employer—that the labour, so far as that labour is concerned, shall be sufficient to pay to the employer a profit on his capital, and a compensation for his risk."[32] Whether the man of money is a seller of money, as he is in *Letters on a Regicide Peace*, or a buyer of labor, as he is in *Thoughts on Scarcity*, it is his needs, risks, and concerns that signify.

The monied men have a right to look to advantage in the investment of their property. To advance their money, they risk it; and the risk is to be included in the price. If they were to incur a loss, that would amount to a tax on that peculiar species of property. In effect, it would be the most unjust and impolitick of all things, unequal taxation.[33]

The needs, risks, and concerns of labor do not register.

> I premise that labour is, as I have already intimated, a commodity, and as such, an article of trade... When any commodity is carried to market, it is not the necessity of the vender, but the necessity of the purchaser that raises the price. . . If the goods at market are beyond the demand, they fall in their value; if below it, they rise. The impossibility of the subsistence of a man, who carries his labour to a market, is totally beside the question in this way of viewing it. The only question is, what is it worth to the buyer?[34]

There is one moment in *Letters on a Regicide Peace* where Burke considers the needs and interests of labor in the setting of prices. After asking why it is so difficult to lure men from their ordinary labors to become soldiers, he concedes that there is "abundant occupation" and "augmented stipend" to be found on farms and villages; such men must be given an incentive to leave. "The price of men for new and untried ways of life must bear a proportion to the profits of that mode of existence from when they are to be bought."[35] What is remarkable about this statement is how isolated it is—this is the only instance of such a consideration anywhere in the essay-length *Thoughts* or in the expansive *Letters*, which took up more than one volume of the earliest editions of Burke's works—and how far it runs counter to most of Burke's economic formulations. Unlike Smith, who applied such considerations to both capital and labor—just as the capitalist must be assured a particular rate of profit, for profit is "the proper fund of his subsistence," so must the worker be assured a particular wage, for it is his "subsistence"[36]—Burke paid almost exclusive attention to the needs of capital. When it comes to determining value, the market fades into the scenery, labor moves to the wings, the man of money strides to center stage.[37]

In these writings, Burke pursues a vision that—depending on which moment of the argument we're looking at—will define either the consensus of neoclassical economics more than a century later (the market as the settler of value) or the economics of the Austrian School of Carl Menger, Ludwig von Mises, and Friedrich Hayek, in which the subjective nature of value and the shaping preferences of capital play a tremendous role.[38]

That Burke should have come to these positions at all—much less when and how he did—is more surprising than we might think. Whether one takes Burke to be arguing that the market settles price and that price is value, or that the men of money determine the price and thus the value of commodities, his position is sharply at odds with the arguments of Adam Smith, whose writings already dominated the age and whose thinking Burke believed to be in harmony with his own.[39] In this respect, as in so many others, Burke wrote less as a conventionalist than as a controversialist, the lead player of a still incipient avant-garde. While Smith was obviously alive to the role of supply and demand, he didn't believe that they alone settled the price or the value of commodities, particularly labor. And while he was alert to the fact that men of money are able to set the price of labor, he did not believe that was an intrinsic feature of markets. Instead, he thought their outsized influence was due to their wealth and power and the favor of the law.

Underlying Smith's writing about the market and market price is the claim that though the price of a good is a manifestation—really, an approximation—of its value, it is not in and of itself the value of that good. For Smith, the real value of a good at market is however much we are willing to give up in the getting of it. While price can be a measure of value, it is not a reliable or consistent measure because the value of money changes over time. Today's dollar is not the same as yesterday's or tomorrow's. There has to be a more reliable measure of value, a fixed "standard by which we can compare the values of different commodities at all times and all places." That standard is labor. Not only is labor "the first price, the original purchase-money that was paid for all things"—i.e., the means by which we originally procured for ourselves all that we needed—but it remains "the only universal, as well as the only accurate measure of value."[40] Labor provides a transhistorical measure of value because it reflects the effort of the human body and what it is like for that body, given its capabilities, to make that effort.

> The real price of every thing, what every thing really costs to the man who wants to acquire it, is the toil and trouble of acquiring it. What every thing is really worth to the man who has acquired it, and who wants to dispose of it or exchange it for something else, is the toil and trouble which it can save to himself, and which it can impose upon other people. What is bought with money or with goods is purchased by labour, as much as what we acquire by the toil of our own body. The money or those goods indeed save us this toil. They contain the value of a certain quantity of labour which we exchange for what is supposed at the time to contain the value of an equal quantity.[41]

Assuming that the body and its capacities, as well as human nature, do not fundamentally change across time, labor provides a reliable standard of value, for the cost of its exertions to the body and the self that inhabits that body remains constant across time.[42]

While labor is the measure of value, it is not for Smith the determinant of value. It is not because an item requires x units of labor in order to become a commodity that we say the value of that commodity is x. Labor is a factor in the cost of that commodity, but so are rent and profit. When Smith says labor is the measure of value he is referring, as the Cambridge historian Phyllis Deane explained, not to "the labour *embodied* in a commodity but to "the labour *commanded* by a commodity."[43] How many units of labor that commodity can be exchanged for, how much labor that commodity saves us or enables us to purchase, is what determines the value of that commodity.

While there is an obvious distinction to be made, then, between the value of a commodity and its price, what is most instructive about Smith's account of the price of labor is his insistence that wages reflect more than what the market will bear. Smith claims that all wages, "even of the lowest species of labour," have a floor, a minimum that can't be breached. He describes that minimum as either a subsistence wage to procure the worker's survival or a family wage enabling a family not only to maintain and reproduce itself but also to advance itself.[44] Not only must wages provide "the necessaries and conveniences of life"; what constitutes those necessities and conveniences will depend upon the overall wealth of a society. As the wealth of society increases, so must the necessities and conveniences of life—and wages, too.[45] Beyond subsistence, maintenance, and convenience, wages must reflect the worker's contribution to society. Workers performing onerous but necessary tasks should enjoy at least the goods provided by those labors. "It is but equity, besides, that they who feed, cloathe and lodge the whole body of the people, should have such a share of their produce of their own labour as to be themselves tolerably well fed, cloathed and lodged."[46] Finally, there must always obtain a certain "proportion" between the rate of profit and the wages of labor.[47]

Wages, Smith acknowledges, often don't conform to these strictures of sustenance, maintenance, contribution, and so on. Some part of that disparity has to do with market disequilibria, the inevitable lag between changes in supply and demand. But Smith identifies two additional factors: the power of employers and the favor of the laws. Were there not such disparities of economic power between labor and capital, and were the laws either neutral between labor and capital or more favorable to labor, markets would settle in such a way that wages would reflect these principles. The natural forces of the market, in other words, are not completely indeterminate, permitting capital to extract whatever it can from labor; if it is working properly, the market should break on terms favorable to labor. (And indeed one of Smith's central justifications for capitalism is that it improves the lot of the laborer and "the lower ranks of the people.")[48]

Smith is highly sensitive to the imbalance of power between labor and capital. There are fewer employers than employees, so employers can combine more easily. Even when they do not coordinate their actions, informal codes and unspoken rules ensure that they will not break with each other. Concert thus comes easily to capital. But more important than concert, capital has capital. Vast reserves of wealth free employers from necessity. Though they ultimately need labor to realize the value of their capital, "ultimately" is a long ways off; in any dispute, capital can afford to wait labor out.[49]

Capital also has the law on its side.

Whenever the legislature attempts to regulate the differences between masters and their workmen, its counsellors are always the masters. When the regulation, therefore, is in favour of the workmen, it is always just and equitable; but it is sometimes otherwise when in favour of the masters.[50]

Capital controls the legislature, so the only laws regulating wages that are allowed are those that put a cap on wages rather than a floor beneath them. Labor is prohibited from acting in concert; capital is not. Should workers summon the wherewithal to defy their employers, the latter will "never cease to call aloud for the assistance of the civil magistrates, and the rigorous execution of those laws which have been enacted with so much severity against the combinations of servants, labourers, and journeymen." As a result, the collective efforts of the workers "generally end in nothing, but the punishment or ruin of the ringleaders."[51]

What ultimately undergirds Smith's specific claims about labor as the measure of value—and concomitant claims about the distortions wrought by capital's power and control of the legislature—is a vision of labor as the prime mover in the world. Insofar as labor is a universal measure of value, it is also a marker of our common humanity: what we, as human beings, have to do in the world in order to secure what we want from the world. It is how we make our way in the world.

> The rich and opulent merchant who does nothing but give a few directions, lives in far greater state and luxury and ease and plenty of all the conveniencies and delicacies of life than his clerks, who do all the business. They too, excepting their confinement, are in a state of ease and plenty far superior to that of the artizan by whose labour these commodities were furnished. The labour of this man too is pretty tollerable; he works under cover protected from the inclemency in the weather, and has his livelihood in no uncomfortable way if we

compare him with the poor labourer. He has all the inconveniencies of the soil and the season to struggle with, is continually exposed to the inclemency of the weather and the most severe labour at the same time. Thus *he who as it were supports the whole frame of society* and furnishes the means of the convenience and ease of all the rest is himself possessed of a very small share and is buried in obscurity. *He bears on his shoulders the whole of mankind,* and unable to sustain the load is buried by the weight of it and thrust down into the lowest parts of the earth, from whence *he supports all the rest.*[52]

That picture, and its details, is different from Burke's. Where Smith insists on distinguishing between value and price, Burke collapses the two. Where Smith sees labor as the measure of value, Burke sees the market as the measure of value. Where Smith sees the needs and contributions of labor as determinants of the price of labor, Burke disclaims any interest in the needs or contributions of labor. The price of labor is a function of capital's demand for labor; any consideration beyond that, says Burke, is "passed out of that department" of commerce and justice and "comes within the jurisdiction of mercy" and Christian charity.[53] Where Smith sees capital using its economic and legal power to extract the most damaging contracts from labor, Burke sees the free market at work. Where Smith seems to countenance those legislative interventions that favor labor—and points out all the ways in which the legislature already favors capital—Burke insists that "the moment that Government appears at market, all the principles of market will be subverted," while remaining silent about all the ways in which the government already appears at market on behalf of capital.[54] And where Smith sees labor as the driving agent of the world, Burke sees capital contributing "all the mind that actuates the whole machine."[55]

On the specific question of value and labor, Burke's views are closer to those of Thomas Pownall, governor of Massachusetts Bay colony and later Member of Parliament, who had written Smith a lengthy critique of *The Wealth of Nations*. In his *Letter from Governor Pownall to Adam Smith*, Pownall declared: "What then is to be the real standard of measure [of value]? Not labour itself. What is to give the respective estimation in which each holds his labour? . . . value cannot be fixed by and in the nature of labour; it will depend upon the nature of the feelings and activity of the persons estimating it."[56] Against Smith, Burke seems to hold, with Pownall, what we now call a subjective theory of economic value. There can be no common measure of value, even one grounded in labor, because there is no universal human nature, no universal response to the facts of the economic world, even to the fact of labor. All we have in the economic world are the disparate responses of disparate individuals to the possibilities on offer in that world. Absent a universal standard of value, we are left with only the subjective preferences of buyers and sellers in the market.

Yet Burke is not quite ready to completely dissolve the economic universe into a market of discrete particulars. When it comes to value creation, there are two coherent blocs in the market: capital and labor. It is capital's role, as a class, "to set a value" on its goods at market, and it is labor's role, as a class, to be the object of capital's estimation: "the only question is, what is it [labor] worth to the buyer."[57] Capital is the maker of value; labor bears its stamp.

Not only are there two coherent blocs—one setting value, the other having its value set—but each possesses a value that transcends the subjective estimations of the market; it is that transcendent or objective value that makes capital the estimator and labor the estimate. This kind of value inheres in the personal qualities of the members of each class. In the case of labor, this is a value that can be measured—not by attending to the distinctive capacities and talents of each individual worker but by abstracting from a group of workers a composite type that represents the whole. To cite this statement from Burke's *Thoughts on Scarcity* again:

> Unquestionably, there is a good deal of difference between the value of one man's labour and that of another, from strength, dexterity, and honest application. But I am quite sure, from my best observation, that any given five men will, in their total, afford a proportion of labour equal to any other five within the periods of life I have stated; that is, that among such five men there will be one possessing all the qualifications of a good workman, one bad, and the other three middling, and approximating to the first and the last. So that in so small a platoon as that of even five, you will find the full complement of all that five men *can* earn. Taking five and five throughout the kingdom, they are equal: therefore, an error with regard to the equalization of their wages by those who employ five, as farmers do at the very least, cannot be considerable.[58]

The value of labor, in this regard, can be properly measured beyond its rate at the market. It is homogenous, and so long as it does not include the old and the infirm, women and children, it can be quantified and abstracted. It is precisely the fact that labor can be measured in this way, beyond the market, that it can be valued at market.

Capital also has common characteristics, which set it apart from labor, in the economy and the polity. In the sphere of employment, capital is the "thinking and presiding principle to the labourer." In the same way that the laborer "is as reason to the beast," so is the employer the reason of the employee. In ancient times, labor was "called the *instrumentum vocale*," a tool that speaks; it belonged within the larger category of tools that included "*instrumentum semivocale*" (farm animals) and "*instrumentum mutum*" (carts, plows, hammers, and hoes). Labor needs a principle of reason to guide it; that principle is to be found in capital. It is thus critical that the hierarchy between capital and labor be maintained: "An attempt to break this chain of subordination in any part is equally absurd."[59]

Within the wider economy and polity, capital contributes its funds to the sustenance of the people and the state. Its "desire of accumulation" and "love of lucre," however vicious and foolish the excesses of those passions may be, is "the grand cause of prosperity to all States." Capital also provides a more direct service to the state, particularly in a time of war. Insofar as they are members of the "higher classes," the men of money "furnish the means" of war—wealth, resources, and equipment—and "contribute all the mind that actuates the whole machine." In the same way that capital provides reason to labor, so do the monied classes apply "a cool, steady, deliberate principle" to the "unthinking alacrity of the common soldier, or common sailor." Theirs is a reason that blends heart and head, that balances temper and temperance, fortitude and forbearance.[60]

Because of the specific genius of these various contributions, the value of capital—not the money that men forward as a loan or an investment but the class of human beings, the men who front the capital—cannot be measured as the value of labor is. Capital's contributions are great—certainly greater than those of labor—but they cannot be abstracted or quantified. Certainly not with the calculators one would use to measure the value of labor. Their value is peculiar to each of them as individuals. It is sui generis.

Thus we have in Burke two views of value. On the one hand, value is subjective, dependent on the wit and whimsy of the men of capital. On the other hand, there is a hierarchy of value that divides and distinguishes rich from poor, capital from labor. That value is objective. In the case of labor, it can be quantified and measured; in the case of capital, it is beyond measure. So it is the task of capital to set the value at market of whatever it is selling and whatever it is buying. The final intimation of Burke, never developed or realized but hinted at and suggested, was of an objective order of ranks and rewards, in which the better man occupied the superior rank, while the worse man occupied the lower one.

Two moves would follow, for Burke, from the blend of subjectivism in the market and objectivism in the social order. The first would be to call into question not the legitimacy of social hierarchy as such, but the composition of the higher orders, to raise the question of who is worthy of membership in the nobility. The second would be the growing sense that the proving ground of that social hierarchy—the determination of higher and lower value, not just in the economy but throughout society—was to be found in the market.

In *A Letter to a Noble Lord*, Burke toys with both moves by calling into question the historical sources of Bedford's and Lauderdale's nobility and their contributions to society as a whole, and by comparing those contributions to his own. It makes for riveting prose, with Burke summoning the full force of his achievements—and stricken fury of his humiliations—in order to stake his claim, his entire rank and reward, on his merits. "Whatever they are," Burke says of his merits, they "are original and personal." "His," he says, with a nod at Bedford, "are derivative."[61]

> I was not, like his grace of Bedford, swaddled, and rocked, and dandled into a legislator; *"Nitor in adversum"* is the motto for a man like me. I possessed not one of the qualities, nor cultivated one of the arts, that recommend men to the favour and

protection of the great. . . At every step of my progress in life (for in every step was I traversed and opposed), and at every turnpike I met, I was obliged to shew my passport, and again and again to prove my sole title to the honour of being useful to my country, by a proof that I was not wholly unacquainted with its laws, and the whole system of its interests both abroad and at home. Otherwise, no rank, no toleration even, for me. I had no arts, but manly arts. On them I have stood.[62]

Throughout the text, Burke resorts to the language of labor, of strain and effort, to demonstrate his singular, non-derivative merits. "I have on a hundred occasions, exerted myself with singular zeal" on behalf of others. Of his efforts in India he says, "They are those on which I value myself the most; most for the importance; most for the judgment; most for constancy and perseverance in the pursuit." Of his defense of Europe's aristocratic order he says, "I have strained every nerve to keep the duke of Bedford in that situation, which alone makes him my superior."[63] Burke mobilizes this record of labor not merely to justify his rewards, but to call into question the record of that "poor rich man" Bedford, the original limousine liberal, defending the French Revolution from the comfort of the House of Lords while questioning the modest pension of a humble servant of the government of Britain. A man like Bedford who inherited everything "can hardly know any thing of publick industry in its exertions, or can estimate it compensations when its work is done." Of course he can't: Bedford was swaddled, rocked, and dandled into a legislator. He did not give birth to anything; he was born with everything.[64]

In Burke's hands, birth and lineage become more than suspect; they are the scene of criminal acts of appropriation. Just before he narrates the story of how Bedford's ancestors came to their lands and title—essentially, they were the reward of Henry VIII's unlawful and violent dispossessions of the older nobility—Burke taunts Bedford with two alternatives: he can allow Bedford's story to be told by "gentle historians," antiquarians who "dip their pens in nothing but the milk of human kindness," or he can plunge the duke's patrimony into the acid baths of real history. Almost gleefully, he opts for the latter: "Let us turn our eyes to history."[65] Never has an inquisition into the past sounded more menacing, save in the annals of Jacobinism.

Against the past and present of Bedford, Burke arrays his own past and present, what he has done and the rewards he has received. His object is to compare the two—"thus stands the account of the comparative merits of the crown grants which compose the due of Bedford's fortune as balanced against mine"— but it is a comparison, he comes to realize, that cannot be made. There is no relationship between Burke's labors and his compensation from the Crown. Not only were his labors so great that no reward could possibly encompass them, but the two—labor and compensation—are animals of different species: "They are quantities incommensurable. Money is made for the comfort and convenience of animal life. It cannot be a reward for what, mere animal life must indeed sustain, but never can inspire."[66] There is the additional fact that whatever the Crown awards is just that: an award. It can be neither merited nor unmerited. It should be received and thought of as a gift from a higher being.[67] Thus, it is nearly impossible to compare Burke's pension with Bedford's title and estate, for there is no relationship between the efforts that garnered his pension and the pension itself.

Burke appears to be caught in a vise. On the one hand, he claims that his labors are demonstrably superior to those of Bedford and that Bedford's title is a wicked and worthless thing, rooted in the "pillage of unoffending men" by a *levelling* tyrant," taken from "possessions voluntarily surrendered by their lawful proprietors with the gibbet at their door."[68] That is the cosmic mismatch of this world, where Bedford is a noble and Burke a pensioner. On the other hand, Burke insists that his labors can be neither gauged nor quantified; they are singular, resisting all measure and comparison. Even more poignant, it is a vise of his own making. Burke firmly believes in the objective value of men, which is found in the system of inherited ranks and orders, yet he also knows that his value, which is far greater than that of inherited men, had to be demonstrated in a system that rewards success and failure, a system that functions in effect as the market sector of aristocratic society.

But Burke cannot go there, to that final intuition of a market determining value. He believes too much in the society of prescribed, inherited ranks. Not long before, he had composed, in the *Reflections on the Revolution in France*, the most rhapsodic of defenses of that society based on rank and privilege; he has devoted his life to "defending the high and eminent."[69] And it is a revolutionary age. Thus is he bound "to defend an order of things, which, like the sun of heaven, shines alike on the useful and the worthless."[70] It is a curious note to end on. Not merely because it registers a shrugging indifference, even agnosticism, about the objective value of the nobility, but also because it sounds so reminiscent of the market subjectivism that that order of ranks is supposed to surround but not succumb to. Far from registering a contrast between aristocratic and market societies, Burke's vocabulary of value suggests a confluence between them, a confluence that even he, try as he might, could not entirely avoid.

In a sense, Burke had been tussling with this conflict between aristocratic modes of preferment and market modes of selection since at least the 1770s. It was then that he first began voicing his misgivings about the East India Company, noting with alarm the ever-growing role of private and unaccountable modes of economic power and reason, the ways in which modern commercial forms were supplanting aristocratic modes of political power and reason.[71] What distinguishes Burke's late writings from these earlier texts is not only his slow warming to those economic modes of reason and power ("all the mind that actuates the whole machine") but also the extent to which they come to stand in, at least potentially, for the lost arts of politics. That is a switch from his earlier writings on India, but it is a switch that might have been warranted, in his mind, by a change in personnel. Where the confrontation between polity and economy in India was conceived by Burke as the insinuation of men of low character yet relatively high standing into the private chambers of Britain's ruling classes—"They marry into your families," said Burke of Hastings and his gang, "they enter your senate; they ease your estate by loans"[72]—it was now being fought against the backdrop of an unprecedented assertion on the part of the laboring classes that it was they who supported "the whole frame of society" and they who bore on their "shoulders the whole of mankind."[73] In that context, it might prove the better part of prudence to embrace the market as the proving ground of a new ruling class.

As I said, Burke couldn't go there. He flirted with the idea but in the end had to pull back from it. He distrusted new money as much as he distrusted new power. That he himself was a creature of both sorts of novelty—his political and financial rewards were founded on a system of value closer to that of the coming society he rejected than they were to that of the dissolving society he mourned—was but one of the many contradictions he could never quite resolve. It would fall to later theorists, most notably the Austrian economists, to take up those contradictions and work out their kinks and implications.

6

In Nietzsche's Margins

"One day," Friedrich Nietzsche wrote in *Ecce Homo*, "my name will be associated with the memory of something tremendous, a crisis without equal on earth, the most profound collision of conscience."[1] It's one of the great ironies of intellectual history that the terms of that collision can best be seen in the rise of a movement Nietzsche in all likelihood would have despised.

The Nobel Prize–winning economist Friedrich Hayek is the leading theoretician of this movement, which is often called neoliberalism but can also be understood as the most genuinely political theory of capitalism the right has managed to produce. The theory does not imagine a shift from government to the individual, as is often claimed by conservatives; nor does it imagine a shift from the state to the market or from society to the atomized individual, as is often claimed by the left. Instead, the theory recasts our understanding of politics and where it might be found. It takes what Nietzsche called *grosse Politik*— a conception of political life as the embodiment of ancient ideals of aristocratic action, aesthetic notions of artistic creation, and a rarefied vision of the warrior—and locates that vision not in high affairs of state but in the operations and personnel of a capitalist economy. The result is an agonistic romance of the market, where economic activity is understood as exciting rather than efficient, as the expression of aristocratic virtues, aesthetic values, and warlike action rather than a repository of bourgeois conceits.

The seedbed of Hayek's theory is the half-century between the Marginal Revolution that changed the field of economics in the late nineteenth century and the collapse of the Hapsburg Monarchy in 1918. It is by now a commonplace of European cultural history that a dying Austro-Hungarian Empire gave birth to modernism, psychoanalysis, and fascism. Yet from the vortex of Vienna came not only Wittgenstein, Freud, and Hitler but also Hayek, who was born and educated in the city, and the Austrian School of economics.

That Nietzsche also figures in this story, less as an influence than a diagnostician, will strike some as an improbable claim: Wasn't Nietzsche contemptuous of capitalists, capitalism, and economics? Yes, he was, and for all his reading in political economy, Nietzsche never wrote a treatise on politics or economics.[2] And despite the long shadow he cast over the fin-de-siècle Vienna avant-garde, he is hardly ever cited by the economists of the Austrian School.

Yet no one understood better than Nietzsche the social and cultural forces that would shape the Austrians: the demise of an ancient ruling class; the raising of the labor question by trade unions and socialist parties; the inability of an ascendant bourgeoisie to crush or contain democracy in the streets; the need for a new ruling class in and for an age of mass politics. The relationship between Nietzsche and the free-market right—which has been seeking to put labor back in its box since the nineteenth century, and has now, with the help of the neoliberal left, succeeded—is thus one of elective affinity rather than direct influence, at the level of idiom rather than policy.[3]

In 1869, Nietzsche was appointed professor of classical philology at Basel University. Like most junior faculty, he was plagued by meager wages and major responsibilities, such as teaching fourteen hours a week, Monday through Friday, beginning at 7 a.m. He also sat on multiple committees and covered for senior colleagues who couldn't make it to their classes. He lectured to the public on behalf of the university. He dragged himself to dinner parties. Yet within three years he managed to complete *The Birth of Tragedy*, a minor masterwork of modern literature, which he dedicated to his close friend and "sublime predecessor" Richard Wagner.[4]

One chapter, however, he withheld from publication. In 1872, Nietzsche was invited to spend the Christmas holidays with Wagner and his wife Cosima, but sensing a potential rift with the composer, he begged off and sent a gift instead. He bundled "The Greek State" with four other essays, slapped a title onto a cover page (*Five Prefaces to Five Unwritten Books*), and mailed the leather-bound text to Cosima as a birthday present. Richard was offended, Cosima unimpressed. "Prof. Nietzsche's manuscript does not restore our spirits," she sniffed in her diary.[5] Though presented as a sop to a fraying friendship, "The Greek State" reflects the larger European crisis of war and revolution that had begun in 1789 and would only come to an end in 1945. More immediately, it bears the stamp of the Franco-Prussian War, which had broken out in 1870, and the Paris Commune, which was declared the following year.

Initially ambivalent about the war, Nietzsche quickly became a partisan of the German cause. "It's about our culture!" he wrote his mother. "And for that no sacrifice is too great! This damned French tiger." He signed up to serve as a medical orderly; Cosima tried to persuade him to stay put in Basel, recommending he send cigarettes to the front instead. But Nietzsche was adamant. In

August 1870 he left for Bavaria with his sister Elisabeth, riding the rails and singing songs. He got his training, headed to the battlefield, and promptly contracted dysentery and diphtheria. He lasted a month.[6]

The war lasted for six. A half million soldiers were killed or wounded, as were countless civilians. The preliminary peace treaty, signed in February 1871, favored the Germans and punished the French, particularly the citizens of Paris who were forced to shoulder the burden of heavy indemnities to the Prussians. Enraged by its impositions—and a quarter century of simmering discontent—workers and radicals in Paris rose up and took over the city in March. Nietzsche was scandalized, his horror at the revolt inversely proportional to his exaltation over the war. Fearing that the Communards had destroyed the Louvre (they hadn't), he wrote:

> The reports of the past few days have been so awful that my state of mind is altogether intolerable. What does it mean to be a scholar in the face of such earthquakes of culture! . . . It is the worst day of my life.[7]

In the quicksilver transmutation of a conventional war between states into a civil war between classes, Nietzsche saw a terrible alchemy of the future: "Over and above the struggle between nations the object of our terror was that international hydra-head, suddenly and so terrifyingly appearing as a sign of quite different struggles to come."[8]

By May, the Commune had been put down at the cost of tens of thousands of lives—much to the delight of the Parisian aesthete-aristocrat Edmond Goncourt.

> All is well. There has been neither compromise nor concili-ation. The solution has been brutal, imposed by sheer force

of arms. The solution has saved everyone from the dangers of cowardly compromise. The solution has restored its self-confidence to the Army, which has learnt in the blood of the Communards that it was still capable of fighting. . . a bleeding like that, by killing the rebellious part of a population, postpones the next revolution by a whole conscription.[9]

Of the man who wrote these words and the literary milieu of which he was a part, Nietzsche would later say: "I know these gentlemen inside out, so well that I have really had enough of them already. One has to be more radical: fundamentally they lack the main thing—'la force.'"[10]

The clash of these competing worlds of war and work echoes throughout "The Greek State." Nietzsche begins by announcing that the modern era is dedicated to the "dignity of work." Committed to "equal rights for all," democracy elevates the worker and the slave. Their demands for justice threaten to "swamp all other ideas," to tear "down the walls of culture." Modernity has made a monster in the working class: a created creator (shades of Marx and Mary Shelley), it has the temerity to see itself and its labor as a work of art. Even worse, it seeks to be recognized and publicly acknowledged as such.[11]

The Greeks, by contrast, saw work as a "disgrace," because the existence it serves—the finite life each of us lives—"has no inherent value." Existence can be redeemed only by art, but art too is premised on work. It is made, and its maker depends on the labor of others; they take care of him and his household, freeing him from the burdens of everyday life. Inevitably, his art bears the taint of their necessity. No matter how beautiful, art cannot escape the pall of its creation. It arouses shame, for in shame "there lurks the unconscious recognition that these conditions" of work "are required for the actual goal" of art to be achieved. For that reason the Greeks properly kept labor and the laborer hidden from view.[12]

Throughout his writing life, Nietzsche was plagued by the vision of workers massing on the public stage—whether in trade unions, socialist parties, or communist leagues. Almost immediately upon his arrival in Basel, the First International descended upon the small city to hold its fourth congress. Nietzsche was petrified. "There is nothing more terrible," he wrote in *Birth of Tragedy*, "than a class of barbaric slaves who have learned to regard their existence as an injustice, and now prepare to avenge, not only themselves, but all generations." Several years after the International had left Basel, Nietzsche convinced himself that it was slouching toward Bayreuth in order to ruin Wagner's festival there. And just weeks before he went mad in 1888 and disappeared forever into his own head, he wrote, "The cause of *every* stupidity today. . . lies in the existence of a labour question at all. About certain things *one does not ask questions*."[13]

One can hear in the opening passages of "The Greek State" the pounding march not only of European workers on the move but also of black slaves in revolt. Hegel was brooding on Haiti while he worked out the master-slave dialectic in the *The Phenomenology of Spirit*. Though generations of scholars have told us otherwise, perhaps Nietzsche had a similar engagement in mind when he wrote, "Even if it were true that the Greeks were ruined because they kept slaves, the opposite is even more certain, that we will be destroyed because we fail to keep slaves." What theorist, after all, has ever pressed so urgently—not just in this essay but in later works as well—the claim that "slavery belongs to the essence of a culture"?[14] What theorist ever had to? Prior to the eighteenth century, bonded labor was an accepted fact. Now it was the subject of a roiling debate, provoking revolutions and emancipations throughout the world. Serfdom had been eliminated in Russia only a decade before—and in some German states, only a generation before Nietzsche's birth in 1844—while Brazil would soon become the last state in the Americas to abolish slavery. An edifice of the ages had been brought down by a mere century's vibrations. Is it so implausible that Nietzsche, attuned to the vectors and velocity of decay as he was, would pause to record the earthquake and insist upon taking the full measure of its effects?

If slavery was one condition of great art, Nietzsche continued in "The Greek State," war and high politics were another. "Political men par excellence," the Greeks channeled their agonistic urges into bloody conflicts between cities and less bloody conflicts within them. Healthy states were built on the repression and release of these impulses. The arena for conflict created by that regimen gave "society time to germinate and turn green everywhere" and allowed "blossoms of genius" periodically to "sprout forth." Those blossoms were not only artistic but also political. Warfare sorted society into lower and higher ranks, and from that hierarchy rose "the military genius" whose artistry was the state itself. The real dignity of man, Nietzsche insisted, lay not in his lowly self but in the artistic and political genius his life was meant to serve and on whose behalf it was to be expended.[15]

Instead of the Greek state, however, Europe had the bourgeois state; instead of aspiring to a work of art, states dedicated themselves to the market at work. Politics, Nietzsche complained, had become "an instrument of the stock exchange" rather than the terrain of heroism and glory. With the "specifically political impulses" of Europe so weakened—even his beloved Franco-Prussian War had not revived the spirit in the way he had hoped—Nietzsche could only "detect dangerous signs of atrophy in the political sphere, equally worrying for art and society."[16] The age of aristocratic culture and high politics was at an end. All that remained was the detritus of the lower orders: the disgrace of the laborer, the paper chase of the bourgeoisie, the barreling threat of socialism. "The Paris commune," Nietzsche would later write in his notebooks, "was perhaps no more than minor indigestion compared to what is coming."[17]

Nietzsche had little, concretely, to offer as a counter-volley to democracy, whether bourgeois or socialist. Despite his appreciation of the political impulse and his studious attention to political events in Germany—from the Schleswig-Holstein crisis of the early 1860s to the imperial push of the late 1880s—he remained leery of programs, movements, and platforms.[18] The best he could muster was a vague principle: that society is "the continuing, painful birth of those exalted men of culture in whose service everything else has to consume itself" and the state a "means of setting" that "process of society in motion and guaranteeing its unobstructed continuation."[19] It was left to later generations to figure out what that could mean in practice—and where it might lead. Down one path might lay fascism; down another, the free market.

Around the time—almost to the year—that Nietzche was launching his revolution of metaphysics and morals, a trio of economists, working separately across three countries, were starting their own. It began with the publication in 1871 of Carl Menger's *Principles of Economics* and Stanley Jevons's *Theory of Political Economy*. Along with Léon Walras's *Elements of Pure Economics*, which appeared three years later, these were the European voices—speaking in German, English, and French—of what would come to be called the Marginal Revolution.

The marginalists focused less on production than on the pulsing demand of consumption. The protagonist was not the landowner or the laborer, working his way through the farm, the factory or the firm; it was the universal man of the market, whose signature act was to consume things. That's how market man increased his utility: by consuming something until he reached the point where consuming one more increment of it gave him so little additional utility that he was better off consuming something else. Of such microscopic calculations at the periphery of our estate was the economy made.

Though the early marginalists helped transform economics from a humanistic branch of the moral sciences into a technical discipline of the social sciences, they were still able to command an audience and influence all too rare in contemporary economics. Jevons may have spent his career as an independent scholar and professor in Manchester and London worrying about his lack of readers—"I am low because my essay on 'Gold' is out, and as yet no one has said a word in its favour except my sister"— but Gladstone invited him over to discuss his work and Mill praised it on the floor of Parliament. Keynes tells us that "for a period of half a century, practically all elementary students both of Logic and of Political Economy in Great Britain and also in India and the Dominions were brought up on Jevons."[20]

According to Hayek, the "immediate reception" of Menger's *Principles* "can hardly be called encouraging." Reviewers seemed not to understand it. Two students at the University of Vienna, however, did. One was Friedrich von Wieser, the other was Eugen Böhm-Bawerk, and both became legendary educators and theoreticians.[21] Their students included Hayek; Ludwig von Mises, who attracted a small but devoted following in the United States and elsewhere; and Joseph Schumpeter, dark poet of capitalism's forces of "creative destruction."[22] Through Böhm-Bawerk and Wieser, Menger's text became the groundwork of the Austrian School, whose reach, due in part to the efforts of Mises and Hayek, now extends across the globe.

The contributions of Jevons and Menger were multiple, yet each of them took aim at a central postulate of economics shared by everyone from Adam Smith to the socialist left: the notion that labor is a—if not *the*—source of value. Though adumbrated in the idiom of prices and exchange, the labor theory of value evinced an almost primitive faith in the metaphysical objectivity of the economic sphere—a faith made all the more surprising by the fact that the objectivity of the rest of the social world (politics, religion, and morals) had been subject to increasing scrutiny since the Renaissance. Commodities may have come wrapped in the pretty paper of the market, but inside, many believed, were the brute facts of nature: raw materials from the earth and the physical labor that turned those materials into goods. Because those materials were only made useful, hence valuable, by labor, labor was the source of value. That, and the fact that labor could be measured in some way (usually time), lent the world of work a kind of ontological status—and political authority—that had been increasingly denied to the world of courts and kings, lands and lords, parishes and priests. As the rest of the world melted into air, labor was crystallizing as the one true solid.

By the time the marginalists came on the scene, the most politically threatening version of the labor theory of value was associated with the left. Though Marx would categorically reject it in his mature writings, the simple notion that labor produces value remained associated with his name—and even more so with that of his competitor Ferdinand Lassalle, about whom Nietzsche read a fair amount—and with the larger socialist and trade union movements of which he was a part.[23] That association helped set the stage for the marginalists' critique.

Admittedly, the relationship between marginalism and antisocialism is complex. On the one hand, there is little evidence to suggest that the first-generation marginalists had heard of, much less read, Marx, at least not at this early stage of their careers.[24] Much more than the threat of socialism underpinned the emergence of marginalist economics, which was as opposed to traditional defenses of the market as it was to the market's critics. By the twentieth century, moreover, many marginalists were on the left, and used their ideas to help construct the institutions of social democracy; even Walras and Alfred Marshall, another early marginalist, were sympathetic to the claims of the left.

On the other hand, Jevons was a tireless polemicist against trade unions, which he identified as "the best example. . . of the evils and disasters" attending the democratic age. Jevons saw marginalism as a critical antidote to the labor movement and insisted that its teachings be widely transmitted to the working classes. "To avoid such a disaster," he argued, "we must diffuse knowledge" to the workers—empowered as they were by the vote and the strike—"and the kind of knowledge required is mainly that comprehended in the science of political economy."[25] Menger interrupted his abstract reflections on value to make the point that while it may "appear deplorable to a lover of mankind that possession of capital or a piece of land often provides the owner a higher income. . . than the income received by a laborer," the "cause of this is not immoral." It was "simply that the satisfaction of more important human needs depends upon the services of the given amount of capital or piece of land than upon the services of the laborer." Any attempt to get around that truth, he warned, "would undoubtedly require a complete transformation of our social order."[26] Finally, there is no doubt that the marginalists of the Austrian School, who would later prove so influential on the American right, saw their project as primarily anti-Marxist and anti-socialist. "The most momentous consequence of the theory," declared Wieser in 1891, "is, I take it, that it is false, with the socialists, to impute to labor alone the entire productive return."[27]

With its division of intellectual labor, the modern academy often separates economics from ethics and philosophy. Earlier economists and philosophers did not make that separation. Even Nietzsche recognized that economics rested upon genuine moral and philosophical premises, many of which he found dubious, and that it had tremendous moral and political effects, all of which he detested. In *The Wanderer and His Shadow*, Nietzsche criticized "our economists" for having "not yet wearied of scenting a similar unity in the word 'value' and of searching after the original root-concept of the word." In his preliminary outline for the summa he hoped to publish on "the will to power," he scored the "nihilistic consequences of the ways of thinking in politics and economics."[28] Nietzsche thus saw in labor's appearance more than an economic theory of goods: he saw a terrible diminution of the good. Morals must be "understood as the doctrine of the relations of supremacy," he wrote in *Beyond Good and Evil*; every morality "must be forced to bow. . . before the order of rank."[29] But like so many before them, including the Christian slave and English utilitarian, the economist and the socialist promoted an inferior human type—and inferior set of values—as the driving agent of the world. Nietzsche saw in this elevation not only a transformation of values but also a loss of value and, potentially, the elimination of value altogether. Conservatives from Edmund Burke to Patrick Devlin have conflated the transformation of values with the end of value. Nietzsche, on occasion, did too: "What does nihilism mean?" he asked himself in 1887. "That the highest values devalu-ate themselves." The nihilism consuming Europe was best under-stood as a democratic "hatred against the order of rank."[30]

Part of Nietzsche's worry was philosophical: how was it pos-sible in a godless world, naturalistically conceived, to deem any-thing of value? But his concern was also cultural and political. Because of democracy, which was "Christianity made natural," aristocracy had lost "its naturalness," that is, the traditional vindication of its power.[31] How then might a hierarchy of excellence, aesthetic and political, reestablish itself, defending itself against the mass, particularly a mass of workers, and dominate that mass? As Nietzsche wrote in the late 1880s:

> A reverse movement is needed—the production of a synthetic, summarizing, justifying man for whose existence this transformation of mankind into a machine is a precondition, as a base on which he can invent his higher form of being.
>
> He needs the opposition of the masses, of the "leveled," a feeling of distance from them. he stands on them, he lives off them. This higher form of aristocracy is that of the future.— Morally speaking, this overall machinery, this solidarity of all gears, represents a maximum of exploitation of man; but it presupposes those on whose account this exploitation has meaning.[32]

Nietzsche's response to that challenge was not to revert or resort to a more objective notion of value; that was neither possible nor desirable. Instead, he embraced one part of the modern understanding of value—its fabricated nature—and turned it against its democratic and Smithian premises. Value was indeed a human creation, Nietzsche acknowledged, and as such could just as easily be conceived as a gift, an honorific bestowed by one man upon another. "Through esteeming alone is there value," Nietzsche has Zarathustra declare; "to esteem is to create."[33] Value was not made with coarse and clumsy hands; it was enacted with an appraising gaze, a nod of the head signifying the matchless abundance of an exquisite sense of taste. It was, in short, aristocratic.

While slaves had once created value in the form of Christianity, they had achieved that feat not through their labor but through their censure and praise. They also had done it unwittingly, act-ing upon a deep and unconscious compulsion: a sense of inferior-ity, a rage against their powerlessness, and a desire for revenge against their betters. That combination of overt impotence and covert drive made them ill-suited to creating values of excellence. "The noble type of man," by contrast, "experiences itself as deter-mining values," Nietzsche wrote in *Beyond Good and Evil*. That self-conscious exercise and enjoyment of power made the noble type a better candidate for the creation of values in the modern world, for these were values that would have to break with the slave morality that had dominated for millennia. Only insofar as "it knows itself to be that which first accords honor to things" can the noble type truly be "value-creating."[34]

Labor belonged to nature, which is not capable of generating value. Only the man who arrayed himself against nature—the artist, the general, the statesman—could claim that role. He alone had the necessary refinements, wrought by "that pathos of dis-tance which grows out of ingrained difference between strata," to appreciate and bestow value: upon men, practices, and beliefs.[35] Value was not a product of the prole; it was an imposition of peer-less taste. In the words of *The Gay Science*:

> Whatever has *value* in our world now does not have value in itself, according to its nature—nature is always value-less, but has been *given* value at some time, as a present—and it was *we* who gave and bestowed it.[36]

That was in 1882. Just a decade earlier, Menger had written, "Value is therefore nothing inherent in goods, no property of them, but merely the importance that we first attribute to the satisfaction of our needs, that is, to our lives and well-being."[37] Jevons's position was identical, and like Nietzsche, Menger and

Jevons thought value was instead a high or low estimation put by a man upon the things of life. But lest that desiring self be reduced to a simple creature of tabulated needs, Menger and Jevons took care to distinguish their positions from traditional theories of utility.

Jevons, for example, was prepared to follow Jeremy Bentham in his definition of utility as "that property in an object, whereby it tends to produce benefit, advantage, pleasure, good, or happiness." He thought this "perfectly expresses the meaning of the word Economy."[38] But Jevons also insisted on a critical rider: "provided that the will or inclination of the person concerned is taken as the sole criterion, for the time, of what is good and desirable."[39] Our expressed desires and aversions are not measures of our objective or underlying good; there is no such thing. Nor can we be assured that those desires or aversions will bring us pleasure or pain. What we want or don't want is merely a representation, a snapshot of the motions of our will—that black box of preference and partiality that so fascinated Nietzsche precisely because it seemed so groundless and yet so generative. Every mind is inscrutable to itself: we lack, said Jevons, "the means of measuring directly the feelings of the human heart." The inner life is inaccessible to our inspections; all we can know are its effects, the will it powers and the actions it propels. "The will is our pendulum," declared Jevons, a representation of forces that cannot be seen but whose effects are nevertheless felt, "and its oscillations are minutely registered in all the price lists of the markets."[40]

Menger thought the value of any good was connected to our needs, but he was extraordinarily attuned to the complexity—and contingency—of that relationship. Needs, wrote Menger, "as least as concern their origin, depend upon our wills or on our habits." Needs are more than the givens of our biology or psyche; they are the desiderata of our volitions and practices, which are idiosyncratic and arbitrary. Only when our needs finally "come into existence"—that is, only when we become aware of them—can we truly say that "there is *no further arbitrary element*" in the process of value formation.[41]

Even then, needs must pass through a series of checkpoints before they can enter the land of value. Awareness of a need, says Menger, entails a comprehensive knowledge of how the need might be fulfilled by a particular good, how that good might contribute to our lives, and how (and whether) command of that good is necessary for the satisfaction of that need. That last bit of knowledge requires us to look at the external world: to ask how much of that good is available to us, to consider how many sacrifices we must bear—how many satisfactions we are willing to forgo—in order to secure it. Only when we have answered these questions are we ready to speak of value, which Menger reminds us is "the importance we attribute to the satisfaction of our needs." Value is thus "a judgment" that "economizing men make about the importance of the goods at their disposal for the maintenance of their lives and well-being." It "does not exist outside the consciousness of men." Even though previous economists had insisted on the "objectification of the value of goods," Menger, like Jevons and Nietzsche, concludes that value "is entirely subjective in nature."[42]

In their war against socialism, the philosophers of capital faced two challenges. The first was that by the early twentieth century, socialism had cornered the market on morality. As Mises complained in his 1932 preface to the second edition of *Socialism*, "Any advocate of socialistic measures is looked upon as a friend of the Good, the Noble, and the Moral, as a disinterested pioneer of necessary reforms, in short, as a man who unselfishly serves his own people and all humanity."[43] Indeed, with the help of kindred notions such as "social justice," socialism seemed to be the very definition of morality. Nietzsche had long been wise to this insinuation; one source of his discontent with religion was his sense that it had bequeathed to modernity an understanding of what morality entailed (selflessness, universality, equality) such that only socialism and democracy could be said to fulfill it. But where Nietzsche's response to the equation of socialism and morality was to question the value of morality, at least as it had been customarily understood, economists like Mises and Hayek pursued a different path, one Nietzsche would never have dared to take: they made the market the very expression of morality.

Moralists traditionally viewed the pursuit of money and goods as negative or neutral; the Austrians claimed it embodies our deepest values and commitments. "The provision of material goods," declared Mises, "serves not only those ends which are usually termed economic, but also many other ends." All of us have ends or ultimate purposes in life: the cultivation of friendship, the contemplation of beauty, the enjoyment of music, a lover's companionship. We enter the market for the sake of those ends. Economic action thus "consists firstly in valuation of ends, and then in the valuation of the means leading to these ends. All economic activity depends, therefore, upon the existence of ends. Ends dominate economy and alone give it meaning."[44] We simply cannot speak, writes Hayek in *The Road to Serfdom*, of "purely economic ends separate from the other ends of life."[45]

This claim, however, could just as easily be enlisted into an argument for socialism. In providing men and women with the means of life—housing, food, health care—the socialist state frees them to pursue the ends of life: beauty, knowledge, wisdom. The Austrians went further, insisting that the very decision about what constitutes means and ends was itself a judgment of value. Any economic situation confronts us with the necessity of choice, of having to deploy our limited resources—whether time, money, or effort—on behalf of some end. In making that choice, we reveal which of our ends matters most to us, which is higher, which is lower. "Every man who, in the course of economic activity, chooses between the satisfaction of two needs, only one of which can be satisfied, makes judgments of value," says Mises.[46]

In order for those choices to reveal our ends, our resources must be finite—unlimited time, for example, would obviate the need for choice—and our choice of ends unconstrained by external interference. The best, indeed only, method for guaranteeing such a situation is if money (or its equivalent in material goods) is the currency of choice—and not just of economic choice but of all of our choices. As Hayek writes in *The Road to Serfdom*:

> So long as we can freely dispose over our income and all our possessions, economic loss will always deprive us only of what we regard as the least important of the desires we were able to satisfy. A "merely" economic loss is thus one whose effect we can still make fall on our less important needs. . . Economic changes, in other words, usually affect only the fringe, the "margin," of our needs. There are many things which are more important than anything which economic gains or losses are likely to affect, which for us stand high above the amenities and even above many of the necessities of life which are affected by the economic ups and downs.[47]

Should the government decide which of our needs is "merely economic," we would be deprived of the opportunity to decide whether these are higher or lower goods, whether they are the marginal or mandatory items of our flourishing. So vast is the gulf between each soul, so separate and unequal are we, it is impossible to assume anything universal about the sources and conditions of human happiness, a point Nietzsche—and Jevons ("every mind is thus inscrutable to every other mind, and no common denominator of feeling is possible")—would have found congenial.[48] The judgment of what constitutes a means, what an end, must be left in the hands of the self. Hayek again:

> Economic control is not merely control of a sector of human life which can be separated from the rest; it is the control of the means for all our ends. And whoever has sole control of the means must also determine which ends are to be served, which values are to be rated higher and which lower—in short what men should believe and strive for.[49]

While the economic is, in one sense readily acknowledged by Hayek, the sphere of our lower needs, it is, in another altogether more important sense, the anvil upon which our sense of what is lower and higher in this world, our morality, is forged. "Economic values," he writes, "are less important to us than many things precisely because in economic matters we are free to decide what to us is more, and what less, important."[50] But we can only be free to make those choices if they are left to us to make—and, paradoxically, if we are forced to make them. If we didn't have to choose, we'd never have to value anything.

By imposing this drama of choice, the economy becomes a theater of self-disclosure, the stage upon which we discover and reveal our ultimate ends. It is not in the casual chatter of a seminar or the cloistered pews of a church that we determine our values; it is in the duress—the ordeal—of our lived lives, those moments when we are not only free to choose but forced to choose. "Freedom to order our own conduct in the sphere where material circumstances force a choice upon us," Hayek wrote, "is the air in which alone moral sense grows and in which moral values are daily re-created."[51]

Where progressives often view this discourse of choice as either dime-store morality or fabricated scarcity, the Austrians saw the economy as the disciplining agent of all ethical action, a moment of—and opportunity for—moral artistry. Freud thought the compressions of the dream world made every man an artist; these other Austrians thought the compulsions of the economy made every man a moralist. It is only when we are navigating its narrow channels—where every decision to expend some quantum of energy requires us to make a calculation about the desirability of its posited end—that we are brought face to face with ourselves and compelled to answer the questions: What do I believe? What do I want in this world? From this life?

While there are precedents for this argument in Menger's theory of value (the fewer opportunities there are for the satisfaction of our needs, Menger says, the more our choices will reveal which needs we value most), its true and full dimensions can best be understood in relation to Nietzsche.[52] As much as Nietzsche railed against the repressive effect of laws and morals on the highest types, he also appreciated how much "on earth of freedom, subtlety, boldness, dance, and masterly sureness" was owed to these constraints.[53] Confronted with a set of social strictures, the diverse and driving energies of the self were forced to draw upon unknown and untapped reserves of ingenuity—either to overcome these obstacles or to adapt to them with the minimum sacrifice. The results were novel, value-creating.

Nietzsche's point was primarily aesthetic. Contrary to the romantic notion of art being produced by a process of "letting go," Nietzsche insisted that the artist "strictly and subtly. . . obeys thousandfold laws." The language of invention—whether poetry, music, or speech itself—is bound by "the metrical compulsion of rhyme and rhythm."[54] Such laws are capricious in their origin and tyrannical in their effect. That is the point: from that unforgiving soil of power and whimsy grows the most miraculous increase. Not just in the arts—Goethe, say, or Beethoven—but in politics and ethics as well: Napoleon, Caesar, Nietzsche himself ("Genuine philosophers. . . are commanders and legislators: they say, 'thus it shall be!'")[55]

One school would find expression for these ideas in fascism. Writers like Ernst Jünger and Carl Schmitt imagined political artists of great novelty and originality forcing their way through or past the filtering constraints of everyday life. The leading legal theorist of the Third Reich, Schmitt looked to those extraordinary instances in politics—war, the "decision," the "exception"—when "the power of real life," as he put it in *Political Theology*, "breaks through the crust of a mechanism that has become torpid by repetition." In that confrontation between mechanism and real life, the man of exception would find or make his moment: by taking an unauthorized decision, ordaining a new regime of law, or founding a political order. In each case, something was "created out of nothingness."[56]

It was the peculiar—and in the long run more significant—genius of the Austrian School to look for these moments and experiences not in the political realm but in the marketplace. Money in a capitalist economy, Hayek came to realize, could be best understood and defended in Nietzschean terms: as "the medium through which a force"—the self's "desire for power to achieve unspecified ends"—"makes itself felt."[57]

The second challenge confronting the philosophers of capital was more daunting. While Nietzsche's transvaluation of values gave pride of place to the highest types of humanity—values were a gift, the philosopher their greatest source—the political implications of marginalism were ideologically more ambidextrous. If on one reading it was the capitalist who gave value to the worker, on another it was the worker—in his capacity as consumer—who gave value to capital. Social democrats pursued the latter argument with great zeal. The result was the welfare state, with its emphasis on high wages and good benefits—as well as unionization—as the driving agent of mass demand and economic prosperity. More than a macroeconomic policy, social democracy (or liberalism, as it was called in America) reflected an ethos of the citizen-worker-consumer as the creator and center of the economy. Long after economists had retired the labor theory of value, the welfare state remained lit by its afterglow. The political economy of the welfare state may have been marginalist, but its moral economy was workerist.

The midcentury right was in desperate need of a response that, squaring Nietzsche's circle, would clear a path for aristocratic action in the capitalist marketplace. It needed not simply an alternative economics but an answering vision of society. Schumpeter provided one, Hayek another.

Schumpeter's entrepreneur is one of the more enigmatic characters of modern social theory. He is not inventive, heroic, or charismatic. "There is surely no trace of any mystic glamour about him," Schumpeter writes in Capitalism, Socialism and Democracy. His instincts and impulses are confined to the office and the counting table. Outside those environs, he cannot "say boo to a goose." Yet it is this nothing, this great inscrutable blank, that will "bend a nation to his will"—not unlike the father figures of a Mann or Musil novel.[58]

What the entrepreneur has—or, better, is—are force and will. As Schumpeter explains in a 1927 essay, the entrepreneur possesses "extraordinary physical and nervous energy." That energy gives him focus (the maniacal, almost brutal, ability to shut out what is inessential) and stamina. In those late hours when lesser beings have "given way to a state of exhaustion," he retains his "full force and originality." By originality Schumpeter means some-thing peculiar: "receptivity to new facts."[59] It is the entrepreneur's ability to recognize that sweet spot of novelty and occasion (an untried technology, a new method of production, a different way to market or distribute a product) that enables him to revolution-ize the way business gets done. Part opportunist, part fanatic, he is "a leading man," Schumpeter suggests in *Capitalism, Socialism and Democracy*, overcoming all resistance in order to create the new modes and orders of everyday life.[60]

Schumpeter is careful to distinguish entrepreneurialism from politics as it is conventionally understood: the entrepreneur's power "does not readily expand. . . into the leadership of nations"; "he wants to be left alone and to leave politics alone."[61] Even so, the entrepreneur is best understood as neither an escape from nor evasion of politics but as the sublimation of politics, the relocation of politics in the economic sphere.

Rejecting the static models of other economists—equilibrium is death, he says—Schumpeter depicts the economy as a dramatic confrontation between rising and falling empires (firms).[62] Like Machiavelli in *The Prince*, whose vision Nietzsche described as "perfection in politics," Schumpeter identifies two types of agents struggling for position and permanence amid great flux: one is dynastic and lawful, the other upstart and intelligent. Both are engaged in a death dance, with the former in the potentially weaker position unless it can innovate and break with routine. [63]

Schumpeter often resorts to political and military meta-phors to describe this dance. Production is "a history of revolu-tions." Competitors "command" and wield "pieces of armor." Competition "strikes" at the "foundations" and "very lives" of firms; entrepreneurs in equilibrium "find themselves in much the same situations as generals would in a society perfectly sure of permanent peace."[64] In the same way that Schmitt imagines peace as the end of politics, Schumpeter sees equilibrium as the end of economics.

Against this backdrop of dramatic, even lethal, contest, the entrepreneur emerges as a legislator of values and new ways of being. The entrepreneur demonstrates a penchant for breaking with "the routine tasks which everybody understands." He overcomes the multiple resistances of his world—"from simple refusal either to finance or to buy a new thing, to physical attack on the man who tries to produce it."

> To act with confidence beyond the range of familiar beacons and to overcome that resistance requires aptitudes that are present in only a small fraction of the population and that define the entrepreneurial type.

The entrepreneur, in other words, is a founder. As Schumpeter describes him in *The Theory of Economic Development*:

> There is the dream and the will to found a private kingdom, usually, though not necessarily, also a dynasty. The modern world really does not know any such position, but what may be attained by industrial and commercial success is still the nearest approach to medieval lordship possible to modern man.[65]

That may be why his inner life is so reminiscent of the Machiavellian prince, that other virtuoso of novelty. All of his energy and will, the entirety of his force and being, is focused outward, on the enterprise of creating a new order.

And yet even as he sketched the broad outline of this legislator of value, Schumpeter sensed that his days were numbered. Innovation was increasingly the work of departments, committees, and specialists. The modern corporation "socializes the bourgeois mind." In the same way that modern regiments had destroyed the "very personal affair" of medieval battle, so did the corporation eliminate the need for "individual leadership acting by virtue of personal force and personal responsibility for success." The "romance of earlier commercial adventure" was "rapidly wearing away."[66] With the entrepreneurial function in terminal decline, Schumpeter's experiment in economics as great politics seemed to be approaching an end.

Hayek offered an alternative account of the market as the proving ground of aristocratic action. Schumpeter had already hinted at it in a stray passage in *Capitalism, Socialism and Democracy*. Taking aim at the notion of a rational chooser, who knows what he wants, wants what is best (for him at any rate), and works efficiently to get it, Schumpeter invoked a half century of social thought—Le Bon, Pareto, and Freud—to emphasize not only "the importance of the extra-rational and irrational element in our behavior" but also the power of capital to shape the preferences of the consumer.

> Consumers do not quite live up to the idea that the economic textbook used to convey. On the one hand their wants are nothing like as definite and their actions upon those wants nothing like as rational and prompt. On the other hand they are so amenable to the influence of advertising and other methods of persuasion that producers often seem to dictate to them instead of being directed by them.[67]

In *The Constitution of Liberty*, Hayek developed this notion into a full-blown theory of the wealthy and the well-born as an avant-garde of taste, as makers of new horizons of value from which the rest of humanity took its bearings. Instead of the market of consumers dictating the actions of capital, it would be capital that would determine the market of consumption—and beyond that the deepest beliefs and aspirations of a people.

The distinction Hayek draws between mass and elite has not received much attention from his critics or his defenders, bewildered or beguiled as they are by his repeated invocations of liberty. Yet a careful reading of Hayek's argument reveals that liberty for him is neither the highest good nor an intrinsic good. It is a contingent and instrumental good (a consequence of our ignorance and the condition of our progress), the purpose of which is to make possible the emergence of a heroic legislator of value.

Civilization and progress, Hayek argues, depend upon each of us deploying knowledge that is available for our use yet inaccessible to our reason. The computer on which I am typing is a repository of centuries of mathematics, science, and engineering. I know how to use it but I don't understand it. Most of our knowledge is like that. We know the "how" of things—how to turn on the computer, call up our word processing program, and type—without knowing the "that" of things: electricity is the flow of electrons, circuits operate through binary choices, and so on. Others possess the latter kind of knowledge; not us. That combination of our know-how and their knowledge advances the cause of civilization. Because they have thought through how a computer can be optimally designed, we are free to ignore its transistors and microchips; instead we can order clothes online, keep up with old friends as if they lived next door, and dive into previously inaccessible libraries and archives in order to produce a novel account of the Crimean War.

We can never know what serendipity of knowledge and know-how will produce the best results, which union of genius and ignoramus will yield the greatest advance. For that reason, individuals—all individuals—must be free to pursue their ends, to exploit the wisdom of others for their own purposes. Allowing for the uncertainties of progress is the greatest guarantor of progress. Hayek's argument for freedom rests less on what we know or want to know than on what we don't know, less on what we are morally entitled to as individuals than on the beneficial consequences of individual freedom to society as a whole.

In fact, Hayek continues, it is not really my freedom that I should be concerned about, nor is it the freedom of my friends and neighbors. It is the freedom of that unknown and untapped figure of invention to whose imagination and ingenuity my friends and I will later owe our greater happiness and flourishing: "What is important is not what freedom I personally would like to exercise but what freedom some person may need in order to do things beneficial to society. This freedom we can assure to the unknown person only by giving it to all."[68]

Deep inside Hayek's understanding of freedom, then, is the notion that the freedom of some is worth more than the freedom of others: "The freedom that will be used by only one man in a million may be more important to society and more beneficial to the majority than any freedom that we all use." Hayek cites approvingly this statement of a nineteenth-century philosopher: "It may be of extreme importance that some should enjoy liberty. . . although such liberty may be neither possible nor desirable for the great majority." That we don't grant freedom only to that individual is due solely to the happenstance of our ignorance: we cannot know in advance who he might be. "If there were omniscient men, if we could know not only all that affects the attainment of our present wishes but also our future wants and desires, there would be little case for liberty."[69]

As this reference to "future wants and desires" suggests, Hayek has much more in mind than producers responding to a preexisting market of demand; he's talking about men who create new markets—and not just of wants or desires but of basic tastes and beliefs. The freedom Hayek cares most about is the freedom of those legislators of value who shape and determine our ends.

The overwhelming majority of men and women, Hayek says, are simply not capable of breaking with settled patterns of thought and practice; given a choice, they would never opt for anything new, never do anything better than what they do now.

> Action by collective agreement is limited to instances where previous efforts have already created a common view, where opinion about what is desirable has become settled, and where the problem is that of choosing between possibilities already generally recognized, not that of discovering new possibilities.[70]

While some might claim that Hayek's argument here is driven less by a dim view of ordinary men and women than his dyspepsia about politics, he explicitly excludes "the decision of some governing elite" from the acid baths of his skepticism.[71] Nor does he hide his misgivings about the individual abilities of wage laborers who comprise the great majority. The working stiff is a being of limited horizons. Unlike the employer or the "independent," both of whom are dedicated to "shaping and reshaping a plan of life," the worker's orientation is "largely a matter of fitting himself into a given framework." He lacks responsibility, initiative, curiosity, and ambition. Though some of this is by necessity—the workplace does not countenance "actions which cannot be prescribed or which are not conventional"—Hayek insists that this is "not only the actual but the preferred position of the majority of the population." The great majority like submitting to the workplace regime because it "gives them what they mainly want: an assured fixed income available for current expenditure, more or less automatic raises, and provision for old age. They are thus relieved of some of the responsibilities of economic life." Simply put, these are people for whom taking orders from a superior is not only a welcome relief but a prerequisite of their fulfillment: "To do the bidding of others is for the employed the condition of achieving his purpose."[72]

It thus should come as no surprise that Hayek believes in an avant-garde of taste-makers, whose power and position give them a vantage from which they can not only see beyond the existing horizon but also catch a glimpse of new horizons.

> Only from an advanced position does the next range of desires and possibilities become visible, so that the selection of new goals and the effort toward their achievement will begin long before the majority can strive for them.[73]

These horizons include everything from "what we regard as good or beautiful" to the ambitions, goals, and ends we pursue in our everyday lives to "the propagation of new ideas in politics, morals, and religion."[74] On all of these fronts it is the avant-garde that leads the way and sets our parameters.

More interesting is how explicit and insistent Hayek is about linking the legislation of new values to the possession of vast amounts of wealth and capital, even—or especially—wealth that has been inherited. Often, says Hayek, it is only the very rich who can afford new products or tastes. Lavishing money on these boutique items, they give producers the opportunity to experiment with better designs and more efficient methods of production. Thanks to their patronage, producers will find cheaper ways of making and delivering these products—cheap enough, that is, for the majority to enjoy them. What was before a luxury of the idle rich—stockings, automobiles, piano lessons, the university—is now an item of mass consumption.

The most important contribution of great wealth, however, is that it frees its possessor from the pursuit of money so that he can pursue non-material goals. Liberated from the workplace and the rat race, the "idle rich"—a phrase Hayek seeks to reclaim as a positive good—can devote themselves to patronizing the arts, subsidizing worthy causes like abolition or penal reform, founding new philanthropies and cultural institutions. Those born to wealth are especially important. Not only are they the beneficiaries of the higher culture and nobler values that have been transmitted across the generations—Hayek insists that we will get a better elite if we allow parents to pass their fortunes on to their children; requiring a ruling class to start fresh with every generation is a recipe for stagnation, for having to reinvent the wheel—but they are immune to the petty lure of money. "The grosser pleasures in which the newly rich often indulge have usually no attraction for those who have inherited wealth."[75] (How Hayek reconciles this position with the agnosticism about value he expresses in *Road to Serfdom* remains unclear.)

The men of capital, in other words, are best understood not as economic magnates but as cultural legislators: "However important the independent owner of property may be for the economic order of a free society, his importance is perhaps even greater in the fields of thought and opinion, of tastes and beliefs." While this seems to be a universal truth for Hayek, it is especially true in societies where wage labor is the rule. The dominance of paid employment has terrible consequences for the imagination, which are most acutely felt by the producers of that imagination: "There is something seriously lacking in a society in which all the intellectual, moral, and artistic leaders belong to the employed classes. . . . Yet we are moving everywhere toward such a position."[76] When labor becomes the norm, in both senses of the term, culture does not stand a chance.

In a virtuoso analysis of what he calls "The Intransigent Right," Perry Anderson identifies four figures of the twentieth-century conservative canon: Schmitt, Hayek, Michael Oakeshott, and Leo Strauss. Strauss and Schmitt come off best in Anderson's analysis (the sharpest, most profound and far-seeing), Oakeshott the worst, and Hayek somewhere in between. This hierarchy of judgment is not completely surprising. Anderson has never taken seriously the political theory of a nation of shopkeepers, so the receptivity of the English to Oakeshott and Hayek, who became a British subject in 1938, makes them almost irresistible targets for his critique. Anderson's cosmopolitan indifference to the indiscreet charms of the Anglo bourgeoisie usually makes him the most sure-footed of guides, but in Hayek's case it has led him astray. So taken with the bravura and brutality of Strauss's and Schmitt's self-styled realism is Anderson that he can't grasp the far greater daring and profundity of Hayek's political theory of shopkeeping—his effort to relocate great politics in the economic relations of capitalism.

What distinguishes the theoretical men of the right from their counterparts on the left, Anderson clams, is that their voices were "heard in the chancelleries."[77] Yet whose voice has been more listened to, across decades and continents, than Hayek's? Schmitt and Strauss have attracted readers from all points of the political spectrum as writers of dazzling if disturbing genius. Yet the two projects with which they are most associated—European fascism and American neoconservatism—have never generated the global traction or gathering energy that neoliberalism has now sustained for more than four decades.

It would be a mistake to draw too sharp a line between the marginal children of Nietzsche, with political man on one branch of the family tree, and economic man on the other. Hayek, at times, could sound the most Schmittian notes. At the height of Augusto Pinochet's power in Chile, Hayek told a Chilean interviewer that when any "government is in a situation of rupture, and there are no recognized rules, rules have to be created."[78] The sort of situation he had in mind was not anarchy or civil war but Allende-style social democracy, where the government pursues "the mirage of social justice" through administrative and increasingly discretionary means. Even in *The Constitution of Liberty*, an extended paean to the notion of a "spontaneous order" that slowly evolves over time, we get a brief glimpse of "the lawgiver" whose "task" it is "to create conditions in which an orderly arrangement can establish and ever renew itself." ("Of the modern German writings" on the rule of law, Hayek also says there, Schmitt's "are still among the most learned and perceptive.")[79] Current events seemed to supply Hayek with an endless parade of candidates. A year after its publication in 1961, he sent *The Constitution of Liberty* to Portuguese strongman António Salazar, with a covering note professing his hope that it might assist the dictator "in his endeavour to design a constitution which is proof against the abuses of democracy."[80] Pinochet's constitution of 1980 is named after the 1961 text.[81]

Still, it's difficult to escape the conclusion that though Nietzschean politics may have fought the battles, Nietzschean economics won the war. After all, the Detlev-Rohwedder-Haus in Berlin, built to house the Luftwaffe during World War II, is now the headquarters of the German Ministry of Finance.

PART 3 American Vistas

7

Metaphysics and Chewing Gum

Saint Petersburg in revolt gave us Vladimir Nabokov, Isaiah Berlin, and Ayn Rand. The first was a novelist, the second a philosopher. The third was neither but thought she was both. Many other people have thought so too. In 1998, readers responding to a Modern Library poll identified *Atlas Shrugged* and *The Fountainhead* as the two greatest novels in English of the twentieth century—surpassing *Ulysses, To the Lighthouse,* and *Invisible Man.* In 1991, a survey by the Library of Congress and the Book-of-the-Month Club found that with the exception of the Bible, no book has influenced more American readers than *Atlas Shrugged.*[1]

One of those readers might well have been Farrah Fawcett. Not long before she died, the actress called Rand a "literary genius" whose refusal to make her art "like everyone else's" inspired Fawcett's own experiments in painting and sculpture. The admiration, it seems, was mutual. Rand watched *Charlie's Angels* each week and, according to Fawcett, "saw something" in the show "that the critics didn't."

She described the show as a "triumph of concept and casting." Ayn said that while *Angels* was uniquely American, it was also the exception to American television in that it was the only show to capture true "romanticism"—it intentionally depicted the world not as it was, but as it should be. Aaron Spelling was probably the only other person to see *Angels* that way, although he referred to it as "comfort television."

So taken was Rand with Fawcett that she hoped the actress (or if not her, Raquel Welch) would play the part of Dagny Taggart in a TV version of *Atlas Shrugged* on NBC. Unfortunately, network head Fred Silverman killed the project in 1978. "I'll always think of 'Dagny Taggart' as the best role I was supposed to play but never did," Fawcett said.[2]

Rand's following in Hollywood has always been strong. Barbara Stanwyck and Veronica Lake fought to play the part of Dominique Francon in the movie version of *The Fountainhead*. Never to be outdone in that department, Joan Crawford threw a dinner party for Rand in which she dressed as Francon, wearing a streaming white gown dotted with aquamarine gemstones.[3] More recently, the author of *The Virtue of Selfishness* and the statement "if civilization is to survive, it is the altruist morality that men have to reject" has found an unlikely pair of fans in the Hollywood humanitarian set.[4] Rand "has a very interesting philosophy," says Angelina Jolie. "You re-evaluate your own life and what's important to you." *The Fountainhead* "is so dense and complex," marvels Brad Pitt, "it would have to be a six-hour movie." (The 1949 film version already has a running time of two hours.) Christina Ricci claims that *The Fountainhead* is her favorite book because it taught her that "you're not a bad person if you don't love everyone." Rob Lowe boasts that *Atlas Shrugged* is "a stupendous achievement, and I just adore it." And any boyfriend of Eva Mendes, the actress says, "has to be an Ayn Rand fan."[5]

But Rand, at least according to her fiction, shouldn't have attracted any fans at all. The central plot device of her novels is the conflict between the creative individual and the hostile mass. The greater the individual's achievement, the greater the mass's resistance. As Howard Roark, architect hero of *The Fountainhead*, puts it:

> The great creators—the thinkers, the artists, the scientists, the inventors—stood alone against the men of their time. Every great new thought was opposed. Every great new invention was denounced. The first motor was considered foolish. The airplane was considered impossible. The power loom was considered vicious. Anesthesia was considered sinful. But the men of unborrowed vision went ahead. They fought, they suffered and they paid.[6]

Rand clearly thought of herself as one of these creators. In an interview with Mike Wallace she declared herself "the most creative thinker alive." That was in 1957, when Arendt, Quine, Sartre, Camus, Lukács, Adorno, Murdoch, Heidegger, Beauvoir, Rawls, Anscombe, and Popper were all at work. It was also the year of the first performance of *Endgame* and the publication of *Pnin, Doctor Zhivago,* and *The Cat in the Hat*. Two years later, Rand told Wallace that "the only philosopher who ever influenced me" was Aristotle. Otherwise, everything came "out of my own mind." She boasted to her friends and to her publisher at Random House, Bennett Cerf, that she was "challenging the cultural tradition of two and a half thousand years." She saw herself as she saw Roark, who said, "I inherit nothing. I stand at the end of no tradition. I may, perhaps, stand at the beginning of one." Yet tens of thousands of fans were already standing with her. In 1945, just two years after its publication, *The Fountainhead* sold 100,000 copies. In 1957, the year of its publication, *Atlas Shrugged* sat on the *New York Times* bestseller list for twenty-one weeks.[7]

Rand may have been uneasy about the challenge her popularity posed to her worldview, for she spent much of her later life spinning tales about the chilly response she and her work had received. She falsely claimed that twelve publishers rejected *The Fountainhead* before it found a home. She styled herself the victim of a terrible but necessary isolation, claiming that "all achievement and progress has been accomplished, not just by men of ability and certainly not by groups of men, but by a struggle between man and mob." But how many lonely writers emerge from their study, having just written "The End" on the last page of their novel, to be greeted by a chorus of congratulations from a waiting circle of fans?[8]

Had she been a more careful reader of her work, Rand might have seen this irony coming. However much she liked to pit the genius against the mass, her fiction always betrayed a secret communion between the two. Each of her two most famous novels gives its estranged hero an opportunity to defend himself in a lengthy speech before the untutored and the unlettered. Roark declaims before a jury of "the hardest faces" that includes "a truck driver, a bricklayer, an electrician, a gardener and three factory workers." John Galt takes to the airwaves in *Atlas Shrugged*, addressing millions of listeners for hours on end. In each instance, the hero is understood, his genius acclaimed, his alienation resolved. And that's because, as Galt explains, there are "no conflicts of interest among rational men"—which is just a Randian way of saying that every story has a happy ending.[9]

The chief conflict in Rand's novels, then, is not between the individual and the masses. It is between the demigod-creator and all those unproductive elements of society—the intellectuals, bureaucrats, and middlemen—that stand between him and the masses. Aesthetically, this makes for kitsch; politically, it bends toward fascism. Admittedly, the argument that there is a connection between fascism and kitsch has taken a beating over the years. Yet surely the example of Rand is suggestive enough to put the question of their connection back on the table.

She was born on February 2, three weeks after the failed revolution of 1905. Her parents were Jewish. They lived in Saint Petersburg, a city long governed by hatred of the Jews. By 1914, its register of antisemitic restrictions ran to nearly 1,000 pages, including one statute limiting Jews to no more than 2 percent of the population. They named her Alissa Zinovievna Rosenbaum.[10]

When she was four or five years old she asked her mother if she could have a blouse like the one her cousins wore. Her mother said no. She asked for a cup of tea like the one being served to the grown-ups. Again her mother said no. She wondered why she couldn't have what she wanted. Someday, she vowed, she would. In later life, Rand would make much of this experience. Her biographer does too: "The elaborate and controversial philosophical system she went on to create in her forties and fifties was, at its heart, an answer to this question."[11]

The story, as told, is pure Rand. There's the focus on a single incident as portent or precipitant of dramatic fate. There's the elevation of a childhood commonplace to grand philosophy. What child, after all, hasn't bridled at being denied what she wants? Though Rand seems to have taken youthful selfishness to its outermost limits—as a child she disliked Robin Hood; as a teenager she watched her family nearly starve while she treated herself to the theater—her solipsism was neither so rare nor so precious as to warrant more than the usual amount of adolescent self-absorption.[12] There is, finally, the inadvertent revelation that one's worldview constitutes little more than a case of arrested development. "It is not that chewing gum undermines metaphysics," Max Horkheimer once wrote about mass culture, "but that it is metaphysics—this is what must be made clear."[13] Rand made it very, very clear.

But the anecdote suggests something additionally distinctive about Rand. Not her opinions or tastes, which were middlebrow and conventional. Rand claimed Victor Hugo as her primary inspiration in matters of fiction; Edmond Rostand's *Cyrano de Bergerac* was another touchstone. She deemed Rachmaninoff superior to Bach, Mozart, and Beethoven. She was offended by a reviewer's admittedly foolish comparison of *The Fountainhead* to *The Magic Mountain*. Mann, Rand thought, was the inferior author, as was Solzhenitsyn.[14]

Nor was it her sense of self that set Rand apart from others. True, she tended toward the cartoonish and the grandiose. She told Nathaniel Branden, her much younger lover and disciple of many years, that he should desire her even if she were eighty and in a wheelchair. Her essays often quote Galt's speeches as if the character were a real person, a philosopher on the order of Plato or Kant. She claimed to have created herself with the help of no one, even though she was the lifelong beneficiary of social democratic largesse. She got a college education thanks to the Russian Revolution, which opened universities to women and Jews and, once the Bolsheviks had seized power, made tuition free. Subsidizing theater for the masses, the Bolsheviks also made it possible for Rand to see cheesy operettas on a weekly basis. After Rand's first play closed in New York City in April 1936, the Works Progress Administration took it on the road to theaters across the country, giving Rand a handsome income of $10 a performance throughout the late 1930s. Librarians at the New York Public Library assisted her with the research for *The Fountainhead*.[15] Still, her narcissism was probably no greater—and certainly no less sustaining—than that of your run-of-the-mill struggling author.

No, what truly distinguished Rand was her ability to translate her sense of self into reality, to will her imagined identity into material fact. Not by being great, but by persuading others, even shrewd biographers, that she was great. Anne Heller, for example, author of *Ayn Rand and the World She Made*, repeatedly praises Rand's "original, razor sharp mind" and "lightning-quick logic," making one wonder how closely she has read Rand's work. She claims that Rand was able "to write more persuasively from a male point of view than any female writer since George Eliot."[16] Does Heller really believe that Roark or Galt is more credible or persuasive than Lawrence Selden or Newland Archer? Or little James Ramsay, who seems to have acquired more psychic depth in his six years than any of Rand's protagonists, male or female, demonstrate throughout their entire lives? Jennifer Burns, an intellectual historian and author of *Goddess of the Market: Ayn Rand and the American Right*, writes that Rand was "among the first to identify the modern state's often terrifying power and to make it an issue of popular concern," which is true only if one sets aside Montesquieu, Godwin, Constant, Tocqueville, Proudhon, Bakunin, Spencer, Kropotkin, Malatesta, and Emma Goldman. Burns claims that Rand disliked the "messiness of the bohemian student protestors" of the sixties because she was "raised in the high European tradition." But what kind of high European tradition includes operettas and Rachmaninoff, melodrama and movies? Burns concludes that "what remains" of enduring value in Rand is her injunction to "be true to yourself." Yet it hardly took Rand to teach us that; indeed, the very same notion figures in a play about a Danish prince written roughly five centuries before Rand's birth.[17]

To understand how Alissa Rosenbaum created Ayn Rand, we need to trace her itinerary not to prerevolutionary Russia, which is the mistaken conceit of her biographers, but to her destination upon leaving Soviet Russia in 1926: Hollywood. For where else but in the dream factory could Rand have learned how to make dreams—about America, capitalism, and herself?

Even before she was in Hollywood, Rand was of Hollywood. In 1925 alone, she saw 117 movies. It was in movies, Burns says, that Rand "glimpsed America"—and, we might add, developed her enduring sense of narrative form. Once there, she became the subject of her very own Hollywood story. She was discovered by Cecil B. DeMille, who saw her mooning about his studio looking for work. Intrigued by her intense gaze, he gave her a ride in his car and a job as an extra, which she quickly turned into a screenwriting gig. Within a few years her scripts were attracting attention from major players, prompting one newspaper to run a story with the headline "RUSSIAN GIRL FINDS END OF RAINBOW IN HOLLYWOOD."[18]

Rand, of course, was not the only European who came to Hollywood during the interwar years. But unlike Fritz Lang, Hanns Eisler, and all the other exiles in paradise, Rand did not escape to Hollywood; she went there willingly, eagerly. Billy Wilder arrived and shrugged his shoulders; Rand came on bended knee. Her mission was to learn, not refine or improve, the art of the dream factory: how to turn a good yarn into a suspenseful plot, an ordinary person into an outsize hero (or villain)—all the tricks of melodramatic narrative designed to persuade millions of viewers that life is really lived at a fever pitch. Most important, she learned how to perform that alchemy upon herself. Ayn Rand was Norma Desmond in reverse: she was small; it was the pictures that got big.

When playing the part of the Philosopher, Rand liked to claim Aristotle as her tutor. "Never have so many"—uncharacteristically, she included herself here—"owed so much to one man."[19] It's not clear how much of Aristotle's work Rand actually read: when she wasn't quoting Galt, she had a habit of attributing to the Greek philosopher statements and ideas that don't appear in any of his writings. One alleged Aristotelianism Rand was fond of citing did appear, complete with false attribution, in the autobiography of Albert Jay Nock, an influential libertarian from the New Deal era. In Rand's copy of Nock's memoir, Burns observes in an endnote, the passage is marked "with six vertical lines."[20]

Rand also liked to cite Aristotle's law of identity or noncontradiction—the notion that everything is identical to itself, captured by the shorthand "A is A"—as the basis of her defense of selfishness, the free market, and the limited state. That particular transport sent Rand's admirers into rapture and drove her critics, even the friendliest, to distraction. Several months before his death in 2002, Harvard philosopher Robert Nozick, the most analytically sophisticated of twentieth-century libertarians, said that "the use that's made by people in the Randian tradition of this principle of logic . . . is completely unjustified so far as I can see; it's illegitimate."[21] In 1961, Sidney Hook wrote in the *New York Times*:

> Since his baptism in medieval times, Aristotle has served many strange purposes. None have been odder than this sacramental alliance, so to speak, of Aristotle with Adam Smith. The extraordinary virtues Miss Rand finds in the law that A is A suggests that she is unaware that logical principles by themselves can test only consistency. They cannot establish truth. . . . Swearing fidelity to Aristotle, Miss Rand claims to deduce not only matters of fact from logic but, with as little warrant, ethical rules and economic truths as well. As she understands them, the laws of logic license her in proclaiming that "existence exists," which is very much like saying that the law of gravitation is heavy and the formula of sugar sweet.[22]

Whether or not Rand read Aristotle, it's clear that he made little impression upon her, particularly when it came to ethics. Aristotle had a distinctive approach to morality, quite out of keeping with modern sensibilities; and while Rand had some awareness of its distinctiveness, its substance seems to have been lost on her. Like a set of faux-leather classics on the living room shelf, Aristotle was there to impress the company—and, in Rand's case, distract from the real business at hand.

Unlike Kant, the emblematic modern who claimed that the rightness of our deeds is determined solely by reason, unsullied by need, desire, or interest, Aristotle rooted his ethics in human nature, in the habits and practices, the dispositions and tendencies, that make us happy and enable our flourishing. And where Kant believed that morality consists of austere rules, imposing unconditional duties upon us and requiring our most strenuous sacrifice, Aristotle located the ethical life in the virtues. These are qualities or states, somewhere between reason and emotion but combining elements of both, that carry and convey us, by the gentlest and subtlest of means, to the outer hills of good conduct. Once there, we are inspired and equipped to scale these lower heights, whence we move onto the higher reaches. A person who acts virtuously develops a nature that wants and is able to act virtuously and that finds happiness in virtue. That coincidence of thought and feeling, reason and desire, is achieved over a lifetime of virtuous deeds. Virtue, in other words, is less a codex of rules, which must be observed in the face of the self's most violent opposition, than it is the food and fiber, the grease and gasoline, of a properly functioning soul.

If Kant is an athlete of the moral life, Aristotle is its virtuoso. Rand, by contrast, is a melodramatist of the moral life. Apprenticed in Hollywood rather than Athens, she has little patience for the quiet habituation in the virtues that Aristotelian ethics entails.

She returns instead to her favored image of a heroic individual confronting a difficult path. Difficulty is never the result of confusion or ambiguity; Rand loathed "the cult of moral grayness," insisting that morality is first and always "a code of black and white."[23] What makes the path treacherous—not for the hero, who seems to have been born fully outfitted for it, but for the rest of us—are the obstacles along the way. Doing the right thing brings hardship, penury, and exile, while doing the wrong thing brings wealth, status, and acclaim. Because he refuses to submit to architectural conventions, Roark winds up splitting rocks in a quarry. Peter Keating, Roark's doppelgänger, betrays everyone, including himself, and is the toast of the town. Ultimately, of course, the distribution of rewards and punishments will reverse: Roark is happy, Keating miserable. But ultimately is always and inevitably a long way off.

In her essays, Rand seeks to apply to this imagery a superficial Aristotelian gloss. She, too, roots her ethics in human nature and refuses to draw a distinction between self-interest and the good, between ethical conduct and desire or need. But Rand's metric of good and evil, virtue and vice, is not happiness or flourishing. It is the stern and stark exigencies of life and death. As she writes in "The Objectivist Ethics":

I quote from Galt's speech: "There is only one fundamental alternative in the universe: existence or nonexistence—and it pertains to a single class of entities: to living organisms. The existence of inanimate matter is unconditional, the existence of life is not: it depends on a specific course of action. Matter is indestructible, it changes its forms, but it cannot cease to exist. It is only a living organism that faces a constant alternative: the issue of life or death. Life is a process of self-sustaining and self-generated action. If an organism fails in that action, it dies; its chemical elements remain, but its life goes out of existence. It is only the concept of 'Life' that makes the concept of 'Value' possible. It is only to a living entity that things can be good or evil."[24]

Rand's defenders like to claim that what Rand has in mind by "life" is not simply biological preservation but the good life of Aristotle's great-souled man, what Rand characterizes as "the survival of man *qua* man."[25] And it's true that Rand isn't much taken with mere life or life for life's sake. That would be too pedestrian. But Rand's naturalism is far removed from Aristotle's. For him life is a fact; for her it is a question, and that very question is what makes life, on its own, such an object and source of reflection.

What gives life value is the ever-present possibility that it might (and one day will) end. Rand never speaks of life as a given or ground. It is a conditional, a choice we must make, not once but again and again. Death casts a pall, lending our days an urgency and weight they otherwise would lack. It demands wakefulness, an alertness to the fatefulness of each and every moment. "One must never act like a zombie," Rand enjoins.[26] Death, in short, makes life dramatic. It makes our choices—not just the big ones but the little ones we make every day, every second—matter. In the Randian universe, it's high noon all the time. Far from being exhausting or enervating, such an existence, at least to Rand and her characters, is enlivening and exciting.

If this idea has any moral resonance, it will be heard neither in the writings of Aristotle nor in the superficially similar existentialism of Sartre, but rather in the drill march of fascism. The notion of life as a struggle against and unto death, of every moment laden with destruction, every choice pregnant with destiny, every action weighed upon by annihilation, its lethal pressure generating moral meaning—these are the watchwords of the European night. In his Berlin Sportpalast speech of February 1943, Goebbels declared, "Whatever serves it and its struggle for existence is good and must be sustained and nurtured. Whatever is injurious to it and its struggle for existence is evil and must be removed and eliminated."[27] The "it" in question is the German nation, not the Randian individual. But if we strip the pronoun of its antecedent—and listen for the background hum of *Sein oder Nichtsein*—the similarities between the moral syntax of Randianism and of fascism become clear. Goodness is measured by life, life is a struggle against death, and only our daily vigilance ensures that one does not prevail over the other.

Rand, no doubt, would object to the comparison. There is, after all, a difference between the individual and the collective. Rand thought the former an existential fundament, the latter—whether it took the form of a class, race, or nation—a moral monstrosity. And where Goebbels talked of violence and war, Rand spoke of commerce and trade, production and economy. But fascism is hardly hostile to the heroic individual. That individual, moreover, often finds his deepest calling in economic activity. Far from demonstrating a divergence from fascism, Rand's economic writings register its presence indelibly.

Here is Hitler speaking to a group of industrialists in Düsseldorf in 1932:

> You maintain, gentlemen, that the German economy must be constructed on the basis of private property. Now such a conception of private property can only be maintained in practice if it in some way appears to have a logical foundation. This conception must derive its ethical justification from the insight that this is what nature dictates.[28]

Rand, too, believes that capitalism is vulnerable to attack because it lacks "a philosophical base." If it is to survive, it must be rationally justified. We must "begin at the beginning," with nature itself. "In order to sustain its life, every living species has to follow a certain course of action required by its nature." Because reason is man's "means of survival," nature dictates that "men prosper or fail, survive or perish in proportion to the degree of their rationality." (Notice the slippage between success and failure and life and death.) Capitalism is the one system that acknowledges and incorporates this dictate of nature. "It is the basic, metaphysical fact of man's nature—the connection between his survival and his use of reason—that capitalism recognizes and protects."[29] Like Hitler, Rand finds in nature, in man's struggle for survival, a "logical foundation" for capitalism.

Far from privileging the collective over the individual or subsuming the latter under the former, Hitler believed that it was the "strength and power of individual personality" that determined the economic (and cultural) fate of the race and nation.[30] Here he is in 1933 addressing another group of industrialists:

> Everything positive, good and valuable that has been achieved in the world in the field of economics or culture is solely attributable to the importance of personality. . . . All the worldly goods we possess we owe to the struggle of the select few.[31]

And here is Rand in *Capitalism: The Unknown Ideal* (1967):

> The exceptional men, the innovators, the intellectual giants. . . . It is the members of this exceptional minority who lift the whole of a free society to the level of their own achievements, while rising further and ever further.[32]

If the first half of Hitler's economic views celebrates the romantic genius of the individual industrialist, the second spells out the inegalitarian implications of the first. Once we recognize "the outstanding achievements of individuals," Hitler says in Düsseldorf, we must conclude that "people are not of equal value or of equal importance." Private property "can be morally and ethically justified only if [we] admit that men's achievements are different." An understanding of nature fosters a respect for the heroic individual, which fosters an appreciation of inequality in its most vicious guise. "The creative and decomposing forces in a people always fight against one another."[33]

Rand's appreciation of inequality is equally pungent. I quote from Galt's speech:

> The man at the top of the intellectual pyramid contributes the most to all those below him, but gets nothing except his material payment, receiving no intellectual bonus from others to add to the value of his time. The man at the bottom who, left to himself, would starve in his hopeless ineptitude, contributes nothing to those above him, but receives the bonus of all their brains. Such is the nature of the "competition" between the strong and the weak of the intellect. Such is the pattern of "exploitation" for which you have damned the strong.[34]

Rand's path from nature to individualism to inequality also ends in a world divided between "the creative and decomposing forces." In every society, says Roark, there is a "creator" and a parasitic "second-hander," each with its own nature and code. The first "allows man to survive." The second is "incapable of survival."[35] One produces life, the other induces death. In *Atlas Shrugged* the battle is between the producer and the "looters" and "moochers." It too must end in life or death.

To find Rand in such company should come as no surprise, for she and the Nazis share a patrimony in the vulgar Nietzscheanism that has stalked the radical right, whether in its libertarian or fascist variants, since the early part of the twentieth century. As both of her biographers show, Nietzsche exerted an early grip on Rand that never really loosened. Her cousin teased Rand that Nietzsche "beat you to all your ideas." When Rand arrived in the United States, *Thus Spake Zarathustra* was the first book in English she bought. With Nietzsche on her mind, she was inspired to write in her journals that "the secret of life" is "you must be nothing but will. Know what you want and do it. Know what you are doing and why you are doing it, every minute of the day. All will and all control. Send everything else to hell!" Her entries frequently include phrases like "Nietzsche and I think" and "as Nietzsche said."[36]

Rand was much taken with the idea of the violent criminal as moral hero, a Nietzschean transvaluator of all values; according to Burns, she "found criminality an irresistible metaphor for individualism." A literary Leopold and Loeb, she plotted out a novella based on the actual case of a murderer who strangled a twelve-year-old girl. The murderer, said Rand, "is born with a wonderful, free, light consciousness—resulting from the absolute lack of social instinct or herd feeling. He does not understand, because he has no organ for understanding, the necessity, meaning or importance of other people."[37] That is not a bad description of Nietzsche's master class in *The Genealogy of Morals*.

Though Rand's defenders claim she later abandoned her infatuation with Nietzsche, there is too much evidence of its persistence. There's the figure of Roark himself: "As she jotted down notes on Roark's personality," writes Burns, "she told herself, 'See Nietzsche about laughter.' The book's famous first line indicates the centrality of this connection: 'Howard Roark laughed.'"[38] And then there's *Atlas Shrugged*, which Ludwig von Mises, one of the presiding eminences of libertarian economics, praised thus:

> You have the courage to tell the masses what no politician told them: you are inferior and all the improvements in your conditions which you simply take for granted you owe to the effort of men who are better than you.[39]

But Nietzsche's influence saturated Rand's writing in a deeper way, one emblematic of the overall trajectory of the right since its birth in the crucible of the French Revolution. Rand was a lifelong atheist with a special animus for Christianity, which she called the "best kindergarten of communism possible."[40] Far from representing a heretical tendency within conservatism, Rand's statement channels a tradition of right-wing suspicion about the insidious effects of religion, particularly Christianity, on the modern world. Where many conservatives since 1789 have rallied to Christianity and religion as an antidote to the democratic revolutions of the eighteenth and nineteenth centuries, a not insignificant subset among them have seen religion, or at least some aspect of religion, as the adjutant of revolution.

Joseph de Maistre was one of the first. An arch-Catholic, he traced the French Revolution to the acrid solvents of the Reformation. With its celebration of "private interpretation" of the Scriptures, Protestantism paved the way for century upon century of regicide and revolt originating in the lower classes.[41]

> It is from the shadow of a cloister that there emerges one of mankind's very greatest scourges. Luther appears; Calvin follows him. The Peasants' Revolt; the Thirty Years' War; the civil war in France . . . the murders of Henry II, Henry IV,

Mary Stuart, and Charles I; and finally, in our day, from the same source, the French Revolution.[42]

Nietzsche, the child of a Lutheran pastor, radicalized this argument, painting all of Christianity—indeed all of Western religion, going back to Judaism—as a slave morality, the psychic revolt of the lower orders against their betters. Before there was religion or even morality, there was the sense and sensibility of the master class. The master looked upon his body—its strength and beauty, its demonstrated excellence and reserves of power—and saw and said that it was good. As an afterthought he looked upon the slave, and saw and said that it was bad. The slave never looked upon himself: he was consumed by envy of and resentment toward his master. Too weak to act upon his rage and take revenge, he launched a quiet but lethal revolt of the mind. He called all the master's attributes—power, indifference to suffering, thoughtless cruelty—evil. He spoke of his own attributes—meekness, humility, forbearance—as good. He devised a religion that made selfishness and self-concern a sin, and compassion and concern for others the path to salvation. He envisioned a universal brotherhood of believers, equal before God, and damned the master's order of unevenly distributed excellence.[43] The modern residue of that slave revolt, Nietzsche makes clear, is found not in Christianity, or even in religion, but in the nineteenth-century movements for democracy and socialism:

> Another Christian concept, no less crazy, has passed even more deeply into the tissue of modernity: the concept of the "equality of souls before God." This concept furnishes the prototype of all theories of equal rights: mankind was first taught to stammer the proposition of equality in a religious context, and only later was it made into morality: no wonder that man

ended by taking it seriously, taking it practically!—that is to say, politically, democratically, socialistically.[44]

When Rand inveighs against Christianity as the forebear of socialism, when she rails against altruism and sacrifice as inversions of the true hierarchy of values, she is cultivating the strain within conservatism that sees religion as not a remedy to, but a helpmate of, the left. And when she looks, however ineptly, to Aristotle for an alternative morality, she is recapitulating Nietzsche's journey back to antiquity, where he hoped to find a master-class morality untainted by the egalitarian values of the lower orders.

Though Rand's antireligious defense of capitalism might seem out of place in today's political firmament, we would do well to recall the recent revival of interest in her books. More than 800,000 copies of her novels were sold in 2008 alone; as Burns rightly notes, "Rand is a more active presence in American culture now than she was during her lifetime." Indeed, Rand is regularly cited as a formative influence upon an entire new generation of Republican leaders; Burns calls her "the ultimate gateway drug to life on the right."[45] Whether or not she is invoked by name, Rand's presence is palpable in the concern, heard increasingly on the right, that there is something sinister afoot in the institutions and teachings of Christianity.

> I beg you, look for the words "social justice" or "economic justice" on your church website. If you find it, run as fast as you can. Social justice and economic justice, they are code words. Now, am I advising people to leave their church? Yes.

That was Glenn Beck on his March 2, 2010 radio show, taking a stand against, well, pretty much every church in the Christian faith: Catholic, Episcopalian, Methodist, Baptist—even his very own Church of Jesus Christ of Latter-day Saints.[46]

On her own, Rand is of little significance. It is only her resonance in American culture—and the unsavory associations her resonance evokes—that makes her of any interest. She's not unlike the "second-hander" described by Roark: "Their reality is not within them, but somewhere in that space which divides one human body from another. Not an entity, but a relation. . . . The second-hander acts, but the source of his actions is scattered in every other living person."[47] For once, it seems, he knew whence he spoke.

But after all the Nietzsche is said and Aristotle is done, we're still left with a puzzle about Rand: How could such a mediocrity, not just a second-hander but a second-rater, exert such a continuing influence on the culture at large?

We possess an entire literature, from Melville to Mamet, devoted to the con man and the hustler, and it's tempting to see Rand as one of the many fakes and frauds that periodically light up the American landscape. But that temptation should be resisted. Rand represents something different, more unsettling. The con man is a liar who can ascertain the truth of things, often better than the rest of us. He has to: if he is going to fleece his mark, he has to know who the mark is and who the mark would like to be. Working in that netherworld between fact and fantasy, the con man can gild the lily only if he sees the lily for what it is. But Rand had no desire to gild anything. The gilded lily was reality. What was there to add? She even sported a lapel pin to make the point: made of gold and fashioned in the shape of a dollar sign, it was bling of the most literal sort.

Since the nineteenth century, it has been the task of the left to hold up to liberal civilization a mirror of its highest values and to say, "You do not look like this." You claim to believe in the rights of man, but it is only the rights of property you uphold. You claim to stand for freedom, but it is only the freedom of the strong to dominate the weak. If you wish to live up to your principles, you must give way to their demiurge. Allow the dispossessed to assume power, and the ideal will be made real, the metaphor will be made material.

Rand believed that this meeting of heaven and earth could be arranged by other means. Rather than remake the world in the image of paradise, she looked for paradise in an image of the world. Political transformation wasn't necessary. Transubstantiation was enough. Say a few words, wave your hands and the ideal is real, the metaphor material. An idealist of the most primitive sort, Rand took a century of socialist dichotomies and flattened them. Small wonder so many have accused her of intolerance: When heaven and earth are pressed so closely together, where is there room for dissent?

Far from needing explanation, her success explains itself. Rand worked in that quintessential American proving ground— alongside the likes of Richard Nixon and Ronald Reagan, Steve Bannon and Glenn Beck—where garbage achieves gravitas and bullshit gets blessed. There she learned that dreams don't come true. They are true. Turn your metaphysics into chewing gum, and your chewing gum is metaphysics. A is A.

8

The Prince as Pariah

"The 1960s are rightly remembered as years of cultural dissent and political upheaval, but they are wrongly remembered as years stirred only from the left," writes George Will in the foreword to a reissued edition of Barry Goldwater's *The Conscience of a Conservative*.[1] Several decades ago, such a claim would have elicited puzzled looks, if not catcalls and jeers. But in the years since, the publication of a slew of books, each advancing the notion that most of the political innovation of the last half-century has come from the right, has led historians to revise the conventional wisdom about postwar America, including the 1960s. The new consensus is reflected in the opening sentence of Ronald Story and Bruce Laurie's *The Rise of Conservatism in America, 1945–2000*: "The central story of American politics since World War II is the emergence of the conservative movement."[2] Yet for some reason, George Will still feels that his kinsmen are insufficiently appreciated and recognized.

Will is hardly the first conservative to believe himself an exile in his own country. A sense of exclusion has haunted the movement from the beginning, when émigrés fled the French Revolution and Edmund Burke and Joseph de Maistre took up their cause. Born in the shadow of loss—of property, standing, memory, inheritance, a place in the sun—conservatism remains a gathering of fugitives. Even when assured of his position, the conservative plays the truant. Whether instrumental or sincere, this fusion of pariah and power is one of the sources of his appeal. As William F. Buckley wrote in the founding statement of *National Review*, the conservative's badge of exclusion has made him "just about the hottest thing in town."[3]

While John Locke, David Hume, and Adam Smith are often cited by the more genteel defenders of conservatism as the movement's leading lights, their writings cannot account for what is truly bizarre about conservatism: a ruling class resting its claim to power upon its sense of victimhood, arguably for the first time in history. Plato's guardians were wise; Aquinas's king was good; Hobbes's sovereign was, well, sovereign. But the best defense of monarchy Maistre could muster was that his aspiring king had attended the "terrible school of misfortune" and suffered in the "hard school of adversity."[4] Maistre had good reason to offer this defense: playing the plebe, we now know, is a critical weapon in the conservative arsenal. Still, it's a confusing defense. After all, if the main offering a prince brings to the table is that he's really a pauper, why not seat the pauper instead?

Conservatives have asked us not to obey them, but to feel sorry for them—or to obey them because we feel sorry for them. Rousseau was the first to articulate a political theory of pity, and for that he has been called the "Homer of the losers."[5] But doesn't Burke, with his overwrought account of Marie Antoinette, have some claim to the title, too?[6]

Marie Antoinette was a particular kind of loser, a person with everything who found herself utterly and at once dispossessed. Burke saw in her fall an archetype of classical tragedy, the great person laid low by fortune. But in tragedy, the most any hero can hope for is to understand his fate: the wheel of time cannot be reversed; suffering cannot be undone. Conservatives, however, are not content with illumination. They want restoration, an opportunity presented by the new forces of revolution and counterrevolution. Identifying as victims, they become the ultimate moderns, adept competitors in a political marketplace where rights and their divestiture are prized commodities.

Reformers and radicals must convince the subordinated and disenfranchised that they have rights and power. Conservatives are different. They are aggrieved and entitled—aggrieved because entitled—and already convinced of the righteousness of their cause and the inevitability of its triumph. They can play victim and victor with a conviction and dexterity the subaltern can only imagine. This makes them formidable claimants on our allegiance and affection. Whether we are rich or poor or somewhere in between, the conservative is, as Hugo Young said of Maggie Thatcher, one of us.[7]

But how do they convince us that we are one of them? By making privilege democratic and democracy aristocratic. The conservative does not defend the Old Regime; he speaks on behalf of old regimes—in the family, the factory, the field. There, ordinary men, and sometimes women, get to play the part of little lords and ladies, supervising their underlings as if they all belong to a feudal estate. Long before Huey Long cried, "Every man a king," a more ambiguous species of democrat spoke virtually the same words, though to different effect: the promise of democracy is to govern another human being as completely as a monarch governs his subjects. The task of conservatism becomes clear: surround these old regimes with fences and gates, protect them from meddlesome intruders like the state or a social movement, and descant on mobility and innovation, freedom and the future.

Making privilege palatable is a permanent project of conservatism, but each generation must tailor that project to fit the contour of its times. Goldwater's challenge was set out in the title of his book: to show that conservatives had a conscience. Not a heart—he lambasted Eisenhower and Nixon for trying to prove that Republicans were compassionate[8]—or a brain, which liberals from John Stuart Mill to Lionel Trilling had doubted, but a conscience. Political movements often have to convince their followers that they can succeed, that their cause is just and their leaders are savvy, but rarely must they prove that theirs is a march of inner lights. Goldwater thought otherwise: to attract new voters and rally the faithful, conservatism had to establish its idealism and integrity, its absolute independence from the beck and call of wealth, from privilege and materialism—from reality itself. If they were to change reality, conservatives would have to divorce themselves, at least in their self-understanding, from reality.[9] In this regard, he was not altogether different from Burke, who warned that while the ruling classes in Britain had "a vast interest to preserve" against the Jacobin threat and "great means of preserving it," they were like an "artificer . . . incumbered by his tools." Possessing vast "resources," Burke concluded, "may be among impediments" in the struggle against revolution.[10]

In recent years, it has become fashionable to dismiss today's Republican as a true believer who betrayed conservatism by abandoning its native skepticism and spirit of mild adjustment. Goldwater was independent and ornery, the argument goes, recoiling from anything so stultifying (and Soviet) as an ideology; Bush (or the neocon or Tea Partier) is rigid and doctrinaire, an enforcer of bright lines and gospel truths. But conservatism has always been a creedal movement—if for no other reason than to oppose the creeds of the left. "The other side have got an ideology," declared Thatcher. "We must have one as well."[11] To counter the left, the right has had to mimic the left. "As small as they are," John C. Calhoun wrote admiringly of the abolitionists, they "have acquired so much influence by the course they have pursued."[12]

Goldwater understood that. During the Gilded Age, conservatives had opposed unions and government regulation by invoking the freedom of workers to contract with their employer. Liberals countered that this freedom was illusory: workers lacked the means to contract as they wished; real freedom required material means. Goldwater agreed, only he turned the same argument against the New Deal: high taxes robbed workers of their wages, rendering them less free and less able to be free. Channeling John Dewey, he asked, "How can a man be truly free if he is denied the means to exercise freedom?"[13] Franklin Delano Roosevelt claimed that conservatives cared more about money than men. Goldwater said the same about liberals. Focusing on welfare and wages, they "look only at the material side of man's nature" and "subordinate all other considerations to man's material well being." Conservatives, by contrast, take in "the whole man," making his "spiritual nature" the "primary concern" of politics and putting "material things in their proper place."[14]

This romantic howl against the economism of the New Deal—similar to that of the New Left—was not a protest against politics or government; Goldwater was no libertarian. It was an attempt to elevate politics and government, to direct public discussion toward ends more noble and glorious than the management of creature comforts and material well-being. Unlike the New Left, however, Goldwater did not reject the affluent society. Instead, he transformed the acquisition of wealth into an act of self-definition through which the "uncommon" man could distinguish himself from the "undifferentiated mass."[15] To amass wealth was not only to exercise freedom through material means, but also a way of lording oneself over others.

In his essay on conservative thought, Karl Mannheim argued that conservatives have never been wild about the idea of freedom. It threatens the submission of subordinate to superior. Because freedom is the lingua franca of modern politics, however, conservatives have had "a sound enough instinct not to attack" it. Instead, they have made freedom the stalking horse of inequality, and inequality the stalking horse of submission. Men are naturally unequal, they argue. Freedom requires that they be allowed to develop their unequal gifts. A free society must be an unequal society, composed of radically distinct, and hierarchically arrayed, particulars.[16]

Goldwater never rejected freedom; indeed, he celebrated it. But there is little doubt that he saw it as a proxy for inequality—or war, which he called "the price of freedom." A free society protected each man's "absolute differentness from every other human being," with difference standing in for superiority or inferiority. It was the "initiative and ambition of uncommon men"—the most different and excellent of men—that made a nation great. A free society would identify such men at the earliest stages of life and give them the resources they needed to rise to preeminence. Against those who subscribed to "the egalitarian notion that every child must have the same education," Goldwater argued for "an educational system which will tax the talents and stir the ambitions of our best students and . . . thus insure us the kind of leaders we will need in the future."[17]

Mannheim also argued that conservatives often champion the group—races or nations—rather than the individual. Races and nations have unique identities, which must, in the name of freedom, be preserved. They are the modern equivalents of feudal estates. They have distinctive, and unequal, characters and functions; they enjoy different, and unequal, privileges. Freedom is the protection of those privileges, which are the outward expression of the group's unique inner genius.[18]

Goldwater rejected racism (though not nationalism). But try as he might, when discussing freedom he could not resist the tug of feudalism. He called states' rights "the cornerstone" of liberty, "our chief bulwark against the encroachment of individual freedom" by the federal government. In theory, states protected individuals rather than groups. But who in 1960 were these individuals? Goldwater claimed that they were anyone and everyone, that states' rights had nothing to do with Jim Crow. Yet even he was forced to admit that segregation "is, today, the most conspicuous expression of the principle" of states' rights.[19] The rhetoric of states' rights threw up a cordon around white racism. While surely the most noxious plank in the conservative platform—eventually, it was abandoned—Goldwater's argument for states' rights fits squarely within a tradition that sees freedom as a shield for inequality and a surrogate for mass feudalism.

Goldwater lost big in the 1964 presidential election. His children and grandchildren went on to win big—by broadening the circle of discontent beyond Southern whites to include husbands and wives, evangelicals and white ethnics, and by continuing to absorb and transmute the idioms of the left.[20] Adapting to the left didn't make American conservatism less reactionary—any more than Maistre's or Burke's recognition that the French Revolution had permanently changed Europe tempered conservatism there. Rather, it made conservatism suppler and more successful. The more it adapted, the more reactionary conservatism became.

Evangelical Christians were ideal recruits to the cause, deftly playing the victim card as a way of rejuvenating the power of whites. "It's time for God's people to come out of the closet," declared a Texas televangelist in 1980. But it wasn't religion that made evangelicals queer; it was religion combined with racism. One of the main catalysts of the Christian right was the defense of

Southern private schools that were created in response to deseg- regation. By 1970, 400,000 white children were attending these "segregation academies." States like Mississippi gave students tuition grants, and until the Nixon administration overturned the practice, the IRS gave donors to these schools tax exemptions.[21] According to New Right and direct-mail pioneer Richard Viguerie, the attack on these public subsidies by civil rights activists and the courts "was the spark that ignited the religious right's involvement in real politics." Though the rise of segregation academies "was often timed exactly with the desegregation of formerly all-white public schools," writes one historian, their advocates claimed to be defending religious minorities rather than white supremacy (initially nonsectarian, most of the schools became evangelical over time). Their cause was freedom, not inequality—not the freedom to associate with whites, as the previous generation of massive resisters had claimed, but the freedom to practice their own embattled religion.[22] It was a shrewd transposition. In one fell swoop, the heirs of slaveholders became the descendants of persecuted Baptists, and Jim Crow a heresy the First Amendment was meant to protect.

The Christian right was equally galvanized by the backlash against the women's movement. Antifeminism was a latecomer to the conservative cause. Through the early 1970s, advocates of the Equal Rights Amendment (ERA) could still count Richard Nixon, George Wallace, and Strom Thurmond as supporters; even Phyllis Schlafly described the ERA as something "between innocuous and mildly helpful." But once feminism entered "the sensitive and intensely personal arena of relations between the sexes," writes historian Margaret Spruill, the abstract phrases of legal equality took on a more intimate and concrete meaning. The ERA provoked a counterrevolution, as we saw in chapter 2, led by Schlafly and other women, that was as grassroots and nearly as diverse as the movement it opposed.[23] So successful was this counterrevolution—not just at derailing the ERA, but at propelling the Republican Party to power—that it seemed to prove the feminist point. If women could be that effective as political agents, why shouldn't they be in Congress or the White House?

Schlafly grasped the irony. She understood that the women's movement had tapped into and unleashed a desire for power and autonomy among women that couldn't simply be quelled. If women were to be sent back to the exile of their homes, they would have to view their retreat not as a defeat, but as one more victory in the long battle for women's freedom and power. As we saw in chapter 2, Schlafly described herself as a defender, not an opponent, of women's rights. The ERA was "a takeaway of women's rights," she insisted, the "right of the wife to be supported and to have her minor children supported" by her husband. By focusing her argument on "the right of the wife in an ongoing marriage, the wife in the home," Schlafly reinforced the notion that women were wives and mothers first; their only need was for the protection provided by their husbands. At the same time, she described that relationship in the liberal language of entitlement rights. "The wife has the right to support" from her spouse, she claimed, treating the woman as a feminist claimant and her husband as the welfare state.[24]

Like their Catholic predecessors in eighteenth-century France, the Christian Right appropriated not just the ideas but the manners and mores of its opponents. Billy Graham issued an album called *Rap Session: Billy Graham and Students Rap on Questions of Today's Youth*. Evangelicals criticized the culture of narcissism— and then colonized it. James Dobson of the Focus on the Family got his start as a child psychologist at the University of Southern California, competing with Dr. Spock as the author of a bestselling child-rearing text. Evangelical bookstores, according to historian

Paul Boyer, "promoted therapeutic and self-help books offering advice on finances, dating, marriage, depression, and addiction from an evangelical perspective." Most audacious of all was the film version of Hal Lindsey's book *The Late Great Planet Earth*. While the book popularized Christian prophecies of the End of Days, the film was narrated by Orson Welles, the original bad boy of the Popular Front.[25]

The most interesting cases of the right's appropriation of the left, however, came from big business and the Nixon administration. The business class saw the student movement as a critical constituency. Using hip and informal language, writes historian Bethany Moreton, corporate spokesmen left "their plaid suits in the closet" in order to sell capitalism as the fulfillment of sixties-style liberation, participation, and authenticity. Reeling from protests against the invasion of Cambodia (and the massacre of four students that ensued), students at Kent State formed a chapter of Students in Free Enterprise (SIFE), one of 150 across the country. They sponsored a "Battle of the Bands," for which one contestant wrote the following lyrics:

> You know I could never be happy
> Just working some nine-to-five.
> I'd rather spend my life poor.
> Than living it as a lie.
> If I could just save my money
> Or maybe get a loan,
> I could start my own business
> And make it on my own.

Small business institutes were set up on college campuses, casting "the businessman as a victim, not a bully." Business brought its Gramscian tactics to secondary schools as well. In Arkansas,

SIFE performed classroom skits of Milton Friedman's PBS series *Free to Choose.* In 1971, Arizona passed a law requiring high school graduates to take a course in economics so that they would have "some foundation to stand on," according to the bill's sponsor, when they came up "against professors that are collectivists or Socialists." Twenty states followed suit. Arizona students could place out of the course if they passed an exam that asked them, among other things, to match the phrase "government intervention in a free enterprise system" with "is detrimental to the free market."[26]

The most ambidextrous of politicians, Nixon was the master of talking left while walking right. Nixon understood that the best response to the Civil Rights Movement was not to defend whites against blacks, but to make whites into white ethnics burdened with their own histories of oppression and requiring their own liberation movements. Where immigrants from Southern and Eastern Europe had jumped into the melting pot and turned white, Nixon and the ethnic revivalists of the 1970s "provided Americans of European descent a new vehicle for asserting citizenship rights at a moment when it grew increasingly illegitimate to make claims on the state on the basis of whiteness," write historian Tom Sugrue and sociologist John Skrentny. Under Nixon's leadership, the Republican Party was transformed into a right-wing version of the Democratic urban machine. Poles and Italians were appointed to high-profile offices in his administration, and Nixon campaigned vigorously in white ethnic neighborhoods. He even told one crowd that "he felt like he had Italian blood." Nixon's efforts occasionally went beyond the symbolic—a 1971 proposal would have extended affirmative action to "members of certain ethnic groups, primarily of Eastern, Middle, and Southern European ancestry, such as Italians, Greeks, and Slavic groups"— but most were rhetorical. That didn't make them less potent: the new vocabulary of white ethnicity helped create "a romanticized past of hard work, discipline, well-defined gender roles, and tight-knit families," providing a new language for a new age—and a very old regime.[27]

Barry Goldwater's mother was a descendant of Roger Williams. His father, who converted to Episcopalianism, was a descendant of Polish Jews. When Goldwater ran in 1964, Harry Golden quipped, "I always knew the first Jew to run for president would be an Episcopalian."[28] If the history of conservatism is any guide, perhaps he should have run as a Jew.

9

Remembrance of Empires Past

In 2000, I spent part of the summer interviewing William F. Buckley and Irving Kristol. I had become interested in the defections to the left of right-wing intellectuals and wanted to hear what the movement's founding fathers thought of their wayward sons. Over the course of our conversations, however, it became clear that Buckley and Kristol were less interested in these ex-conservatives than they were in the sorry state of the conservative movement and the uncertain fate of the United States as a global empire. The end of Communism and the triumph of the free market, they told me, were mixed blessings. While they were conservative victories, these developments had rendered the United States ill-equipped for the post-Cold War era. Americans now possessed the most powerful empire in history. At the same time, they were possessed by one of the most antipolitical ideologies in history: the free market.

According to its idealists, the free market is a harmonious order, promising an international civil society of voluntary exchange, requiring little more from the state than the occasional enforcement of laws and contracts. For Buckley and Kristol, this was too bloodless a notion upon which to found a national order, much less a global empire. It did not provide the passion and élan, the gravitas and authority, that the exercise of American power truly required, at home and abroad. It encouraged triviality and small-minded politics, self-interest over the national interest—not the most promising base from which to launch an empire. What's more, the right-wingers in charge of the Republican Party didn't seem to realize this.

"The trouble with the emphasis in conservatism on the market," Buckley told me, with an unknowing nod at Burke's theory of the sublime, "is that it becomes rather boring. You hear it once, you master the idea. The notion of devoting your life to it is horrifying if only because it's so repetitious. It's like sex." Conservatism, Kristol added, "is so influenced by business culture and by business modes of thinking that it lacks any political imagination, which has always been, I have to say, a property of the left." Kristol confessed to a deep yearning for an American empire: "What's the point of being the greatest, most powerful nation in the world and not having an imperial role? It's unheard of in human history. The most powerful nation always had an imperial role." But, he continued, previous empires were not "capitalist democracies with a strong emphasis on economic growth and economic prosperity." Because of its commitment to the free market, the United States lacked the fortitude and vision to wield imperial power.

"It's too bad," Kristol lamented. "I think it would be natural for the United States . . . to play a far more dominant role in world affairs. Not what we're doing now but to command and to give orders as to what is be done. People need that. There are many parts of the world, Africa in particular, where an authority willing to use troops can make a very good difference, a healthy difference." But with public discussion moderated by accountants, Kristol thought it unlikely that the United States would take its rightful place as the successor to empires past. "There's the

Republican Party tying itself into knots. Over what? Prescriptions for elderly people? Who gives a damn? I think it's disgusting that . . . presidential politics of the most important country in the world should revolve around prescriptions for elderly people. Future historians will find this very hard to believe. It's not Athens. It's not Rome. It's not anything."[1]

Since 9/11, I've had many occasions to recall these conversations. September 11, we were told in the aftermath, shocked the United States out of the complacent peace and prosperity that set in after the Cold War. It forced Americans to look beyond their borders, to understand at last the dangers that confront a world power. It reminded us of the goods of civic life and of the value of the state, putting an end to that fantasy of creating a public world out of private acts of self-interested exchange. It restored to our woozy civic culture a sense of depth and seriousness, of things "larger than ourselves." Most critical of all, it gave the United States a coherent national purpose and focus for imperial rule. A country that seemed for a time unwilling to face up to its international responsibilities was now prepared, once again, to bear any burden, pay any price, for freedom. This changed attitude, the argument went, was good for the world. It pressed the United States to create a stable and just international order. It was also good for the United States. It forced us to think about something more than peace and prosperity, reminding us that freedom was a fighting faith rather than a cushy perch.

Like any historical moment, 9/11—not the terrorist attacks or the day itself, but the new wave of imperialism it spawned—had multiple dimensions. Some part of this rejuvenated imperial political culture was the product of a surprise attack on civilians and the efforts of U.S. leaders to provide some measure of security to an apprehensive citizenry. Some part of it flowed from the subterranean political economy of oil, from the desire of U.S. elites to secure access to energy reserves in the Middle East and Central Asia, and to wield oil as an instrument of geopolitics. But while these factors played a role in determining U.S. policy, they do not explain entirely the politics and ideology of the imperial moment itself. To understand that dimension, we must look to the impact on American conservatives of the end of the Cold War, of the fall of Communism and the ascendancy of the free market as the organizing principle of the domestic and international order. For it was conservative dissatisfaction with that order that drove, in part, their effort to create a new one.

As we have come to learn, conservatives' envisioned imperium could not provide such an easy resolution to the challenges confronting the United States. The cultural and political renewal that many conservatives imagined 9/11 would produce proved to be a chimera, the victim of a free-market ideology that shows no sign of abating. 9/11 did not—and, in all truth, could not—fulfill the role ascribed to it by the neocons of empire.

Immediately following the attacks on the World Trade Center and the Pentagon, intellectuals, politicians, and pundits—not on the radical left, but mainstream conservatives and liberals—breathed an audible sigh of relief, almost as if they welcomed the strikes as a deliverance from the miasma Buckley and Kristol had been criticizing. The World Trade Center was still on fire and the bodies entombed there scarcely recovered when Frank Rich announced that "this week's nightmare, it's now clear, has awakened us from a frivolous if not decadent decade-long dream." What was that dream? The dream of prosperity, of surmounting life's obstacles with money. During the 1990s, Maureen Dowd wrote, we hoped "to overcome flab with diet and exercise, wrinkles with collagen and Botox, sagging skin with surgery, impotence with Viagra, mood swings with anti-depressants, myopia with laser surgery, decay with human growth hormone, disease with stem cell research and bioengineering." We "renovated our kitchens," observed David Brooks, "refurbished our home entertainment systems, invested in patio furniture, Jacuzzis and gas grills"—as if affluence might free us of tragedy and difficulty.[2] This ethos had terrible domestic consequences. For Francis Fukuyama, it encouraged "self-indulgent behavior" and a "preoccupation with one's own petty affairs." It also had international repercussions. According to Lewis "Scooter" Libby, the cult of peace and prosperity found its purest expression in Bill Clinton's weak and distracted foreign policy, which made "it easier for someone like Osama bin Laden to rise up and say credibly 'The Americans don't have the stomach to defend themselves. They won't take casualties to defend their interests. They are morally weak.'" According to Brooks, even the most casual observer of the pre-9/11 domestic scene, including Al Qaeda, "could have concluded that America was not an entirely serious country."[3]

But after that day in September, more than a few commentators claimed, the domestic scene was transformed. America was now "more mobilized, more conscious and therefore more alive," wrote Andrew Sullivan. George Packer remarked upon "the alertness, grief, resolve, even love" awakened by 9/11. "What I dread now," Packer confessed, "is a return to the normality we're all supposed to seek." For Brooks, "the fear that is so prevalent in the country" after 9/11 was "a cleanser, washing away a lot of the self-indulgence of the past decade." Revivifying fear eliminated the anxiety of prosperity, replacing a disabling emotion with a bracing passion. "We have traded the anxieties of affluence for the real fears of war."[4]

Now upscalers who once spent hours agonizing over which Moen faucet head would go with their copper farmhouse-kitchen sink are suddenly worried about whether the water coming out of pipes has been poisoned. People who longed for Prada bags at Bloomingdales are suddenly spooked by unattended bags at the airport. America, the sweet land of liberty, is getting a crash course in fear.[5]

After the attacks, Brooks concluded, "commercial life seems less important than public life. . . . When life or death fighting is going on, it's hard to think of Bill Gates or Jack Welch as particularly heroic."[6]

Writers repeatedly welcomed the moral electricity now coursing through the body politic. They described it as a pulsing energy of public resolve and civic commitment, which would restore trust in government—perhaps, according to some liberals, even authorize a revamped welfare state—and bring about a culture of patriotism and connection, a new bipartisan consensus, the end of irony and the culture wars, a more mature, more elevated presidency.[7] According to a reporter at *USA Today*, President Bush was especially keen on the promise of 9/11, offering himself and his generation as Exhibit A in the project of domestic renewal. "Bush has told advisors that he believes confronting the enemy is a chance for him and his fellow baby boomers to refocus their lives and prove they have the same kind of valor and commitment their fathers showed in WWII." And while the specific source of Christopher Hitchens's elation may have been peculiarly his own, his self-declared schadenfreude was not: "I should perhaps confess that on September 11 last, once I had experienced all the usual mammalian gamut of emotions, from rage to nausea, I also discovered that another sensation was contending for mastery. On examination, and to my own surprise and pleasure, it turned out to be exhilaration. Here was the most frightful enemy—theocratic barbarism—in plain view. . . . I realized that if the battle went on until the last day of my life, I would never get bored in prosecuting it to the utmost."[8] With its shocking spectacle of fear and death, 9/11 offered a dead or dying culture the chance to live again.

Internationally, 9/11 forced the United States to reengage the world, to assume the burden of empire without embarrassment or confusion. Where the first George Bush and Bill Clinton had fumbled in the dark, searching for a doctrine to guide the exercise of U.S. power after the collapse of the Soviet Union, the mission of the United States was now clear: to defend civilization against barbarism, freedom against terror. As Condoleezza Rice told the *New Yorker*, "I think the difficulty has passed in defining a role. I think September 11th was one of those great earthquakes that clarify and sharpen. Events are in much sharper relief." An America thought to be lost in the quicksand of free markets, individualism, and isolation was now recalled to a consciousness of a world beyond its borders, and inspired to a commitment to sustain casualties on behalf of a U.S.-led global order. As Clinton's former undersecretary of defense concluded, "Americans are unlikely to slip back into the complacency that marked the first decade after the Cold War." They now understood, in the words of Brooks, that "evil exists" and that "to preserve order, good people must exercise power over destructive people."[9]

More than fifteen years later, it's difficult to recapture, let alone fathom, the mindset of that moment. Not just because it disappeared so quickly, with the country relapsing to its strange and sour partisanship before Bush's first term had even ended. More bewildering is how so many writers and politicians could open their arms to the fallout from mass death, taking 9/11 as an opportunity to express their apparently long-brewing contempt for the very peace and prosperity that preceded it. On September 12, one might have expected expressions of sorrow over the bursting of bubbles—economic, cultural, and political. Instead, many saw

9/11 as a thunderous judgment upon, and necessary corrective to, the frivolity and emptiness of the 1990s. We would have to reach back almost a century—to the opening days of World War I, when the "marsh gas of boredom and vacuity" enveloping another free-trading, globalizing fin de siècle exploded—to find a remotely exact parallel.[10]

To understand this spirit of exuberant relief, we must revisit the waning days of the Cold War, when American elites first saw that the United States would no longer be able to define its mission in terms of the Soviet menace. While the end of the Cold War unleashed a wave of triumphalism, it also provoked an anxious uncertainty about U.S. foreign policy. With the defeat of Communism, many asked, how should the United States define its role in the world? Where and when should it intervene in foreign conflicts? How big a military should it field?

Underlying these arguments was a deep unease about the size and purpose of American power. The United States seemed to be suffering from a surfeit of power, which made it difficult for elites to formulate any coherent principles to govern its use. As Richard Cheney, then serving as the first President Bush's secretary of defense, acknowledged in February 1992, "We've gained so much strategic depth that the threats to our security, now relatively distant, are harder to define." Almost a decade later, the United States would still seem, to its leaders, a floundering giant. As Condoleezza Rice noted during the 2000 presidential campaign, "The United States has found it exceedingly difficult to define its 'national interest' in the absence of Soviet power." So uncertain about the national interest did political elites become that a top Clinton defense aide—and later dean of Harvard's Kennedy School—eventually threw up his hands in defeat, declaring the national interest to be whatever "citizens, after proper deliberation, say it is"—an abdication simply unthinkable during the Cold War reign of the Wise Men.[11]

When Clinton assumed office, he and his advisers took stock of this unparalleled situation—where the United States possessed so much power that it faced, in the words of Clinton National Security Advisor Anthony Lake, no "credible near-term threat to [its] existence"—and concluded that the primary concerns of American foreign policy were no longer military but economic. After summarily rehearsing the various possible military dangers to the United States, President Clinton declared in a 1993 address, "We still face, *overarching everything else*, this amorphous but profound challenge in the way humankind conducts its commerce." The great imperative of the post–Cold War era was to organize a global economy where citizens of the world could trade across borders. For that to happen, the United States had to get its own economic house in order—"renewal starts at home," said Lake—by reducing the deficit (in part through reductions in military spending), lowering interest rates, supporting high-tech industry, and promoting free trade agreements. Because other nations would also have to conduct a painful economic overhaul, Lake concluded that the primary goal of the United States was the "enlargement of the world's free community of market democracies."[12]

Clinton's assessment of the challenges facing the United States was partially inspired by political calculation. He had just won an election against a sitting president who not only had led the United States through victory in the Cold War, but also had engineered a stunning rout over the Iraqi military. A Southern governor with no foreign policy experience—and a draft-dodger to boot—Clinton concluded that his victory over Bush meant that questions of war and peace no longer resonated with American voters the way they might have in an earlier age.[13]

But Clinton's vision also reflected a conviction, common to the 1990s, that the globalization of the free market had undermined the efficacy of military power and the viability of traditional empires. Force was no longer the sole, or most effective, instrument of national will. Power now hinged upon the dynamism and success of a nation's economy and the attractiveness of its culture. As Joseph Nye, Clinton's assistant secretary of defense, would come to argue, "soft power"—the cultural capital that made the United States so admired around the globe—was as important to national preeminence as military power. In perhaps a first for a U.S. official, Nye invoked Gramsci to argue that the United States would only maintain its hegemony if it persuaded—rather than forced—others to follow its example. "If I can get you to *want* to do what I want," wrote Nye, "then I do not have to force you to do what you do *not* want to do."[14] To maintain its standing in the world, the United States would have to out-compete other national economies, all the while ensuring the spread of its free market model and pluralist culture. The greatest danger confronting the United States was that it would not reform its economy or that it would abuse its military superiority and provoke international hatred. The problem was not that the United States did not have enough power, but that it had too much. To render the world safe for globalization, the United States would have to be defanged or, at a minimum, significantly curtailed in its imperial aspirations.

For conservatives who yearned for and then celebrated socialism's demise, Clinton's promotion of easygoing prosperity was a horror. Affluence produced a society without difficulty and adversity. Material satisfaction induced a loss of social depth and political meaning, a lessening of resolve and heroic verve. "In that age of peace and prosperity," David Brooks would write, "the top sitcom was *Seinfeld,* a show about nothing." Robert Kaplan emitted barb after barb about the "healthy, well fed" denizens of "bourgeois society," too consumed with their own comfort and pleasure to lend a hand—or shoulder a gun—to make the world a safer place. "Material possessions," he concluded, "encourage docility."[15] Throughout the 1990s, the lead item of intellectual complaint, across the political spectrum, was that the United States was insufficiently civic-minded or martial, its leaders and citizens too distracted by prosperity and affluence to take care of its inherited institutions, common concerns, and worldwide defense. Respect for the state was supposed to be dwindling, as were political participation and local volunteerism.[16] Indeed, one of the most telling signs of the waning imperative of the Cold War was the fact that the 1990s began and ended with two incidents—the Clarence Thomas–Anita Hill controversy and the Supreme Court decision *Bush v. Gore*—that cast scandalous suspicion on the nation's most venerated political institution.

For influential neocons, Clinton's foreign policy was even more anathema. Not because the neocons were unilateralists arguing against Clinton's multilateralism, or isolationists or realists critical of his internationalism and humanitarianism.[17] Clinton's foreign policy, they argued, was too driven by the imperatives of free market globalization. It was proof of the oozing decadence taking over the United States after the defeat of the Soviet Union, a sign of weakened moral fiber and lost martial spirit. In an influential manifesto published in 2000, Donald and Frederick Kagan could barely contain their contempt for "the happy international situation that emerged in 1991," which was "characterized by the spread of democracy, free trade, and peace" and which was "so congenial to America" with its love of "domestic comfort." According to Kaplan, "the problem with bourgeois societies" like our own "is a lack of imagination." The soccer mom, for instance, so insistently championed by Republicans and Democrats alike, does not care about the world outside her narrow confines. "Peace," he complained, "is pleasurable, and pleasure is about momentary satisfaction." It can be obtained "only through a form of tyranny, however subtle and mild." It erases the memory of bracing conflict, robust disagreement, the luxury of defining ourselves "by virtue of whom we were up against."[18]

Though conservatives are often reputed to favor wealth and prosperity, law and order, stability and routine—all the comforts of bourgeois life—Clinton's conservative critics hated him for his pursuit of these very virtues. Clinton's free-market obsessions betrayed an unwillingness to embrace the murky world of power and violent conflict, of tragedy and rupture. His foreign policy was not just unrealistic; it was insufficiently dark and brooding. "The striking thing about the 1990s zeitgeist," complained Brooks, "was the presumption of harmony. The era was shaped by the idea that there were no fundamental conflicts anymore." Conservatives thrive on a world filled with mysterious evil and unfathomable hatreds, where good is always on the defensive and time is a precious commodity in the cosmic race against corruption and decline. Coping with such a world requires pagan courage and an almost barbaric *virtú*, qualities conservatives embrace over the more prosaic goods of peace and prosperity.[19]

But there was another reason for the neocons' dissatisfaction with Clinton's foreign policy. Many of them found it insufficiently visionary and consistent. Clinton, they claimed, was reactive and ad hoc, rather than proactive and forceful. He and his advisers were unwilling to imagine a world where the United States shaped, rather than responded to, events. Breaking again with the usual stereotype of conservatives as nonideological pragmatists, figures like Paul Wolfowitz, Libby, Kaplan, Perle, Frank Gaffney, Kenneth Adelman, and the father-and-son teams of Kagan and Kristol called for a more ideologically coherent projection of US power, where the "benign hegemony" of American might would spread "the zone of democracy" rather than just extend the free market. They wanted a foreign policy that was, in words that Robert Kagan would later use to praise Senator Joseph Lieberman, "idealistic but not naïve, ready and willing to use force and committed to a strong military, but also committed to using American power to spread democracy and do some good in the world."

As early as the first Bush administration, the neocons were insisting that the United States ought, in Cheney's words, "to shape the future, to determine the outcome of history," or, as the Kagans would later put it, "to intervene decisively in every critical region" of the world, "whether or not a visible threat exists there." They criticized those Republicans, in Robert Kagan's words, who "during the dumb decade of the 1990s" suffered from a "hostility to 'nation-building,' the aversion to 'international social work' and the narrow belief that 'superpowers don't do windows.' "[20] What these conservatives longed for was an America that was genuinely imperial—not just because they believed it would make the United States safer or richer, and not just because they thought it would make the world better, but because they wanted to see the United States *make* the world.

At the most obvious level, 9/11 confirmed what conservatives had been saying for years: the world is a dangerous place, filled with hostile forces that will stop at nothing to see the United States felled. More important, 9/11 gave conservatives an opportunity to articulate, without embarrassment, the vision of imperial America they had been quietly nourishing for decades. Unlike empires past, they argued, this one would be guided by a benign, even beneficent vision of worldwide improvement. Because of America's sense of fair play and benevolent purpose—unlike Britain or Rome, the United States had no intention of occupying or seizing territory of its own—this new empire would not generate the backlash that all previous empires had generated. As a *Wall*

Street Journal writer said, "we are an attractive empire, the one everyone wants to join." In the words of Rice, "Theoretically, the realists would predict that when you have a great power like the United States it would not be long before you had other great powers rising to challenge it. And I think what you're seeing is that there's at least a predilection this time to move to productive and cooperative relations with the United States, rather than to try to balance the United States."[21] In creating an empire, the United States would no longer have to respond to immediate threats, to "wait upon events while dangers gather," as President Bush put it in his 2002 state of the union address. It would now "shape the environment," anticipate threats, thinking not in months or years, but in decades, perhaps centuries. The goals were what Cheney, acting on the advice of Wolfowitz, first outlined in the early 1990s: to ensure that no other power ever arose to challenge the United States and that no regional powers ever attained preeminence in their local theaters. The emphasis was on the preventive and predictive, to think in terms of becoming rather than in terms of being. As Richard Perle put it, vis-à-vis Iraq: "What is essential here is not to look at the opposition to Saddam as it is today, without any external support, without any realistic hope of removing that awful regime, but to look at what could be created."[22]

For conservatives, the two years after 9/11 were a heady time, a moment when their simultaneous commitment and hostility to the free market could finally be satisfied. No longer hamstrung by the numbing politics of affluence and prosperity, they believed they could count on the public to respond to the call of sacrifice and destiny, confrontation and evil. With "danger" and "security" the watchwords of the day, the American state would be newly sanctified—without opening the floodgates to economic redistribution. 9/11 and the American empire, they hoped, would at last resolve the cultural contradictions of capitalism that Daniel Bell had noticed long ago but which had only truly come to the fore after the defeat of Communism.

What a difference a decade and a half makes—or for that matter, a couple of years. Long before the United States would essentially have to declare victory in Iraq and (kind of) go home, long before George W. Bush left his office in disgrace, long before the war in Afghanistan proved to be far more than the American people could stomach, it was clear that the neocon imperium rested upon a shaky foundation. In late October and early November 2001, after mere weeks of bombing had failed to dislodge the Taliban, critics started murmuring their fears that the war in Afghanistan would be a reprise of the Vietnam quagmire.[23] As soon as the war in Iraq seemed to be not quite the cakewalk its defenders had proclaimed it would be, Democrats began to probe, however tentatively, the edges of acceptable criticism. As early as the 2004 presidential campaign, voicing criticism of the war became something of a litmus test among the Democratic candidates.

None of these critics, of course, would challenge the full-throttle military premise of Bush's policies—and even under Obama and now Trump, few would question the basic premises of America's global reach—but the periodic appearance of such critics, particularly in times of trouble or defeat, suggests that the imperial vision is politically viable only so long as it is successful. This is as it must be: because the centerpiece of the imperial promise is that the United States can govern events, that it can determine the outcome of history, the promise stands or falls on success or failure. With any suggestion that events lie beyond the empire's control, the imperial vision blurs. Indeed, it only took a week in March 2002 of horrific bloodshed in Israel and the Occupied Territories—and the resulting accusations that "Bush fiddles in the White House or Texas, playing Nero as the Mideast burns"—for the planned empire to be called into question. No sooner had violence in the Middle East begun to escalate then even the administration's defenders began jumping ship, suggesting that any invasion of Iraq would have to be postponed indefinitely. As one of Reagan's high-level national security aides put it, "The supreme irony is that the greatest power the world has ever known has proven incapable of managing a regional crisis." The fact, this aide added, that the administration had been so maniacally "focused on either Afghanistan or Iraq"—the two key outposts of imperial confrontation—while the Middle East was going up in flames, "reflects either appalling arrogance or ignorance."[24]

Ironically, insofar as the Bush administration avoided those conflicts, such as that between the Israelis and Palestinians, where it might fail, it was forced to forgo the logic of imperialism it sought to avow. Premised as it was on the ability of the United States to control events, the neocon imperial vision could not accommodate failure. But by avoiding failure, the imperialists were forced to acknowledge that they could not control events. As former Secretary of State Lawrence Eagleburger observed of the Israeli-Palestinian conflict, Bush realized "that simply to insert himself into this mess without any possibility of achieving any success is, in and of itself, dangerous, because it would demonstrate that in fact we don't have any ability right now to control or affect events"[25]—precisely the admission the neocons could not afford to make. This Catch-22 was no mere problem of logic or consistency: it betrayed the essential fragility of the imperial position itself.

That fragility also reflected the domestic hollowness of the neocons' imperial vision. Though the neocons saw imperialism as the cultural and political counterpart to the free market, they have never come to terms—even fifteen years later—with how the conservative opposition to government spending and the commitment to tax cuts render the United States unlikely to make the necessary investments in nation-building that imperialism requires.

Domestically, there is little evidence to suggest that the political and cultural renewal imagined by most commentators—the revival of the state, the return of shared sacrifice and community, the deepening of moral awareness—ever took place, even in the headiest days of the aftermath of 9/11. Of all the incidents one could cite from that time, two stand out. In March 2002, sixty-two senators, including nineteen Democrats, rejected higher fuel-efficiency standards in the automobile industry, which would have reduced dependence upon Persian Gulf oil. Missouri Republican Christopher Bond felt so unencumbered by the need to pay homage to state institutions in a time of war that he claimed on the Senate floor, "I don't want to tell a mom in my home state that she should not get an S.U.V. because Congress decided that would be a bad choice." Even more telling was how vulnerable proponents of higher standards were to these anti-statist arguments. John McCain, for example, was instantly put on the defensive by the notion that the government would be interfering with people's private market choices. He was left to argue that "no American will be forced to drive any different automobile," as if that would have been a dreadful imposition in this new era of wartime sacrifice and solidarity.[26]

A few months earlier, Ken Feinberg, head of the September 11 Victims' Compensation Fund, announced that families of victims would receive compensation for their loss based in part on the salary each victim was earning at the time of his or her death. After the attacks on the World Trade Center and the Pentagon, Congress had taken the unprecedented step of assuming national responsibility for restitution to the families of the victims. Though the inspiration for this decision was to forestall expensive lawsuits against the airline industry, many observers took it as a signal of a new spirit in the land: in the face of national tragedy, political leaders were finally breaking with the market survivalism of the Reagan-Clinton years. But even in death, the market was the only language America's leaders knew how to speak. Abandoning the notion of shared sacrifice, Feinberg opted for the actuarial tables to calculate appropriate compensation packages. The family of a single sixty-five-year-old grandmother earning $10,000 a year—perhaps a minimum-wage kitchen worker—would draw $300,000 from the fund, while the family of a thirty-year-old Wall Street trader would get $3,870,064. The men and women killed on September 11 were not citizens of a democracy; they were earners, and rewards would be distributed accordingly. Virtually no one—not even the commentators and politicians who denounced the Feinberg calculus for other reasons—criticized this aspect of his decision.[27]

Even within and around the military, the ethos of patriotism and shared destiny remained secondary to the ideology of the market. In a little-noticed October 2001 article in the *New York Times*, military recruiters confessed that they still sought to entice enlistees not with the call of patriotism or duty but instead with the promise of economic opportunity. As one recruiter said, "It's just business as usual. We don't push the 'Help our country' routine." When the occasional patriot burst into a recruiting office and said, "I want to fight," a recruiter explained, "I've got to calm them down. We're not all about fighting and bombing. We're about jobs. We're about education."[28] Recruiters admitted that they continued to target immigrants and people of color, on the assumption that it was these constituencies' lack of opportunity that drove them to the military. The Pentagon's publicly acknowledged goal, in fact, was to increase the number of Latinos in the military from 10 percent to 22 percent. Recruiters even slipped into Mexico, with promises of instant citizenship to poor noncitizens willing to take up arms on behalf of the United States. According to one San Diego recruiter, "It's more or less common practice that some recruiters go to Tijuana to distribute pamphlets, or in some cases they look for someone to help distribute information on the Mexican side."[29] In December 2002, as the United States prepared to invade Iraq, New York Democratic congressman Charles Rangel decided to confront this issue head-on by proposing a reinstatement of the draft. Noting that immigrants, people of color, and the poor were shouldering a greater percentage of the military burden than their numbers in the population warranted, Rangel argued that the United States should distribute the domestic costs of empire more equitably. If middle-class white kids were forced to shoulder arms, he claimed, the administration and its supporters might think twice before going to war. The bill went nowhere.

The fact that the war never imposed the sort of sacrifices on the population that normally accompany national crusades provoked significant concern among political and cultural elites. "The danger, over the long term," wrote the *Times*'s R. W. Apple before he died, "is loss of interest. With much of the war to be conducted out of plain sight by commandos, diplomats and intelligence agents, will a nation that has spent decades in easy self-indulgence stay focused?" Not long after he had declared the age of glitz and glitter over, Frank Rich found himself publicly agonizing that "you'd never guess this is a nation at war." Prior to 9/11, "the administration said we could have it all." Since 9/11, the administration had been saying much the same thing. A former aide to Lyndon Johnson told the *New York Times*, "People are going to have get involved in this. So far it's a government effort, as it should be, but people aren't engaged."[30] Without consecrating the cause in blood, observers feared, Americans would not have their commitment tested, their resolve deepened.

In what may have been the strangest spectacle of the entire war, the nation's leaders wound up scrambling to find things for people to do—not because there was much to be done, but because without something to do, the ardor of ordinary Americans would grow cold. Since these tasks were unnecessary, and mandating them would have violated the norms of market ideology, the best the president and his colleagues could come up with was to announce Web sites and toll-free numbers where enterprising men and women could find information about helping out the war effort. As Bush declared in North Carolina the day after his 2002 state of the union address, "If you listened to the speech last night, you know, people were saying, 'Well, gosh, that's nice, he called me to action, where do I look?' Well, here's where: at usafreedomcorps.gov. Or you can call this number—it sounds like I'm making a pitch, and I am. This is the right thing to do for America. 1-877-USA-CORPS." The government couldn't even count on its citizens to pay for the call.[31]

10

Affirmative Action Baby

Until his death on February 13, 2016, Antonin Scalia had been, along with Clarence Thomas, the most conservative justice on the Supreme Court. He also loved the television show 24. "Boy, those early seasons," he told his biographer, "I'd be up to two o'clock, because you're at the end of one [episode], and you'd say, 'No, I've got to see the next.'" Scalia was especially taken with Jack Bauer, the show's fictional hero played by Kiefer Sutherland. Bauer is a government agent at a Los Angeles counterterrorism unit who foils mass-murder plots by torturing suspects, kidnapping innocents, and executing colleagues. Refusing to be bound by the law, he fights a two-front war against terrorism and the Constitution. And whenever he bends a rule or breaks a bone, Scalia swooned.

> Jack Bauer saved Los Angeles. . . . He saved hundreds of thousands of lives. . . . Are you going to convict Jack Bauer? Say that criminal law is against him? You have the right to a jury trial? Is any jury going to convict Jack Bauer? I don't think so. So the question is really whether we really believe in these absolutes. And ought we believe in these absolutes?[1]

Yet Scalia spent the better part of his career as a lawyer, professor, and jurist insisting that the Constitution is an absolute, in which we must believe, even when—particularly when—it tells us something we do not want to hear. Scalia's Constitution is not a warming statement of benevolent purpose, easily adapted to our changing needs. His Constitution is cold and dead, its prohibitions and injunctions frozen in time. Phrases like "cruel and unusual punishment" mean what they meant when they were written into the Constitution. If that produces objectionable results—say, the execution of children and the intellectually disabled—too bad. "I do not think," Scalia wrote in *Nixon v. Missouri Municipal League*, that "the avoidance of unhappy consequences is adequate basis for interpreting a text."[2]

Scalia took special pleasure in unhappy consequences. He relished difficulty and disliked anyone who would diminish or deny it. In *Hamdi v. Rumsfeld*, a plurality of the Court held to what Scalia thought was a squishy position on executive power during wartime. The Court ruled that the Authorization for the Use of Military Force, passed by Congress after 9/11, empowered the president to detain U.S. citizens indefinitely as "illegal enemy combatants" without trying them in a court of law. It also ruled, however, that such citizens were entitled to due process and could challenge their detention before some kind of tribunal.

Scalia was livid. Writing against the plurality—as well as the Bush administration and fellow conservatives on the Court—he insisted that a government at war, even one as unconventional as the war on terror, had two, and only two, ways to hold a citizen: try him in a court of law or have Congress suspend the writ of habeas corpus. Live by the rules of due process, in other words, or suspend them. Take a stand; make a choice.

But the Court weaseled out of that choice, making life easier for the government and itself. Congress and the president could act as if habeas corpus were suspended, without having to suspend it, and the Court could act as if the writ hadn't been suspended thanks to a faux due process of military tribunals. More than its coloring outside the lines of the Constitution, it was the Court's "Mr. Fix-It Mentality," in Scalia's words, its "mission to Make Everything Come Out Right," that enraged him.[3]

Scalia's mission, by contrast, was to make everything come out wrong. A Scalia opinion, to borrow a phrase from *New Yorker* writer Margaret Talbot, is "the jurisprudential equivalent of smashing a guitar on stage."[4] Scalia may have once declared the rule of law to be the law of rules—leading some to mistake him for a stereotypical conservative—but rules and laws had a particular frisson for him. Where others look to them for stabilizing checks or reassuring supports, Scalia saw exhilarating impediments and vertiginous barriers. Where others seek security, Scalia sought sublimity. Rules and laws make life harder, and harder is everything. "Being tough and traditional is a heavy cross to bear," he told one reporter. *"Duresse oblige."*[5]

That, and not fidelity to the text or conservatism as it is conventionally understood, is the idée fixe of Scalia's jurisprudence—and the source of his apparent man-crush on Jack Bauer. Bauer never makes things easy for himself; indeed, he goes out of his way to make things as hard as possible. He volunteers for a suicide mission when someone else would do (and probably do it better); he turns himself into a junkie as part of an impossibly baroque plan to stop an act of bioterrorism; he puts his wife and daughter at risk, not once but many times, and then beats himself up for doing so. He loathes what he does but does it anyway. That is his nobility—some might say masochism—and why he warmed Scalia's heart.

It means something, of course, that Scalia identified the path of most resistance in fidelity to an ancient text, while Bauer finds it in the betrayal of that text. But not as much as one might think: as we've come to learn from the marriages of our right-wing preachers and politicians, fidelity is often another word for betrayal.

Scalia was born in Trenton, New Jersey, in March 1936, but had been conceived the previous summer in Florence, Italy. (His father, a doctoral student in romance languages at Columbia, had won a fellowship to travel there with his wife.) "I hated Trenton," Scalia said; his heart belonged to Florence. A devotee of opera and hunting—"he loves killing unarmed animals," observes Clarence Thomas—Scalia liked to cut a Medicean profile of great art and great cruelty. He peppered his decisions with stylish allusions to literature and history. Once upon a time, he enjoyed telling audiences, he was too much the "faint-hearted" originalist to uphold the eighteenth century's acceptance of ear notching and flogging as forms of punishment. Not anymore. "I've gotten older and crankier," he said, ever the diva of disdain.[6]

When Scalia was six, his parents moved to the Elmhurst section of Queens. His lifelong conservatism is often attributed to his strict Italian Catholic upbringing there; alluding to Burke, he called it his "little platoon." He attended Xavier High School, a Jesuit school in Manhattan, and Georgetown, a Jesuit university in Washington, D.C. In his freshman year at Georgetown, the senior class voted Senator Joseph McCarthy as the Outstanding American.[7]

But Scalia came to his ethnicity and religion with an attitude, lending his ideology a defiant edge. He claimed he didn't get into Princeton, his first choice, because "I was an Italian boy from Queens, not quite the Princeton type." Later, after Vatican II liberalized the liturgy and practices of the Church, including his neighborhood church in suburban Washington, D.C., he insisted on driving his brood of seven children miles away to hear Sunday

Mass in Latin. Later still, in Chicago, he did the same thing, only this time with nine children in tow. Commenting on how he and his wife managed to raise conservative children during the sixties and seventies—no jeans in the Scalia household—he said:

> They were being raised in a culture that wasn't supportive of our values, that was certainly true. But we were helped by the fact that we were such a large family. We had our own culture . . . The first thing you've got to teach your kids is what my parents used to tell me all the time, "You're not everybody else. . . . We have our own standards and they aren't the standards of the world in all respects, and the sooner you learn that the better."[8]

Scalia's conservatism, it turns out, is less a little platoon than a Thoreauvian counterculture, a retreat from and rebuke to the mainstream, not unlike the hippie communes and groupuscules he once tried to keep at bay. It is not a conservatism of tradition or inheritance: his parents had only one child, and his mother-in-law often complained about having to drive miles and hours in search of the one true church. "Why don't you people ever seem to live near churches?" she would ask Scalia and his wife.[9] It is a conservatism of invention and choice, informed by the very spirit of rebellion he so plainly loathed—or thought he loathed—in the culture at large.

In the 1970s, while teaching at the University of Chicago, Scalia liked to end the semester with a reading from *A Man for All Seasons*, Robert Bolt's play about Thomas More. While the play's anti-authoritarianism would seem at odds with Scalia's conservatism, its protagonist, at least as he is portrayed by Bolt, is not. Literally more Catholic than the pope, More is a true believer in the law who refuses to compromise his principles in order to accommodate the wishes of Henry VIII. He pays for his integrity with his life.

Scalia's biographer introduces this biographical tidbit with a revealing aside: "Yet even as Scalia in middle age was developing a more rigid view of the law, he still had bursts of idealism."[10] That "yet" is misplaced. Scalia's rigidity was not opposed to his idealism; it was his idealism. His ultraconservative reading of the Constitution reflects neither cynicism nor conventionalism; orthodoxy and piety were, for him, the essence of dissidence and iconoclasm. No charge grieved him more than the claim, rehearsed at length in his 1995 Tanner Lectures at Princeton, that his philosophy is "wooden," "unimaginative," "pedestrian," "dull," "narrow," and "hidebound."[11] Call him a bastard or a prick, a hound from hell or a radical in robes. Just don't say he's a suit.

Scalia's philosophy of constitutional interpretation—variously called originalism, original meaning, or original public meaning—is often confused with original intention. While the first crew of originalists in the 1970s did claim that the Court should interpret the Constitution according to the intentions of the Framers, later originalists like Scalia wisely recast that argument in response to criticisms it received. The intentions of a single author are often unknowable, and in the case of many authors, practically indeterminate. And whose intentions should count: those of the 55 men who wrote the Constitution, the 1,179 men who ratified it, or the even greater number of men who voted for the men who ratified it? From Scalia's view, it is not intentions that govern us. It is the Constitution, the text as it was written and rewritten through amendment. That is the proper object of interpretation.

But how does one go about recovering the meaning of a text that can career from terrifying generality in one sentence ("the executive Power shall be vested in a President") to an uneventful precision (presidential terms are four years) in the next? Look to the public meaning of the words at the time they were adopted, says Scalia. See how they were used: consult dictionaries, other usages in the text, influential writings of the time. Consider the context of their utterance, how they were received. From these sources, construct a bounded universe of possible meanings. Words don't mean one thing, Scalia concedes, but neither do they mean anything. Judges should read the Constitution neither literally nor loosely but "reasonably"—that is, in such a way that each word or phrase is construed "to contain all that it fairly means." And then, somehow or other, apply that meaning to our own much different times.[12]

Scalia justified his originalism on two grounds, both negative. In a constitutional democracy it is the job of elected representatives to make the law, the job of judges to interpret it. If judges are not bound by how the law, including the Constitution, was understood at the time of its enactment—if they consult their own morals or their own interpretations of the country's morals—they are no longer judges but lawmakers, and often unelected lawmakers at that. By tying the judge to a text that does not change, originalism helps reconcile judicial review with democracy and protects us from judicial despotism.

If Scalia's first concern is tyranny from the bench, his second is anarchy on the bench. Once we abandon the idea of an unchanging Constitution, he says, we open the gates to any and all modes of interpretation. How are we to understand a Constitution that evolves? By looking at the polls, the philosophy of John Rawls, the teachings of the Catholic Church? If the Constitution is always changing, what constraints can we impose on what counts as an acceptable interpretation? None, Scalia says. When "every day" is "a new day" in the law, it ceases to be law.[13]

This mix of tyranny and anarchy is no idle fantasy, Scalia and other originalists insist. In their view, for a brief, terrible time—from the Warren Court of the 1960s to the Burger Court of the 1970s—it was a reality. In the name of a "living Constitution," left-wing judges remade (or tried to remake) the country in their own image, forcing an agenda of welfare, sexual liberation, gender equality, racial integration, and moral relativism down the country's throat. Ancient words acquired new implications and insinuations: suddenly "due process of law" entailed a "right to privacy," code words for birth control and abortion (and later gay sex); "equal protection of the laws" required one man, one vote; the ban against "unreasonable searches and seizures" meant that evidence obtained unlawfully by the police could not be admitted in court; the proscription against the "establishment of religion" forbade school prayer. With each law it overturned and right it discovered, the Court seemed to invent a new ground of action. It was a constitutional Carnival, where exotic theories of adjudication were paraded with libidinous abandon. For originalists, what was most outrageous about this revolution from above—beyond the left-wing values it foisted upon the nation—was its radical departure from how the Court traditionally justified its decisions to strike down laws.

Prior to the Warren Court, Scalia said, or the 1920s (it's never clear when exactly the rot set in), everyone was an originalist.[14] That's not quite true. Expansive constructions of constitutional meaning are as old and august as the founding itself. And the theoretical self-consciousness Scalia and his followers bring to the table is a decidedly twentieth-century phenomenon. Scalia, in fact, often sounds like he's a comp lit student circa 1983. He says it is a "sad commentary" that "American judges have no intelligible theory of what we do most" and "even sadder" that the legal profession is "by and large . . . unconcerned with the fact that we have no intelligible theory."[15]

Conservatives used to mock that kind of theory fetishism as the mark of an inexperienced and artless ruling class; even an avowed originalist like Robert Bork conceded that "self-confident legal institutions do not require so much talking about." But Scalia and Bork forged their ideas in battle against a liberal jurisprudence that was self-conscious and theoretical, and, like so many of their predecessors on the right, they have come out of it looking more like their enemies than their friends. Bork, in fact, freely admits that it is not John Marshall or Joseph Story—the traditional greats of judicial review—to whom he looks for guidance; it is Alexander Bickel, arguably the most self-conscious of the twentieth-century liberal theoreticians, who "taught me more than anyone else about this subject."[16]

Like many originalists, Scalia claimed that his jurisprudence had nothing to do with his conservatism. "I try mightily to prevent my religious views or my political views or my philosophical views from affecting my interpretation of the laws." Yet he also said that he learned from his teachers at Georgetown never to "separate your religious life from your intellectual life. They're not separate." Only months before Ronald Reagan nominated him to the Supreme Court in 1986, he admitted that his legal views were "inevitably affected by moral and theological perceptions."[17]

And, indeed, in the deep grammar of his opinions lies a conservatism that, if it has little to do with advancing the immediate interests of the Republican Party, has even less to do with averting the threats of judicial tyranny and judicial anarchy. It is a conservatism that would have been recognizable to Social Darwinists of the late nineteenth century, one that mixes freely of the premodern and the postmodern, the archaic and the advanced. It is not to be found in the obvious places—Scalia's opinions about abortion, say, or gay rights—but in a dissenting opinion about that most un-Scaliaesque of places: the golf course.

Casey Martin was a champion golfer who because of a degenerative disease could no longer walk the eighteen holes of a golf course. After the PGA Tour refused his request to use a golf cart in the final round of one of its qualifying tournaments, a federal court issued an injunction, based on the Americans with Disabilities Act (ADA), allowing Martin to use a cart. Title III of the ADA states that "no individual shall be discriminated against on the basis of disability in the full and equal enjoyment of the goods, services, privileges, advantages, or accommodations of any place of public accommodation by any person who owns, leases (or leases to), or operates a place of public accommodation." By the time the case reached the Supreme Court in 2001, the legal questions had boiled down to these: Is Martin entitled to the protections of Title III of the ADA? Would allowing Martin to use a cart "fundamentally alter the nature" of the game? Ruling 7–2 in Martin's favor—with Scalia and Thomas in dissent—the Court said yes to the first and no to the second.

In answering the first question, the Court had to contend with the PGA's claims that it was operating a "place of exhibition or entertainment" rather than a public accommodation; that only a customer of that entertainment qualified for Title III protections; and that Martin was not a customer but a provider of entertainment. The Court was skeptical of the first two claims. But even if they were true, the Court said, Martin would still be protected by Title III because he was in fact a customer of the PGA: he and the other contestants had to pay $3,000 to try out for the tournament. Some customers paid to watch the tournament, others to compete in it. The PGA could not discriminate against either.

Scalia was incensed. It "seems to me quite incredible," he exploded, that the majority would treat Martin as a "'custome[r]' of 'competition'" rather than as a competitor. The PGA sold entertainment, the public paid for it, the golfers provided it; the qualifying rounds were their application for hire. Martin was no more a customer than is an actor who shows up for an open casting call. He was an employee, or potential employee, whose proper recourse, if he had any, was not Title III of the ADA, which covered public accommodations, but Title I, which covered employment. But Martin wouldn't have that recourse, admitted Scalia, because he was essentially an independent contractor, a category of employee not covered by the ADA. Martin would thus wind up in a legal no man's land, without any protection from the law.

In the majority's suggestion that Martin was a customer rather than a competitor, Scalia saw something worse than a wrongly decided opinion. He saw a threat to the status of athletes everywhere, whose talent and excellence would be smothered by the bosomy embrace of the Court, and also a threat to the idea of competition more generally. It was as if the Homeric rivals of ancient Greece were being plucked from their manly games and forced to walk the aisles of a modern boutique.

Games held a special valence for Scalia: they are the space where inequality rules. "The very nature of competitive sport is the measurement," he wrote, "of unevenly distributed excellence." That inequality is what "determines the winners and losers." In the noonday sun of competition, we cannot hide our superiority or inferiority, our excellence or inadequacy. Games make our unequal natures plain to the world; they celebrate "the uneven distribution of God-given gifts."

In the Court's transposition of competitor into customer, Scalia saw the forced entry of democracy (a "revolution," actually) into this antique preserve. With "Animal Farm determination"—yes,

Scalia does go there—the Court had destroyed our one and only opportunity to see how unequal we truly are, how unfairly God has chosen to bestow his blessings upon us. "The year was 2001," reads the last sentence of Scalia's dissent, "and 'everybody was finally equal.'"

Like the Social Darwinists and Nietzsche, Scalia was too much a modernist, even a postmodernist, to pine for the lost world of feudal fixities. Modernity has seen too much flux to sustain a belief in hereditary status. The watermarks of privilege and privation are no longer visible to the naked eye; they must be identified, again and again, through struggle and contest. Hence the appeal of a game. In sports, unlike law, every day is a new day. Every competition is a fresh opportunity for mixing it up, for throwing our established hierarchies into anarchic relief and allowing a new face of supremacy or abjection to emerge. It thus offers the perfect marriage of the feudal and the fallible, the unequal and the unsettled.

To answer the second question—does riding in a golf cart "fundamentally alter the nature" of golf—the majority undertook a thorough history of the rules of golf. It then formulated a two-part test for determining whether riding in a cart would change the nature of golf. The dutifulness and care, the seriousness with which the majority took its task, both amused and annoyed Scalia.

It has been rendered the solemn duty of the Supreme Court of the United States . . . to decide What Is Golf. I am sure that the Framers of the Constitution, aware of the 1457 edict of King James II of Scotland prohibiting golf because it interfered with the practice of archery, fully expected that sooner or later the paths of golf and government, the law and the links, would once again cross, and that the judges of this august Court would some day have to wrestle with that age-old jurisprudential question, for which their years of study in the law have so well prepared them: Is someone riding around a golf course from shot to shot really a golfer?

Scalia is clearly enjoying himself here, but his mirth is a little mystifying. The ADA defines discrimination as

> a failure to make reasonable modifications in the policies, practices, or procedures, when such modifications are necessary to afford such goods, services, facilities, privileges, advantages, or accommodations to individuals with disabilities, unless the entity can demonstrate that making such modifications would fundamentally alter the nature of such goods, services, facilities, privileges, advantages, or accommodations that the entity provides.

Any determination of discrimination requires a prior determination about whether the "reasonable modification" would "fundamentally alter the nature" of the good in question. The language of the statute, in other words, compels the Court to inquire into and decide What is Golf.

But Scalia wouldn't have any of it. Refusing to be bound by the text, he preferred to meditate on the futility and fatuity of the Court's inquiry. In seeking to discover the essence of golf, the Court is looking for something that does not exist. "To say that something is 'essential,'" he writes, "is ordinarily to say that it is necessary to the achievement of a certain object." But games "have no object except amusement." Lacking an object, they have no essence. It's thus impossible to say whether a rule is essential. "All are arbitrary," he writes of the rules, "none is essential." What makes a rule a rule is either tradition or, "in more modern times," the edict of an authoritative body like the PGA. In an unguarded moment, Scalia entertains the possibility of there being "some point at which the rules of a well-known game are changed to such a degree that no reasonable person would call it the same game." But he quickly pulls back from that foray into essentialism. No Plato for him; he's with Nietzsche all the way.[18]

It is difficult to reconcile this almost Rortyesque hostility to the idea of golf's essence with Scalia's earlier statements about "the very nature of competitive sport" being the revelation of divinely ordained inequalities. (It's also difficult to reconcile Scalia's indifference to the language of the statute with his textualism, but that's another matter.) Left unresolved, however, the contradiction reveals the twin poles of Scalia's faith: a belief in rules as arbitrary impositions of power—reflecting nothing (not even the will or standing of their makers) but the flat surface of their locutionary meaning—to which we must nevertheless submit; and a belief in rules, zealously enforced, as the divining rod of our ineradicable inequality. Those who make it past these blank and barren gods are winners; everyone else is a loser.

In the United States, Tocqueville observed, a federal judge "must know how to understand the spirit of the age." While the persona of a Supreme Court Justice may be "purely judicial," his "prerogatives"—the power to strike down laws in the name of the Constitution—"are entirely political."[19] If he is to exercise those prerogatives effectively, he must be as culturally nimble and socially attuned as the shrewdest pol.

How then to explain the influence of Scalia? Here is a man who proudly, defiantly, proclaimed his disdain for "the spirit of the age"—that is, when he was not embarrassingly ignorant of it (when the Court voted in 2003 to overturn state laws banning gay sex, Scalia saw the country heading down a slippery slope to masturbation.)[20] In 1996, he told an audience of Christians that "we must pray for the courage to endure the scorn of the sophisticated world," a world that "will not have anything to do with miracles." We have "to be prepared to be regarded as idiots."[21] In a dissent from that same year, Scalia declared, "Day by day, case by case, [the Court] is busy designing a Constitution for a country I do not recognize."[22] As Maureen Dowd wrote, "He's so Old School, he's Old Testament."[23]

And yet, according to Elena Kagan, who was appointed by Barack Obama to the Supreme Court in 2010, Scalia "is the justice who has had the most important impact over the years on how we think and talk about the law." John Paul Stevens, the man Kagan replaced and until his retirement the most liberal Justice on the Court, said that Scalia "made a huge difference, some of it constructive, some of it unfortunate." Scalia's influence, moreover, will in all likelihood extend into the future. "He is in tune with many of the current generation of law students," observed Ruth Bader Ginsburg, another Court liberal, a while back.[24]

It is not Scalia's particular positions that have prevailed on the Court. Indeed, some of his most famous opinions—against abortion, affirmative action, and gay rights; in favor of the death penalty, prayer in school, and sex discrimination—were dissents. (With the addition of John Roberts to the Court in 2005 and Samuel Alito in 2006, however, that has begun to change; the ascension of Neil Gorsuch in 2017 will likely push things more in Scalia's direction.) Scalia's hand is more evident in the way his colleagues—and other jurists, lawyers, and scholars—make their arguments.

For many years, originalism was derided by the left. As William Brennan, the Court's liberal titan of the second half of the twentieth century, declared in 1985: "Those who would restrict claims of right to the values of 1789 specifically articulated in the Constitution turn a blind eye to social progress and eschew adaptation of overarching principles to changes of social circumstance." Against the originalists, Brennan insisted that "the genius of the Constitution rests not in any static meaning it might have had in a world that is dead and gone, but in the adaptability of its great principles to cope with current problems and current needs."[25]

Just a decade later, however, the liberal Laurence Tribe, paraphrasing the liberal Ronald Dworkin, would say, "We are all originalists now."[26] That's even truer today. Where yesterday's generation of constitutional scholars looked to philosophy—Rawls, Hart, occasionally Nozick, Marx, or Nietzsche—to interpret the Constitution, today's looks to history, to the moment when a word or passage became part of the text and acquired its meaning. That happens not just on the right, but also on the left: Bruce Ackerman, Akhil Amar, and Jack Balkin are just three of the most prominent liberal originalists writing today.

Liberals on the Court have undergone a similar shift. In his *Citizens United* dissent, Stevens wrote a lengthy excursus on the "original understandings," "original expectations," and "original public meaning" of the First Amendment with regard to corporate speech. Opening his discussion with a dutiful sigh of obligation—"Let us start from the beginning"—Stevens felt compelled by Scalia, whose voice and name were present throughout, to demonstrate that his position was consistent with the original meaning of freedom of speech.[27]

Other scholars and jurists have helped bring about this shift, but it is Scalia who kept the flame at the highest reaches of the law. Not by tact or diplomacy. Scalia was often a pig, mocking his colleagues' intelligence and questioning their integrity. Sandra Day O'Connor, who sat on the Court from 1981 to 2006, was a frequent object of his ridicule and scorn. Scalia characterized one of her arguments as "devoid of content." Another, he wrote, "cannot be taken seriously." Whenever he was asked about his role in *Bush v. Gore* (2000), which put George W. Bush in the White House through a questionable mode of reasoning, he sneered, "Get over it!"[28] Nor, contrary to his camp followers, did Scalia dominate the Court by force of his intelligence. ("How bright is he?" exhaled one representative admirer.)[29] On a Court where everyone is a graduate of Harvard, Yale, or Princeton, and Ivy League professors sit on either side of the bench, there are plenty of brains to go around.

Several other factors explain Scalia's dominance of the Court. For starters, Scalia had the advantage of a straightforward philosophy and nifty method. While he and his army marched through the archives, rifling through documents on the right to bear arms, the commerce clause, and much else, the legal left remains "confused and uncertain," in the words of Yale law professors Robert Post and Reva Siegel, "unable to advance any robust theory of constitutional interpretation" of its own.[30] In an age when the left lacks certainty and will, Scalia's self-confidence can be a potent and intoxicating force.

Second, there's an elective affinity, even a tight fit, between the originalism of *duresse oblige* and Scalia's idea of the game. And that is Scalia's vision of what the good life entails: a daily and arduous struggle, where the only surety, if we leave things well enough alone, is that the strong shall win and the weak shall lose. Scalia, it turns out, was not nearly the iconoclast he thought he was. Far from telling "people what they don't like to hear," as he claimed, he told the power elite exactly what they want to hear: that they are superior and that they have a seat at the table because they are superior.[31] Tocqueville, it seems, was right after all. It was not the alienness but the appositeness of Justice Scalia, the way he reflected rather than refracted the spirit of the age, that explains, at least in part, his influence.

But there may be one additional, albeit small and personal, reason for Scalia's outsized presence in our Constitutional firmament. And that is the patience and forbearance, the general decency and good manners, his liberal colleagues showed him. While he ranted and raved, smashing guitars and strafing his enemies, they tended to respond with an indulgent shrug, a "that's just Nino," as O'Connor was wont to say.[32]

The fact may be small and personal, but the irony is large and political. For Scalia preyed on and profited from the very culture of liberalism he claimed to abhor: the toleration of opposing views, the generous allowances for other people's failings, the "benevolent compassion" he derides in his golf course dissent. Indeed, as two close observers of the Court have noted (in an article aptly titled "Don't Poke Scalia!"), whenever advocates before the bench subjected him to the gentlest of gibes, he was quickly rattled and thrown off his game.[33] Prone to tantrums, coddled by a different set of rules: now that's an affirmative action baby.

Ever since the 1960s, it has been a commonplace of our political culture that liberal niceties depend upon conservative not-so-niceties. A dinner party on the Upper West Side requires a police force that doesn't know from Miranda, the First Amendment a military that doesn't know from Geneva. That, of course, is the conceit of 24 (not to mention a good many other Hollywood productions like A Few Good Men). But that formulation may have it exactly backward: without his more liberal colleagues having indulged and protected him, Scalia—like Jack Bauer—would have had a much more difficult time. The conservatism of duresse oblige depends upon the liberalism of noblesse oblige, not the other way around. That is the real meaning of Justice Scalia.

11

A Show About Nothing

But in the desert you shall be invincible and shall achieve the goal.
—**Arnold Schoenberg,** *Moses und Aron*

In *The Art of the Deal*, Donald Trump tells us—twice—that he doesn't do lunch. By the end of the first 100 pages, he's gone out to lunch three times. Later on, Trump claims that he doesn't take architecture critics seriously. On the very next page, he admits, "I'm not going to kid you: it's also nice to get good reviews." Warm encomiums—or detailed objections—to various reviews follow. Elsewhere, Trump says the Wharton School at the University of Pennsylvania is "the place to go" to become a great entrepreneur. In the next paragraph, he states that a Wharton degree "doesn't prove very much."[1]

Inconsistency has long been Trump's style.[2] But where Trump's critics seize on that inconsistency as evidence of his unique liabilities, yet another instance of the difference between him and his respectable predecessors on the right, a happy avowal of contradiction has been a feature of the conservative tradition since the beginning. Originally, that avowal assumed a tonier form: as a counter to the simpleminded rationalism that was supposed to animate the left.[3] Against the belief that politics and society could be reduced to and made consistent with the austere rules of logic and reason, the conservative sought what Walter Bagehot called, in a different vein, "truth as a succession of perpetual oscillations, like the negative and positive signs of an alternate series, in which you were constantly more or less denying or affirming the same proposition."[4] The capacity to inhabit the twin poles of a proposition and its negation, without attempting to reconcile or overcome them, helped one appreciate and preserve the subtle textures of society. A complex social order, layered by centuries of submission and rule, would be ruined—made smaller, more tractable, less grand—by the leveling reason of the left. "He claims that a constitution does not exist unless he can put it in his pocket," sniffed Joseph de Maistre as he leafed through Thomas Paine's various plans to remake the world. They were all so legible and transparent, so slight. Burke had their measure, decades before anyone had even heard of Paine: "A clear idea is therefore another name for a little idea."[5]

Trump neither knows nor nods to this tradition. Yet as he ambles from one contradiction to the next, it's hard to avoid the suspicion that his indifference to consistency, his refusal to bow before the god of the flip-flop, is part of his appeal on the right. It advertises the image of the non-stuffed shirt that he, like so many conservatives before him, has long cultivated.[6] "Most people are surprised by the way I work," he says in *The Art of the Deal*. "I play it very loose. . . . You can't be imaginative or entrepreneurial if you've got too much structure. I prefer to come to work each day and just see what develops."[7] Trump doesn't need to make things tidy and neat. He's not afraid of a little chaos or disorder. He's also not afraid to give offense. He's as willing to defy the norms of political correctness as he is the rule of reason; those norms are a limitation on freedom as constraining as any socialist design.[8] Like George W. Bush, whose cowboy affect inspired the gushing

title "Rebel in Chief," Trump plays the part of the happy bucca-
neer, forever impolitic, thumbing his nose at the prissy professor
of principle—a part that invokes the right's age-old hostility to
political arithmetic and moral geometry.[9] "Sometimes," as Trump
says, "it pays to be a little wild."[10]

While Trump's racism, irregularity, and populism, and the
ambient violence that trails him and his entourage, are often cited
as the symptoms of a novel disease on the right, these are, as we
have seen throughout this book, the telltale signs of conservatism
across the ages. The racism of the Trumpist right is nastier than its
most recent predecessors—though certainly not nastier or more
violent than the movement's battle against civil rights in the 1960s
and 1970s, in the courts, legislatures, and streets. It's also more
focused on Muslims and Mexicans than on African Americans.
But the weaponization of racism and nativism under Trump is
an intensification of a well-established tradition on the right, as
studies of American conservatism from the 1920s through the
Tea Party have shown, and as earlier chapters here have argued.[11]
Likewise, the erratic nature of Trump's White House, the free-
wheeling disregard of norms and rules, reflect a longstanding conservative animus to the customary and the conventional—even,
in the case of Antonin Scalia, the lawful and the constitutional—
as do Trump's jabs against the establishment. And while there are
important innovations in Trump's populist appeals, populism has
been a critical element of the right from its inception.

Trump, however, is no mere carbon copy of his predecessors.
In at least two respects he has revised the right's script. First,
Trump reflects a tension between two visions on the right: what
we might call the political and the economic. One vision prizes
heroism, glory, and elite action, and is associated with the battlefield, high politics, and the hard affairs of state. The other celebrates the market and trade, the accumulation of wealth and

exchange of commodities, and is associated with unfettered capitalism. The conflict between the warrior and the businessman is an old one, predating the rise of the right and capitalism.[12] But since the eighteenth century, that conflict has produced on the right an intense ambivalence about capitalism. One side of the right has propped up the spheres of war and high politics as antidotes to or escapes from the deadening effects of capitalism. Here, capitalism is not so much eliminated as it is downgraded, its place in society diminished in order to make room for what Nietzsche called *grosse Politik*. The other side, of which there are glimmerings in Burke and a more developed picture in Schumpeter and Hayek, has not denigrated capitalism but recast it. No longer the province of the comfortable bourgeois trader, capitalism comes to look, in this view, like the agonistic political world its early defenders and critics thought capitalism might displace. The businessman ceases to be an antidote to the warrior or the aristocrat; he becomes their sublimation.

The Cold War allowed—or forced—the right to hold these tensions between the warrior and the businessman in check. Against the backdrop of the struggle against communism abroad and welfare-state liberalism at home, the businessman became a warrior and the warrior a businessmen.[13] With the end of the Cold War, that conflation or confusion of roles became difficult to sustain. In one precinct of the right, the market returned to its status as a deadening activity that stifled greatness, whether of the nation or the elite. In another precinct of the right, market activities were revalorized as acts of heroism by an economic class that saw itself and its work as the natural province of rule. Donald Trump hails from the second precinct, but with a twist: he suggests that its self-understanding can no longer be sustained.

Trump's second innovation upends the always-delicate relationship on the right between elite and mass, privilege and populism.

Conservatism is an elitist movement of the masses, an effort to create a new-old regime that, in one way or another, makes privilege popular. Sometimes, conservatism has multiplied the ranks of privilege, creating ever-finer gradations between the worse off and the worst off. Here the model is the American firm, with its many tiers of middle and lower management.[14] Sometimes, conservatism has simplified those ranks into two: the white race and the black race of the white supremacist imagination. Sometimes, it has offshored society's inequalities, seeing in the people of an imperial state a unified rank of superiors, "a kind of nobility among nations" subjugating less civilized peoples abroad.[15] And sometimes it has turned elites into victims, encouraging the masses to see their abjection reflected in the higher misery of those above them. Regardless of the means, conservatism has always found a way to conscript the lower orders into its regime of lordly rule.

Trump's ascendancy suggests that the lower orders are no longer satisfied with the racial and imperial privileges the movement has offered them. The right has reversed many of the gains of the Civil Rights Movement: the schools that African Americans in the South attend today are more segregated than they were under Richard Nixon; the racial wealth gap has tripled since 1984; and in several states, voting rights for African Americans are under attack.[16] Yet a combination of stagnating wages, rising personal and household debt, and increasing precarity—coupled with the tormenting symbolism of a black president and the greater visibility of black and brown faces in the culture industries—has made the traditional conservative offering seem scant to its white constituents. The future of the United States as a minority-majority nation exacerbates this anxiety. Racial dog whistles no longer suffice; a more brazen sound is required.[17]

Trump is that sound. Not just the overt racism and nativism of his rhetoric and his policies, but also the economic populism of his rhetoric. (His economic policies, as some of his disillusioned supporters are beginning to discover, are a different matter.)[18] Trump's critics often dismiss the anti-elitism of his economic rhetoric as incidental if not irrelevant. Yet Trump's critique of plutocracy, defense of entitlements, and articulated sense of the market's wounds were among the more noteworthy rhetorical innovations of his campaign—at least with respect to recent victorious strands of the electoral right (one can find precedents for Trump's mix of racial and economic populism in the less electorally successful campaigns of Father Coughlin, George Wallace, and Pat Buchanan).[19] If nothing else, those rhetorical innovations signal that the sun of Reaganomics—which saw in the unfettered market the answer to the political, economic, and cultural stagflation of the 1970s—no longer warms the lower orders of the right.[20] It's not "morning in America," Trump declared in a recent campaign book, invoking Reagan's famous tag line from 1984; we are now *"mourning for America."*[21]

What these two innovations tell us is that the tensions that long buttressed the right—the countervailing pressures of the political versus the economic, elite versus mass—are no longer as taut as they once were. Those pressures don't support the movement; they don't give it the buoyancy it once had. The reason is the disappearance of the right's traditional antagonists—the freedom movements of the left, those subaltern assertions of agency and will, from the French Revolution through civil rights and women's lib, that sought individual emancipation through collective liberation and vice versa. "Conservatism does its best," the right-wing British philosopher Roger Scruton has written, "in times of crisis." For the right, the crisis is a dynamic and vibrant left, the challenge of movements of revolution or reform that force the right to think harder and better, to act smarter and with greater discipline and intentionality: not out of any Millian desire to get the better of an argument but out of dread necessity, the need to defend power and privilege in the face of a movement seeking their elimination. When the left is ascendant and genuinely threatening, the right gets tough, intellectually and politically; when the left is in abeyance, the right grows sclerotic and complacent, rigid and lazy. According to Hayek, the defense of the free market "became stationary when it was most influential." It "progressed" only when it was "on the defensive." While there are stirrings on the left—Occupy, Black Lives Matter, LGBTQ movements, and the Sanders campaign—none of these movements has yet achieved sufficient velocity or institutional traction to awaken and discipline a new right that would be able to do what its predecessors did. The right's greatest "burst of creative energy," according to Frank Meyer, one of its leading midcentury action intellectuals, occurred "simultaneously with a continuing spread of the influence of Liberalism in the practical political sphere."[22] Without a formidable enemy on the left, without an opponent to discipline and tutor the right, the long-standing fissures of the conservative movement are allowed to deepen and expand.

That absent tutelage is most visibly embodied in Trump, whose whims are as unlettered as his mind is untaught. Yet it would be a mistake to read Trump's deficiencies as his and his alone. Trump is a window onto the dissolution of the conservative whole, a whole that is dissolving because its victories have been so great, a whole that can allow itself to collapse because it has achieved so much. Battling its way to hegemony in the second half of the twentieth century, the American right would never have chosen a Trump—not because it was more intelligent or virtuous, not because it was less racist or violent, but because it was disciplined by its task of destroying the left. Having achieved that task, it can now afford, can now allow itself, the luxury of irresponsibility. Or so it believes; as we have already seen in the opening months of the Trump presidency, the conservative regime—despite its command of all three elected branches of the national government and a majority of state governments—is extraordinarily unstable, even weak, thanks to a number of self-inflicted wounds. That weakness, however, is a symptom not of its failures but its success.

Donald Trump didn't write *The Art of the Deal*, his breakout memoir of 1987. Ghostwriter Tony Schwartz did. But that didn't stop Trump, in announcing his presidential campaign, from declaring, "We need a leader that wrote *The Art of the Deal*." On the *New York Times* best-seller list for 48 weeks after it came out, the book catapulted Trump from outer-borough disrepute to international fame and, ultimately, a successful run for the White House. Much to Schwartz's regret: "I put lipstick on a pig," he told *The New Yorker* in the summer of 2016. "I feel a deep sense of remorse that I contributed to presenting Trump in a way that brought him wider attention and made him more appealing than he is."[23] Schwartz's disavowal is perplexing, though. *The Art of the Deal* is not a flattering or even outsized portrait of Trump. It's a devastating—if unintentional—deflation of not only Trump the man but also the movement, party, and nation he now leads.

The peculiarity of *The Art of the Deal*—and what lent Trump's candidacy such puzzling appeal (a plutocrat denouncing plutocrats, an effect of wealth decrying the effects of wealth, a man of the market denigrating the virtue of the market)—is how it simultaneously advances the right's competing visions of the market. On the one hand, it celebrates the economy as the sphere of great men, where the strong dominate the weak. On the other hand, it mounts a persistent, almost poignant, questioning of the value of capitalism, suggesting that economic pursuits are frivolous if not meaningless, that a society should be about something more than making money. In the words of Steve Bannon—Trump's senior advisor whose fate in the administration remains, as of this writing, unclear—"A country's more than an economy. We're a civic society."[24] Where postwar American conservatives had mostly refused that hierarchy between the state and the economy, between the warrior statesman and the bourgeois businessman—preferring to pivot back and forth from paeans to the market to professions of God and country—it is a sign of the movement's current difficulties that it has turned to someone who sets out both visions so starkly, elevating neither the one nor the other but allowing both to exist side by side, each calling the other into question.[25]

Most of The Art of the Deal is a testimonial to the first vision: the capitalist as warrior prince. Just as the battlefield or the palace was once the plain upon which great men revealed themselves to the world and to each other, the economy is now the sphere where men prove their mettle. There are strong men; there are weak men. There are men who think big and men who think small. But how do these men reveal themselves, how can we know them? By how much they are willing to spend in the market, by how much they are willing financially to commit to their vision of things. "The dollar," writes Trump, "always talks in the end." Money is a truth-teller. It shows how much of ourselves we have to give—and how much of ourselves we have to give up in pursuit of our dreams. If it's a little money, the dream must not be fervently felt; that person is play-acting, pretending to want something he's not willing to pay for. If it's a lot of money, the dream is exigent. That person is more than a dreamer: he's a doer. "All my life," Trump says, "I've believed in paying for the best."[26]

One of Trump's great dreams was to build a fantastic atrium. He poured millions into a vast court at Trump Tower; no expense was spared. His competitors were enthralled by what they saw. They wanted it, too. Then they saw the bill.

> What they discovered is that the bronze escalators were going to cost a million dollars extra, and the waterfall was going to cost two million dollars, and the marble was going to cost many millions more. They saw that it all added up to many millions of dollars, and all of a sudden these people with these great ambitions would decide, well, let's forget about the atrium.[27]

The maintenance of that atrium also cost a bundle. The suits at Equitable Real Estate Group, who co-owned Trump Tower, weren't happy about that:

> One day this fellow called me up and said, "Mr. Trump, I've just been looking over the books, and I'd like you to explain why we're spending so much on the maintenance of Trump Tower." We were, in fact, spending nearly $1 million a year, which is almost unheard of. But the explanation was very simple. When you set the highest possible standards, they're expensive to maintain. As one simple example, my policy was to have all of the brass in the atrium polished twice a month. Why, this fellow asked, couldn't we save some money by polishing once every couple of months?[28]

That was the end of Equitable.

Money, Trump makes clear in the first sentence of *The Art of the Deal*, is not the goal or the end of business: "I don't do it for the money." Nor is money, he explains in the second sentence, a means to an end: "I've got enough, much more than I'll ever need." Trump has never been satisfied "just to earn a good living."

Money is a medium, a way of declaring something about himself. Spending is expressive; it's a way of talking. And it ain't cheap. "I was looking to make a statement. I was out to build something monumental—something worth a big effort."[29]

When it comes to saying something with buildings, however, Trump is less concerned with their size and scale than with their surfaces. Where Ayn Rand, another conservative much taken with building, cared about the engineering and design of a structure, its materials and workmanship, Trump makes almost no mention of design, engineering, or even architecture. This is a man incapable of focusing on any one item for too long: in the 43-page account of his workweek that comprises the first chapter of his book, he flits from meeting to phone call—often a hundred a day, he tells us—from room to room, deal to deal. "It never stops," he exhales, "and I wouldn't have it any other way." But show him a window treatment, mention a slab of stone or pane of burnished glass, and his attention is rapt. Suddenly he becomes the most observant diarist, recording detail after loving detail of the beauty he sees and its effects upon him:

Der, Ivana, and I looked at hundreds of marble samples. Finally, we came upon something called Breccia Perniche, a rare marble in a color none of us had ever seen before—an exquisite blend of rose, peach, and pink that literally took our breath away. . . it was a very irregular marble. When we went to the quarry, we discovered that much of the marble contained large white spots and white veins. That was jarring to me and took away from the beauty of the stone. So we ended up going to the quarry with black tape and marking off the slabs that were the best. . . .

The effect was heightened by the fact that we used so much marble—on the floors and for the walls six full floors up. It created a very luxurious and a very exciting feeling. Invariably, people comment that the atrium—and the color of the marble particularly—is friendly and flattering, but also vibrant and energizing—all things you want people to feel when they shop. . . [30]

Amid a complex account of the financial challenges of retail and how those challenges might play out in a suburban mall versus Trump Tower, Trump can't help noticing that one of his atrium's tenants sells leather pants that are "soft and buttery."[31]

The attention to external detail, to the surface of things, is not confined to Trump's business career; it informs his political judgments as well. One of Trump's most heartfelt criticisms of Obama was that rather than hosting a celebration for foreign dignitaries in a lavish ballroom, he served dinner to them in "an old, broken, rotten-looking tent" on the White House lawn. "That's no way for America to host important meetings and dinners with world leaders and dignitaries. We should project our nation's power and beauty with a proper facility and ballroom." So enraged was Trump at this failed aesthetics of power that he called the White House and, patched through to Obama senior strategist David Axelrod, offered to build a ballroom there for free: "If there's one thing I know how to build, it's a grand ballroom." Axelrod never got back to him on his offer—yet one more sign, wrote a bitter Trump, of "what's wrong with this country."[32]

Now in office, Trump has set things right. According to an early report in the New York Times:

Visitors to the Oval Office say Mr. Trump is obsessed with the décor. . . He will linger on the opulence of the newly hung golden drapes, which he told a recent visitor were once used by Franklin D. Roosevelt but in fact were patterned for Bill Clinton. For a man who sometimes has trouble concentrating on policy memos, Mr. Trump was delighted to page through a book that offered him 17 window covering options.[33]

Trump's sensibility, it turns out, is less monumental than ornamental. That sensibility is not simply personal or psychological. It's a rococo aesthetic that dominated New York fashion and museum culture in the 1980s—when *The Art of the Deal* appeared— and that cultural historian Debora Silverman, in *Selling Culture: Bloomingdale's, Diana Vreeland, and the New Aristocracy of Taste in Reagan's America*, identifies as the true cultural front of the Reagan administration (Nancy Reagan was personally connected to Bloomingdale and Vreeland).[34] This faux-aristocratic ethos found expression in dresses, exhibits, jewelry, and costumes that made nods to an ancient régime of which it had no knowledge and to which it had no connection. It was opulent and ostentatious, loud and luxurious, vicious and vulgar. It was a world made for Donald Trump, the world that made Donald Trump.

Trump is not unaware of the political provenance of his aesthetic: "What I'm doing is about as close as you're going to get, in the twentieth century, to the quality of Versailles."[35] But he tucks those insights inside a family romance. Trump's father had little time for his son's soft and buttery tastes. To the hard-driving Fred Trump, it was all a waste of money.

I still remember a time when my father visited the Trump Tower site, midway through construction. Our façade was a glass curtain wall, which is far more expensive than brick. In addition, we were using the most expensive glass you can buy—bronze solar. My father took one look, and he said to me, "Why don't you forget about the damn glass? Give them four or five stories of it and then use common brick for the rest. Nobody is going to look anyway."

That was his father, says Trump: always "trying to save a few bucks." His mother, on the other hand, spurned the penny-pinching ways of her bourgeois husband. Her passions were more regal.

> Looking back, I realize now that I got some of my sense of showmanship from my mother. She always had a flair for the dramatic and the grand. She was a very traditional housewife, but she also had a sense of the world beyond her. I still remember my mother, who is Scottish by birth, sitting in front of the television set to watch Queen Elizabeth's coronation and not budging for an entire day. She was just enthralled by the pomp and circumstance, the whole idea of royalty and glamour. I also remember my father that day, pacing around impatiently. "For Christ's sake, Mary," he'd say. "Enough is enough, turn it off. They're all a bunch of con artists." My mother didn't even look up. They were total opposites in that sense. My mother loves splendor and magnificence, while my father, who is very down-to-earth, gets excited only by competence and efficiency.[36]

Trump is his mother's son. But where Mary Trump could only pine for the ways of the British monarchy, Trump understood, like his father, that being an aristocrat, expressing oneself in a princely way, costs money. Unlike his father, he was willing to pay it.

No matter how medieval or monarchical their attachments, conservatives reject the staid and static traditionalism of the feudal worldview. Their conception of power is more dynamic, their notions of supremacy more agonistic. They believe in domination, but it is a domination laden with struggle: either among equals, along the lines of what Nietzsche sets out in "Homer's Contest," or between superiors and subordinates.[37] Conservatives want a ruling elite, but it must be one that has been tested, that has won its place at the table through personal displays of fortitude. That fortitude is what makes these ruling elites men of distinction and value as opposed to the lads and layabouts so often found among the sons of the ruling class, the Lauderdales and Bedfords to whom Burke took such exception in his *Letter to a Noble Lord*.[38]

Trump's rhetoric is suffused with this conception of economic life as a struggle of the best men for power and position. Nothing provokes his ire more than the time-server, whether in the family or the firm. One of the men Trump has great admiration for is Conrad Hilton, who built a hotel empire on his own. Hilton believed "that inherited wealth destroys moral character and motivation." Trump agrees (in theory; from his earliest years, he had a trust fund, and he campaigned against the estate tax). That is why he takes such a jaundiced view of Hilton's son, who despite Conrad's warnings about inheritance, came to a position of great power in his father's industry. "It had nothing to do with merit," says Trump; "it's called birthright." Hilton's son was "a member of what I call the Lucky Sperm Club." Like so many to the manor born, he "doesn't try enough." The name of Hilton's son, incidentally, is Barron.[39]

In business, Trump prefers to deal with "the sharpest, toughest, and most vicious people in the world. I happen to love to go up against these guys, and I love to beat them." This is the other side of what money reveals: how much better you are than your competitor: "Money was never a big motivation for me, except as a way to keep score." Like the bloody battles of ancient Greece or medieval Europe, moments of economic combat belong to the more excellent, superior man. Not better in the sense of meritocratic achievement—institutional measures of worth can reward only the institution man—or in terms of an economic contribution—a new product, more jobs, higher shareholder value—but in the sense of besting another in the field of battle. Those moments reveal the "instincts" of the self. Those instincts may entail "a certain intelligence," but more important, they reflect a driving will to overcome, to overpower, to win. There are some who have great talent but who "will never find out how great they could have been. Instead, they'll be content to sit and watch stars perform on television." Such individuals "are afraid of success, afraid of making decisions, afraid of winning." The great man has no such compunctions; he has a driving will to win, to put that greatness into effect, to show it off to the world. And that, says Trump, is not something one can learn or develop; it is "an ability you're born with." It is what truly belongs to the original and originating self.[40]

Trump views these economic contests between businessmen the way Scalia views games: as the divining rod of a natural inequality, a sorting mechanism for distinguishing the drab from the great.[41] Not the wealthy from the poor, but the large from the small.

> I like thinking big. I always have. To me it's very simple: if you're going to be thinking anyway, you might as well think big. Most people think small, because most people are afraid of success, afraid of making decisions, afraid of winning. And that gives people like me a great advantage.[42]

And like Scalia, he believes the outcome of those contests can never be known in advance. That is what is so exciting about them.

Life is very fragile, and success doesn't change that. If anything, success makes it more fragile. Anything can change, without warning. . . The real excitement is playing the game.[43]

Failure must always remain a prospect if success is to mean something, anything. (Two decades later, Trump told an audience at one of his motivational speeches in Colorado: "I love losers because they make me feel so good about myself.")[44] And that is why Trump is so in thrall to the art of the deal. Why does he do it? "I do it to do it. Deals are my art form. Other people paint beautifully on canvas or write wonderful poetry. I like making deals, preferably big deals."[45] The buildings are ornamental. It's the deal that's monumental.

Yet there is an unexpected sigh of emptiness, even boredom, at the end of Trump's celebration of economic combat: "If you ask me exactly what the deals I'm about to describe all add up to in the end, I'm not sure I have a very good answer." In fact, he has no answer at all. He says, hopefully, "I've had a very good time making them," and wonders, wistfully, "If it can't be fun, what's the point?"[46] But the quest for fun is all that he has to offer—a dispiriting narrowness that Max Weber anticipated more than a century ago when he wrote that "in the United States, the pursuit of wealth, stripped of its religious and ethical meaning, tends to become associated with purely mundane passions, which often actually give it the character of sport."[47] Ronald Reagan could marvel, "You know, there really is something magic about the marketplace when it's free to operate. As the song says, 'This could be the start of something big.'"[48] But there is no magic in Trump's marketplace. Everything—save those buttery leather pants—is a bore.[49]

That admission affords Trump considerable freedom to say things about the moral emptiness of the market—and to enact that moral emptiness in his presidency—that no credible aspirant to the Oval Office on the right (or, for the most part, the left) would say. In his objection to people who oppose casinos, Trump says there's only one difference between gambling and the socially acceptable investing that fuels capitalism: "the players" in the New York Stock Exchange "dress in blue pinstripe suits and carry leather briefcases." Bets are a way to make money; casinos are just another market. Such statements, collapsing profit into profiteering, used to be taboo among the ruling classes: they were too explosive. "No man of spirit will consent to remain poor if he believes his betters to have gained their goods by lucky gambling," Keynes warned. "The business man is only tolerable so long as his gains can be held to bear some relations to what, roughly and in some sense, his activities have contributed to Society." Any suggestion to the contrary, any hint that one's reward depends upon gambling, would "strike a blow at capitalism," destroying "the psychological equilibrium which permits the perpetuance of unequal rewards."[50] Trump's genius is to recognize the truth of Keynes's dictum, but rather than run away from it in fear of revolutionary retribution, Trump affirms it, knowing full well there is no revolution in the offing. The more likely consequence is that people will want to know Trump's secrets. Or elect him president.

Ironically, what is so unsettling about Trump's talk, what makes it so pertinent and resonant as a political vision, is not its lies but its brutal honesty.

The final key to the way I promote is bravado. I play to people's fantasies. People do not always think big themselves, but they can still get very excited by those who do. That's why a little hyperbole never hurts. People want to believe that something is the biggest and the greatest and the most spectacular.

I call it truthful hyperbole.[51]

That fakery, that play to fantasy and bravado, is not a sideshow to the economy, to the sphere of real production or honest exchange. It is the economy. "A lot of attention," says Trump, "alone creates value."[52] A lot of attention—not the productivity of labor, design of the engineer, vision of the entrepreneur, risk of the investor, or genius of the advertiser—that *alone* creates value. At the heart of his celebration of economic combat and struggle is a dim awareness that its only justification is itself. The game is the game. And even that desperate grab for meaning is compromised. As he says, "If there's one thing I've learned about the rich, it's that they have a very low threshold for even the mildest discomfort."[53]

This is what makes Trump's economic philosophy, such as it is, so peculiar and of its moment. An older generation of economic Darwinists—from William Graham Sumner to Ayn Rand—believed, without reservation, in the market's revelations. It wasn't just the contest that was glorious; the outcome was, too. That conviction burned in them like a holy fire. Trump, by contrast, subscribes and unsubscribes to that vision. The market is a moment of truth—and an eternity of lies. It reveals; it hides. It is everything; it is nothing. It shall be all; it is naught. Rand grounded her vision of capitalism in A is A; Trump grounds his in A is not A.

In his recent study of Marx's *Capital*, the political theorist William Roberts argues that Marx modeled his masterwork on Dante's *Inferno*. In the same way that Dante's pilgrim journeys through the various layers of hell on his path toward salvation, so does Marx lead his reader—the modern worker—through the social hell that is capitalism. The journey from the market to the workplace to the netherworld of primitive accumulation, says Roberts, is a proletarian's progress. It is a journey downward, through darkness, because it is only through the darkness that the worker will reach the light.[54]

The Art of the Deal is a parody of that journey. The promise is that if you accompany Trump through a week in his life, with side trips to his past, the secrets of his success will be revealed. The premise is that Trump, the happy warrior, is a man whose life is to be envied and whose work is to be studied. Trump is the guide—and the tour. The stops will be one fabulous deal after another, one "character"—Trump loves characters—after another. What the traveler gets instead is the failed Convention Center project, the time Trump bought the Commodore Hotel, negotiations with Bonwit Teller, the housing complex he flipped in Cincinnati, the decision to use brine rather than Freon at Wollman Rink in Central Park. It's about as interesting as the memoir J. Peterman sets out to write, in that episode of *Seinfeld*, based entirely on the stories he's bought from Kramer.

The secret of Trump is that there is no secret. That is the truth about capitalism that is revealed in *The Art of the Deal*: there is no truth. It's a show about nothing.

Trump is by no means the first man of the right (though he may be the first president, at least since Teddy Roosevelt) to reach that conclusion about capitalism. A great many neoconservatives, as we saw in chapter 9, found themselves stranded on the same beach after the end of the Cold War. As had many conservatives before that. Those conservatives, however, always found a redeeming vision in the state. Not the welfare state or the nanny state but The State of high politics, national greatness, imperial leadership, and war. Given the thrumming menace of Trump's rhetoric, his impatience with routine, his fetish for pomp and love of grandeur, this state, too, would seem the natural terminus of his predilections. As Bannon said, "A country's more than an economy. We're a civic society." Yet on closer inspection, the state of Trump's imagination looks less like The State than the deals he's not sure have added up to much.

Trump's 2011 proto-campaign statement *Time to Get Tough*—repackaged for the 2016 campaign with a new subtitle, *Make America Great Again!*®—plots this trajectory to a tee. It opens on that note of wounded nationalism for which Trump has come to be famous—

> Every day in business I see America getting ripped off and abused. We have become a laughingstock, the world's whipping boy, blamed for everything, credited for nothing, given no respect.[55]

—and it never lets up. Across nearly 200 pages, it recounts an epoch of national humiliation, presided over by decadent leaders like Barack Obama and—shades of McCarthyites talking about Dean Acheson—his band of "cream puff 'diplomats.'" We're sinking like a stone, growls Trump, we come to the rest of the world "on bended knee," Obama "practices 'pretty please' diplomacy," his statements are "drenched in weakness," China is our enemy, Obama is a traitor, we have to get tough, Let's Make America Great Again![56] So committed is Trump to America First that, after acknowledging that no American wants to drill for oil in his backyard, he cites as yet another example of our national humiliation the fact that we allow other nations to drill in their backyards. Like George C. Scott's General "Buck" Turgidson in *Dr. Strangelove*—"Mr. President, we must not allow. . . a mineshaft gap!"—Trump complains "the holes are going to get drilled into the planet anyway," so "we should drill them on our soil."[57] Trump's extended aria to our collective pain and suffering here seems to have at least some of the elements of that "passionate nationalism" that historian Robert Paxton describes as the essence of fascism: a sense of grievous dishonor and shame, played out across oceans and continents; the stab in the back from cosmopolitan elites (Obama is "economist to the world" who commits "economic treason"); a longing for re-enchantment of the state; a desire for national restoration and global domination.[58]

For all the apparent violence and statism of the rhetoric, what's remarkable about Trump's political vision is how economistic it can be, especially at moments when he hews most closely to a hard image of the state. Where anti-market conservatives historically flew into the arms (in both senses) of the state as an end run around the market, Trump often sees in matters of state nothing but the transactions of the market. Money is the instrument of state power. Money is the end of state power. Anyone aspiring to wield state power should be an adept of money: success or failure in the business world is the best test of one's political mettle. Even when Trump tries to talk the language of hard power—violence, coercion, rule—he cannot avoid sliding back into the idioms of the market he knows so well.

"China is our enemy," Trump says, and "the military threat from China is gigantic." As a result, "we've got to have a president who knows how to get tough with China."[59] Does that entail an arms race, more aggressive deployments in East Asia, nuclear brinksmanship? No, just the opposite.

We need a president who will sign the bipartisan legislation to force a proper valuation of China's currency. We need a president who will slap the Chinese with a 25 percent tax on all their products entering America if they don't stop undervaluing the yuan. We need a president who will crack down on China's massive and blatant intellectual property theft that allows China to pirate our products (maybe if Obama didn't view entrepreneurs and businesspeople as the enemy he'd be more aggressive about this). Most of all, we need a president who is smart and tough enough to recognize the national security threat China poses in the new frontier of cyber warfare.[60]

Having emphasized the military nature of China's threat to the United States, Trump makes no mention of a military response, save for a glancing reference to cyberwarfare. The antidote to the rising power of China is not a swaggering warrior speaking softly or carrying a big stick (Trump wonders "why we don't speak more loudly"); it is a leader who knows "how to out-negotiate the Chinese." And what is the final victory Trump envisions over China? A company in Georgia that will provide, one day, 150 jobs to Americans making chopsticks—which they will "ship. . . to China! How great is that?"[61] Instead of carrying a big stick, Trump wants to make chopsticks.

America fought a catastrophic war in Iraq. The main catastrophe of that war, for Trump, is not the false pretenses on which it was fought, not the failure to secure basic war aims or to plan for reconstruction, not the fact that it was a long-term strategic disaster. It's that "we should have hammered out the repayment plan with the Iraqis. . . *before* we launched the war." The Iraq War, in other words, was a bad deal. The Iraqis "should pay us back." With oil. If they don't, the United States should "implement a cost-sharing arrangement with Iraq." Trump has a lot of fun with the threatening call "Take the oil." It was a frequent refrain on the campaign trail, and it's the title of the second chapter of *Time to Get Tough*. But notice how he proposes to take the oil.

Why are we footing the bill [in Iraq] and getting nothing in return?

I'll give you the answer. It's because our so-called "leaders" in Washington know absolutely nothing about negotiation and dealmaking. Look, I do deals—big deals—all the time. I know and work with all the toughest operators in the world of high-stakes global finance. These are hard-driving, vicious, cutthroat financial killers, the kind of people who leave blood all over the boardroom table and fight to the bitter end to gain maximum advantage. And guess what? Those are *exactly* the kind of negotiators the United States needs. . . .

The closest Trump gets to violence in this epic moment of confrontation between two international powers is a metaphor drawn from the trading floor of the market.[62]

Trump has certainly surrounded himself and his administration with generals and officers, though whether that tilts his foreign policy in a more militaristic direction than has previous US policy remains to be seen.[63] It may simply be that Trump is as enamored with the shiny medals of the top brass as he is with smooth peach marble. Trump also will make the infrequent and passing nod to military power, often sandwiched between an emphasis on other modes of power and contest: "A smart negotiator would use the leverage of our dollars, our laws, and our armed forces to get a better deal from OPEC." But no sooner does he mention hard power than he's racing back to the other side of the table, almost as if he's scared himself with all the military talk and is more comfortable with the conversation about economics that's going on over there:

> Operate from strength. That means we have to maintain the strongest military in the world, by far. We have to demonstrate a willingness to use our economic strength to reward those countries that work with us and punish those countries that don't. That means going after the banks and financial institutions that launder money for our enemies. . . .

The most coercive instrument he has in mind is that time-honored method of the hard bargain: get up from the table. Rather than threatening his opponent with a rain of bombs or even sanctions, Trump says the problem with American negotiators is that "we don't threaten to walk away. And, more important, we don't walk away."[64]

Trump's other favorite instrument of state power is the tool of trade he perfected in real estate: the lawsuit. How should the United States "take on the oil thugs?" he asks. "We can start by suing OPEC for violating antitrust laws." Quoting a former White House adviser, Trump asks, "Isn't starting a lawsuit better than starting a war?"[65] In his business career, Trump has been a plaintiff or defendant in more than 4,000 lawsuits. He loves to brag about his willingness to take his enemies to court, but the truth is that he often settles and is more skilled at threatening litigation (and spinning his losses) than winning it. In one of his most hard-fought and expensive lawsuits, a federal court awarded him a mere $1 in damages.[66] His penchant for the tough talk of litigation has followed Trump into the White House. When a federal judge put a stay on his travel ban, the strongest response Trump could muster was a plaintive tweet: "I'll see you in court." Indeed, for all the fear that Trump poses a threat to the independence of the judiciary or the rule of law, his primary mode of opposing court rulings has been, like virtually every one of his predecessors in the Oval Office, to appeal those rulings. And now, having lost so many of these appeals, he and his advisers seem to have decided, at least on the question of the travel ban, that rather than railing against the judiciary, the best course of action is to quietly wait on the Supreme Court.[67] Whether he wins or loses, whether the sphere is domestic politics or international affairs, Trump's primary conception of power remains the swagger of the lawsuit.

Part of the reason for this slippage from the political to the economic, from the violent to the legal, is rooted in history. As far back as the nineteenth century, capitalism assumed a militaristic guise, with references to captains of industry, industrial titans, and the like. The businessman was often depicted as a general. It seems natural, then, that given the chance to play an actual commander in chief, the businessman would continue to speak the language of his original milieu. "Dealmaker in chief," in fact, is Trump's preferred term for the president.[68] But there's another reason, of more recent vintage, for Trump's slippage, and that is that politics has increasingly assumed an economistic guise. As Wendy Brown has argued, neoliberalism is, among other things, the conquest of political argument by economic reason.[69] The dominant rationale for public policy is not drawn from the idiom of political philosophy but from the literature on economics: choice, efficiency, competition, exchange. (Among liberals, the most sought-after feature of Obama's healthcare plan was the failed attempt to create a "public option"—itself a confluence of political and economic metaphors—to compete with private insurance markets.) In 1975, Jimmy Carter helped launch the neoliberal turn in American politics by campaigning on the claim "I ran the Georgia government as well as almost any corporate structure in this country is run."[70] Four decades later, managing a firm no longer provides a standard of leadership. It is the substance of leadership.

Given this economistic view of politics, the consistent evasion of the hard ways of state, it's no small irony that as soon as Trump became a serious contender for the Republican nomination, the comparisons to Hitler began.[71] Since Trump's election, they've continued. Though some historians of fascism have cautioned against the comparison, others have found it illuminating.[72] The reasons for the comparison are obvious: the bullying rhetoric, the hatred of racial and ethnic minorities, the xenophobia, the violence of Trump's rallies and his freelance supporters throughout the country, the hostility to dissent, and, for a time, the invocations of American workers humiliated and mangled by the workings of a global capitalism that did not have their interests at heart. Yet if fascism's achievement was to mobilize a mass base of the nation or race, consolidate the state apparatus, clear the political field of opposition and dissent through terror from above and violence from below, and thereby pursue its program with maximal leverage and authority, it's plain that Trump has fallen short of the ideal—if that was ever the ambition in the first place (the economism of Trump's vision, as Paxton has recently and rightly argued, would suggest a serious constraint upon that ideal).[73] At almost every step—from his opening salvo of a travel ban to his attempt to repeal Obamacare to his effort to build a wall to his budget proposal for the remainder of fiscal year 2017 and plans to overhaul the tax code—Trump's plans and purposes have been checked by opposition in the streets, the courts, the Democratic Party, and uncertainty and division within his own party.[74] Less than five months into his term, his voting base—whites, men, and white men and women without college degrees—has begun to erode.[75] With the important exceptions of rolling back his predecessor's regulatory regime and pushing a punitive immigration policy—the latter being an area where all presidents have independent power, a power the last two Democrats in the White House exercised with decreasing restraint[76]—Trump's program, thus far, has been mostly stymied. And despite Trump's campaign promise, repeated in his Inaugural Address, to govern as a new type of conservative, defending the interests of the working man, his practice has been overwhelmingly consistent with mainstream pro-business Republicanism.[77]

While the fissiparous nature of American institutions has helped stop Trump, it's important to remember that those institutions have often served the agents of tyranny—from the defenders of slavery and Jim Crow to the forces of McCarthyism and COINTELPRO—remarkably well.[78] And while Trump's rule has generated much opposition, other presidents have faced similar if not more robust resistance, which they nevertheless managed to turn to their favor. A good deal of Franklin Roosevelt's initial program of recovery was struck down by the courts, which then became the occasion and rationale for FDR's even more frontal assault upon the established institutions of the American state.[79] Bill Clinton parlayed the Republican shutdown of 1995–1996 into higher approval ratings and his reelection, while Nixon could scarcely contain his growling references to rioters and hippies and peaceniks, so potent was that opposition as a legitimating source of his rule.[80] Neither of the latter two presidents, moreover, had majorities in Congress.[81] Something else must explain Trump's inability to achieve full- or even partial-spectrum dominance of the political field—at least thus far: while the opening months of a four-year term are traditionally a moment of great if not the greatest potency for a president, Trump's ebbing fortunes could always improve.

When Hitler came to power in 1933, he was a government novice but an experienced political operative. Not only had he helped build an effective political machine from the most inauspicious parts, not only had he provided that machine with its ideological grease and gasoline, but he also had seen to it that the core of the party's membership and paramilitary swore an oath of personal loyalty directly to him.[82] Trump, by contrast, came to the conservative movement and the Republican Party long after it had been built. He didn't work his way through the arguments or ranks of the right. He had neither government nor political experience. He was rejected by a majority of voters in his party's primaries—the first president since Jimmy Carter to enter the Oval Office with that millstone around his neck—and was only able to secure the nomination thanks to a vacuum within the party and the inability of its leadership to rally around an alternative. Both the vacuum and the inability are symptomatic of a party/movement that has achieved much of what, going back to the 1930s, it set out to achieve.[83]

Hitler fought his way to power as the culmination of a decade-long ascendancy of the right battling back a triumphant left. Trump, by contrast, assumes the leadership of the conservative movement, the Republican Party, and the American government at a difficult moment for the right. It's true that the Republican Party controls all the elected branches of the federal government, all the elected branches of 25 state governments, and the legislatures of seven other states.[84] Yet we should remember that less than two years before the election of Ronald Reagan and the Republican realignment, the Democrats also were at the peak of their control over the state: leading all the elected branches of the federal government—and by far greater margins in the House and Senate than the Republicans do today—and all the elected branches of government in 27 states, and the legislatures of nine other states.[85] More important, between 1968 and 1988, the GOP won five out of six presidential elections. Since 1992, it has won only three out of seven presidential elections—twice without the popular vote. On these latter occasions, it was the Electoral College, not the majority of voters, that put the Republican candidate into office, something that had not occurred in this country since the nineteenth century. One of those occasions also required the intervention of the Supreme Court. Richard Nixon, who first rode the hard-right racial populism of the conservative movement into the White House, was reelected with 61% of the popular vote.

At the height of his power, Ronald Reagan received 59% of the popular vote. At the height of his power, George W. Bush received 51% of the popular vote. Trump has come into office with 46% of the popular vote, and his approval ratings throughout his first months in office have been the worst of any modern president's.[86]

Whatever this means for the electoral prospects of the GOP, it's clear that something has happened to conservatism in the last quarter-century. While conservatism aims to be an elitist movement of the masses, in recent years the popular elements of its rule have been attenuated. Nixon, Reagan, and Bush achieved their upward redistribution of rights and privileges by mobilizing a majority of the electorate based on some combination of muted racism, militaristic and/or Christian nationalism, and market populism.[87] In the face of a still-present New Deal and Civil Rights Movement, populism served the counterrevolution well: across the socioeconomic divide, white men and women could sign up for the right's advancing army of restorative glory.

In recent years, that fusion of elitism and populism has grown brittle. Movement elites no longer find in the electoral majority such a wide or ready response to their populist calls. Like many movements struggling to hold onto power, conservative activists and leaders compensate for their dwindling support in the population by doubling down on their program, issuing ever more strident and racist calls for a return to a white, Christian, free-market nation. Part of the party's elected officialdom subscribes to that program, precluding all concessions or compromise, as we saw during the Obamacare repeal fiasco of March 2017. Wings of the base—and beyond the party's base, the extramural sectors of the alt-right—take the question of white privilege into their own hands, finding a more genuine populism in marauding acts of violence against people of color, religious minorities, and leftist demonstrators.[88] Other parts of the base begin to wonder if they're getting a return for their vote. The populism remains, albeit in truncated form; whether it serves the elite in the way it once it did has become a vexing question. That is the conundrum that conservatism finds itself in today.

As these currents of right-wing discontent proliferate, separating into ever more streams, the leadership of the movement finds itself in need of a steadier flow of power, a more consolidated source of energy. Unable to fund its project on the basis of the masses, at least not nearly to the extent it once did, the right increasingly relies upon the most anti-democratic elements of the state: not merely the Electoral College and the Supreme Court but also restrictions on the vote. As it tries to overcome this deficit of the popular by means of the unpopular—as opposed to its heyday, when it overcame the popular by means of a counter-popular—today's conservative movement calls to mind its predecessor in early-nineteenth-century, pre-Reform Britain, dependent upon a combination of rotten boroughs and stale rhetoric.[89]

This is the movement Trump has led to power. How he will lead it while he is in power—more precisely, whether he can lead it—is an open question. Thus far, it seems the answer is: not well, maybe not even at all. Though again that may change. What seems clear, however, is that by the measure of his own words, two of Trump's ideological options—a celebration of the entrepreneur, a worship of the warrior state—are vastly compromised. Racism and nativism can motivate his base, but the electoral history since Nixon and Trump's performance over his first several months suggest that the base as a whole is shrinking. What's more, on two of Trump's signature campaign issues, which were supposed to herald the arrival of a new racialized economic populism of the right—restrictive immigration and protectionist trade—opinion polls show that rather than rallying a new electoral majority, these positions have growing increasingly unpopular since Trump's election.[90]

That leaves Trump with the one resource that has proven his most reliable ally throughout his career: his mercurial personality. A quicksilver madness has been the right's friend since Burke, who believed that to counter the left, the right would need the "generous wildness of Quixotism." Against a revolutionary challenge, "the madness of the wise" was always "better than the sobriety of fools." Nixon, too, subscribed to this reactionary credo of power: "Never get mad unless it's on purpose."[91] But where conservatives in the past deployed rage strategically, understanding its utility as a mobilizing device against a mobilized left, the rage of Trump is undisciplined, entirely his own, arrayed against anyone and everyone who is not Trump. That is why his rage seems so personal and narcissistic (even though the charge of narcissism has dogged virtually every modern president) as opposed to collective and empowering.[92] Facing dispossession from the left, the privileged classes used to find their madness echoed in a swelling chorus of the lower ranks. But when Trump rants, he does not make common cause with the lower ranks. Instead, he declares his victimhood singular and exceptional: "This is the single greatest witch hunt of a politician in American history!" he tweeted in response to the Russia controversy. "No politician . . . has been treated worse or more unfairly."[93] Amid the vast desert of deprivation that is the Trumpian self, there appears to be no room for anyone else. Trump's rage, like Scalia's, helped catapult him to power, giving him leverage over his timid comrades on the right. But as came to be true of Scalia on the Court, Trump's madness now threatens to make him and his movement marginal. Without a genuinely emancipatory left to oppose, Trump's rage seems to be nothing more than what it is: the ranting and raving of an old man.

Once upon a time, fascism—like the New Right of the 1970s and 1980s—possessed the freshness and vigor of youth. Fascism "was the major political innovation of the twentieth century," explains Paxton. Liberals and leftists found their arguments moldering in the graves of centuries past; fascism was novel. The aging Hindenburg evoked a war—and a zeppelin—that failed. Hitler brazenly traveled the country by plane. "In an era when air travel was considered dangerous," writes Claudia Koonz, "Hitler literally descended from the clouds to address audiences of between 120,000 and 300,000 at major cities." That inventiveness and creativity, that youthful spirit of daring and originality, are what gave fascism its élan and esprit de corps.[94]

It's telling that Trump has repeated—more than once—the stunt of landing from the skies.[95] Not because it reveals him to be a fascist, but rather because it shows that he's forsaken one of the advantages fascism had the first time around: its originality. Nor is Trump the only person in and around his administration whose creativity seems to be challenged. Beginning with his wife Melania's address to the Republican National Convention in August 2016, Trump's team has been plagued by one plagiarism scandal after another: Monica Crowley, Neil Gorsuch, and later, Sheriff David Clarke.[96] Conservatism, as we've seen, has always borrowed from its enemies on the left. But where that borrowing once signified a supple and shrewd awareness of the moment, an ability to repurpose the enemy for the sake of a friend, the Trumpist theft of words and borrowing of gestures signify a conservatism that is exhausted, paradoxically marooned and unmoored.

Most politicians, says Trump, sound "as if they are speaking from a script titled 'How Boring Can I Possibly Be?'"[97] Trump's promise, like that of so many on the right before him, is that he won't bore you. He can bat away the fact that he's a liar, a narcissist, a sexual predator, a financial miscreant, an incompetent, and a naïf. He even thinks—and he may be right—that he could "stand in the middle of 5th Avenue and shoot somebody" without losing any support.[98] But the one charge Trump can't afford is the claim that he's dull, reading from a script. Alas, history may be working against him. Whatever rhetorical innovations he seemed initially to offer, Trump lacks the warrant to see those innovations through. A reversion to the Republican status quo may continue to be his only option.[99] Unless and until there is a genuine new left to oppose, unless and until there is a real emancipation of the lower orders and dispossession of the higher orders to contend with and against, Trump and his brethren will be reading from a script.

Preface to the Second Edition

1. Mark Landler, "Trump's Foreign Policy Quickly Loses Its Sharp Edge," *New York Times* (February 11, 2017), A1; Tom Phillips, "Trump agrees to support 'One China' policy in Xi Jinping call," *The Guardian* (February 10, 2017), https://www.theguardian.com/world/2017/feb/10/donald-trump-agrees-support-one-china-policy-phone-call-xi-jinping; John Wagner, Damian Paletta, and Sean Sullivan, "Trump's Path Forward Only Gets Tougher after Health-Care Fiasco," *Washington Post* (March 25, 2017), https://www.washingtonpost.com/politics/trumps-path-forward-only-gets-tougher-after-health-care-fiasco/2017/03/25/eaf2f3b2-10be-11e7-9b0d-d27c98455440_story.html; Steven Mufson, "Trump's Budget Owes a Huge Debt to This Right-Wing Washington Think Tank," *Washington Post* (March 27, 2017), https://www.washingtonpost.com/news/wonk/wp/2017/03/27/trumps-budget-owes-a-huge-debt-to-this-right-wing-washington-think-tank/; Julie Hirschfeld Davis and Allen Rappeport, "After Calling NAFTA 'Worst Trade Deal,' Trump Appears to Soften Stance," *New York Times* (March 31, 2017), A12; Shane Goldmacher, "White House on edge as 100-day judgment nears," *Politico* (April 10, 2017), http://www.politico.com/story/2017/04/donald-trump-first-100-days-237053; David Lauder, "Trump backs away from labeling China a currency manipulator," Reuters (April 13, 2017), http://www.reuters.com/article/us-usa-trump-currency-idUSKBN17E2L8; Abby Phillip and John Wagner, "Trump as 'Conventional Republican'? That's What Some in GOP Establishment Say They See," *Washington Post* (April 13, 2017), https://www.washingtonpost.com/politics/gop-establishment-sees-trumps-flip-flops-as-move-toward-a-conventional-republican/2017/04/13/f9ce03f6-205c-11e7-be2a-3a1fb24d4671_story.html; Ryan Koronowski, "14 ways Trump lost bigly with the budget deal," *Think Progress* (May 1, 2017), https://thinkprogress.org/14-ways-trump-lost-bigly-with-the-budget-deal-fbe42e852730; Shawn Donnan, "Critics pan Trump's 'early harvest' trade deal with China," *Financial Times* (May 14, 2017), https://www.ft.com/content/

16a9b978-3766-11e7-bce4-9023f8c0fd2e; Ben White, "Wall Street gives up on 2017 tax overhaul," *Politico* (May 17, 2017), http://www.politico.com/story/2017/05/17/tax-reform-wall-street-238474; Kristina Peterson, "Congressional Republicans Face Ideological Rifts Over Spending Bills," *Wall Street Journal* (May 29, 2017), https://www.wsj.com/articles/congressional-republicans-face-ideological-rifts-over-spending-bills-1496059200 ; Richard Rubin, "GOP Bid to Rewrite Tax Code Falters," *Wall Street Journal* (May 30, 2017); Julie Hirschfeld Davis and Kate Kelley, "Trump Plans to Shift Infrastructure Funding to Cities, States and Business," *New York Times* (June 4, 2017), A18.

2. Jenna Johnson, Juliet Eilperin, and Ed O'Keefe, "Trump Is Finding It Easier to Tear Down Old Policies than to Build His Own," *Washington Post* (June 4, 2017), https://www.washingtonpost.com/politics/trump-is-finding-it-easier-to-tear-down-old-policies-than-to-build-his-own/2017/06/04/3d0bcdb2-47c5-11e7-a196-a1bb629f64cb_story.html; Kristina Peterson and Richard Rubin, "Intraparty Disputes Stall Republicans' Legislative Agenda," *Wall Street Journal* (June 27, 2017), https://www.wsj.com/articles/intraparty-disputes-stall-republicans-legislative-agenda-1498608305.

Chapter 1

1. At the turn of the twentieth century, 98% of the overwhelmingly Republican—and anti-union—federal judiciary came from "the very top of the nation's class and status hierarchies." William E. Forbath, *Law and the Shaping of the American Labor Movement* (Cambridge, Mass.: Harvard University Press, 1991), 33.

2. Even today, marital rape is punished with less severity—and requires prosecutors to mount greater obstacles—than nonmarital rape. According to one scholar, "The marital rape exemption survives in some substantial form in a majority of states." Jill Elaine Hasday, "Contest and Consent: A Legal History of Marital Rape," *California Law Review* 88 (October 2000), 1375, 1490; Rebecca M. Ryan, "The Sex Right: A Legal History of the Marital Rape Exemption," *Law & Social Inquiry* 20 (Autumn 1995), 941–942, 992–995; Nancy F. Cott, *Public Vows: A History of Marriage and the Nation* (Cambridge, Mass.: Harvard University Press, 2000), 211.

3. It should be pointed out that before the marital rape exemption was eliminated, sexual violence had come to be considered one of the few legitimate grounds for divorce. Hasday, "Contest and Consent," 1397–1398, 1475–1484; Ryan, "Sex Right," 941; Cott, *Public Vows*, 195, 203.

4. Karen Orren, *Belated Feudalism: Labor, the Law, and Liberal Development in the United States* (New York: Cambridge University Press, 1991); Robert J. Steinfeld, *Coercion, Contract, and Free Labor in the Nineteenth Century* (New York: Cambridge University Press, 2001); Forbath, *Shaping of the American Labor Movement*.

5. Greg Grandin, *The Last Colonial Massacre: Latin America in the Cold War* (Chicago: University of Chicago Press, 2004), 56–57. The outbreak of political speech among those without power was also, according to a disgruntled Democrat writing to liberal Senator Paul Douglas in the 1960s, the great evil of the Great Society: "I feel Mr. Johnson is much responsible for the present riot by his constant encouragement for the Negro to take any measure to assert himself & DEMAND his rights." Rick Perlstein, *Nixonland: The Rise of a President and the Fracturing of America* (New York: Scribner, 2008), 117.

6. John C. Calhoun, "Speech on the Admission of California—and the General State of the Union" (March 4, 1850), in *Union and Liberty: The Political Philosophy of John C. Calhoun*, ed. Ross M. Lence (Indianapolis: Liberty Fund, 1992), 583–585.

7. Alexander Keyssar, *The Right to Vote: The Contested History of Democracy in the United States* (New York: Basic, 2000), 112.

8. Jeremy Brecher, *Strike!* (Cambridge, Mass.: South End Press, 1997), 34, 126. Also see Kim Phillips-Fein, *Invisible Hands: The Businessmen's Crusade against the New Deal* (New York: Norton, 2009), 87–114.

9. Forbath, *Shaping of the American Labor Movement*, 65.

10. James Boswell, *Life of Johnson*, ed. R. W. Chapman and J. D. Fleeman (New York: Oxford University Press, 1998), 1017.

11. Edmund Burke, *Reflections on the Revolution in France*, ed. J. C. D. Clark (Stanford, Calif.: Stanford University Press, 2001), 205–206. Burke's curious focus on hairdressers—of all occupations—as the object of his anti-democratic sentiment has a fascinating backstory, which Don Herzog explores in his *Poisoning the Minds of the Lower Orders* (Princeton: Princeton University Press, 1998), 455–504.

12. Ibid., 217–218.

13. Cited in Daniel T. Rodgers, *Age of Fracture* (Cambridge, Mass.: Harvard University Press, 2011), 207.

14. Friedrich Hayek, *Law, Legislation and Liberty*, vol. 2, *The Mirage of Social Justice* (Chicago: University of Chicago Press, 1976), 84–85; Robert Nozick, *Anarchy, State, and Utopia* (New York: Basic Books, 1974), 235–238.

15. G. A. Cohen, *Self-Ownership, Freedom, and Equality* (New York: Cambridge University Press, 1995), 28–32, 53–59, 98–115, 236–238.

16. Cited in Friedrich A. Hayek, *The Constitution of Liberty* (Chicago: University of Chicago Press, 1960), 424; also see 16–19.

17. Elizabeth Cady Stanton, "Home Life," in *The Elizabeth Cady Stanton–Susan B. Anthony Reader*, ed. Ellen Carol DuBois (Boston: Northeastern University Press, 1981, 1992), 132. Also see Cott, *Public Vows*, 67; Amy Dru Stanley, *From Bondage to Contract: Wage Labor, Marriage, and the Market in the Age of Slave Emancipation* (New York: Cambridge University Press, 1998), 177–178.

18. Sometimes the transcript is not so hidden. Point Four of the 1948 platform of Strom Thurmond's States' Rights Democratic Party—the

Dixiecrats—weaves together the public and private in a seamless and visible whole: "We stand for the segregation of the races and the racial integrity of each race; the constitutional right to choose one's associates; to accept private employment without governmental interference, and to earn one's living in any lawful way. We oppose the elimination of segregation, the repeal of miscegenation statutes, the control of private employment by Federal bureaucrats called for by the misnamed civil rights program. We favor home-rule, local self-government and a minimum interference with individual rights." *The Rise of Conservatism in America, 1945–2000: A Brief History with Documents*, ed. Ronald Story and Bruce Laurie (Boston: Bedford/St. Martin's, 2008), 39.

19. James Baldwin, "They Can't Turn Back," in *The Price of the Ticket: Collected Nonfiction, 1948–1985* (New York: St. Martin's Press, 1985), 215. I am grateful to Jason Frank for bringing this essay to my attention.

20. Peter Kolchin, *American Slavery 1619–1877* (New York: Hill and Wang, 1993, 2003), 100–102, 105, 111, 115, 117.

21. Thomas Roderick Dew, *Abolition of Negro Slavery*, and William Harper, *Memoir on Slavery*, in *The Ideology of Slavery: Proslavery Thought in the Antebellum South, 1830–1860*, ed. Drew Gilpin Faust (Baton Rouge: Louisiana State University Press, 1981), 65, 100.

22. Neil R. McMillen, *Dark Journey: Black Mississippians in the Age of Jim Crow* (Urbana: University of Illinois Press, 1989), 7.

23. Kolchin, *American Slavery*, 118–120, 123–124, 126; Ira Berlin, *Many Thousands Gone: The First Two Centuries of Slavery in North America* (Cambridge, Mass.: Harvard University Press, 1998), 94–95, 112, 128–132, 149–150, 174–175, 188–189.

24. Calhoun, "Speech on the Reception of Abolition Petitions" (February 6, 1837), in *Union and Liberty*, 473; also see Dew, "Abolition of Negro Slavery," 23–24, 27; Kolchin, *American Slavery*, 170, 181–182, 184, 189.

25. Cited in Kolchin, *American Slavery*, 198.

26. Steven Hahn, *A Nation under Our Feet: Black Political Struggles in the Rural South from Slavery to the Great Migration* (Cambridge, Mass.: Harvard University Press, 2003), 218; McMillen, *Dark Journey*, 125.

27. Patrick Allitt, *The Conservatives: Ideas & Personalities Throughout American History* (New Haven, Conn.: Yale University Press, 2009), 19.

28. Edmund Burke, "Speech on the Army Estimates" (February 9, 1790), in *The Portable Edmund Burke*, ed. Isaac Kramnick (New York: Penguin, 1999), 413–414.

29. Edmund Burke, letter to Earl Fitzwilliam (1791), cited in Daniel L. O'Neill, *The Burke-Wollstonecraft Debate: Savagery, Civilization, and Democracy* (University Park: Pennsylvania State University Press, 2007), 211.

30. Cited in Conor Cruise O'Brien, *The Great Melody: A Thematic Biography of Edmund Burke* (Chicago: University of Chicago Press, 1992), 418–419.

31. Edmund Burke, *Letters on a Regicide Peace* (Indianapolis: Liberty Fund, 1999), 127.

32. John Adams, letter to James Sullivan (May 26, 1776), in *The Works of John Adams*, vol. 9, ed. Charles Francis Adams (Boston: Little Brown, 1854), 375.

33. Abigail Adams, letter to John Adams (March 31, 1776), in *The Letters of John and Abigail Adams* (New York: Penguin, 2004), 148–49.

34. John Adams, letter to Abigail Adams (April 14, 1776), in *Letters*, 154.

35. John Adams, letter to James Sullivan (May 26, 1776), in *Works*, 378.

36. John Adams, *A Defense of the Constitutions of Government of the United States of America*, and *Discourses on Davila*, in *The Political Writings of John Adams*, ed. George A. Peck Jr. (Indianapolis: Hackett, [1954] 2003), 148–149, 190.

37. Cited in Susan Moller Okin, *Justice, Gender, and the Family* (New York: Basic Books, 1989), 18.

38. Keyssar, *Right to Vote*, xxi.

39. Linda K. Kerber, *No Constitutional Right to be Ladies: Women and the Obligations of Citizenship* (New York: Hill and Wang, 1998), 3–46, 124–220; Ira Berlin, Barbara J. Fields, Steven F. Miller, Joseph P. Rediy, and Leslie S. Rowland, *Slaves No More: Three Essays on Emancipation and the Civil War* (New York: Cambridge University Press, 1992), 5, 15, 20, 48, 54–59.

40. "The ultimate operative unit in our society is the family, not the individual." Milton Friedman, *Capitalism and Freedom* (Chicago: University of Chicago Press, 1962, 1982, 2002), 32; also see 13. "It would be a mistake of major proportions to assume that legal rules are a dominant force in shaping individual character; family, school, and church are much more likely to be powerful influences. The people who run these institutions will use their influence to advance whatever conception of the good they hold, no matter what the state of the law." Richard A. Epstein, "Libertarianism and Character," in *Varieties of Conservatism in America*, ed. Peter Berkowitz (Stanford, Calif.: Hoover Institution Press, 2004), 76. For earlier statements, see William Graham Sumner, "The Family Monopoly," in *On Liberty, Society, and Politics: The Essential Essays of William Graham Sumner*, ed. Robert C. Bannister (Indianapolis, Liberty Fund, 1929), 136; William Graham Sumner, *What the Social Classes Owe to Each Other* (Caldwell, Idaho: Caxton Press, 2003), 63; Ludwig von Mises, *Socialism: An Economic and Sociological Analysis* (Indianapolis: Liberty Fund, 1981), 74–91. More generally, see Okin, *Justice, Gender*, 74–88.

41. Edmund Burke, letter to Earl Fitzwilliam (1791), in O'Neill, *Burke-Wollstonecraft Debate*, 211.

42. James Fitzjames Stephen, *Liberty, Equality, Fraternity*, ed. Stuart D. Warner (Indianapolis: Liberty Fund, 1993), 173.

43. David Farber, *The Rise and Fall of Modern American Conservatism: A Short History* (Princeton, N.J.: Princeton University Press, 2010), 10.

44. Thomas Paine, *Rights of Man, Part I*, in *Political Writings*, ed. Bruce Kuklick (New York: Cambridge University Press, 2000), 130; Lionel Trilling, *The Liberal Imagination* (Garden City, N.Y.: Doubleday Anchor, 1950), 5; Robert O. Paxton, *The Anatomy of Fascism* (New York: Knopf, 2004), 42.

45. Michael Freeden, *Ideologies and Political Theory* (New York: Oxford University Press, 1996), 318.

46. Cited in Russell Kirk, "Introduction," in *The Portable Conservative Reader*, ed. Russell Kirk (New York: Penguin, 1982), xxiii.

47. Mark F. Proudman, "'The Stupid Party': Intellectual Repute as a Category of Ideological Analysis," *Journal of Political Ideologies* 10 (June 2005), 201–202, 206–207.

48. George H. Nash, *The Conservative Intellectual Movement in America since 1945* (Wilmington, Del.: Intercollegiate Studies Institute), xiv; Roger Scruton, *The Meaning of Conservatism* (London: Macmillan, 1980, 1984), 11.

49. "Problem: How did the exhausted come to make the laws about values? Put differently: How did those come to power who are the last?" Friedrich Nietzsche, *The Will to Power*, trans. Walter Kaufmann and R. J. Hollingdale (New York: Vintage, 1968), 34.

50. Kevin Mattson, *Rebels All! A Short History of the Conservative Mind in Postwar America* (Newark, N.J.: Rutgers University Press, 2008), 121–125.

51. Burke, *Reflections*, 243; Russell Kirk, "The Conservative Mind," in *Conservatism in America since 1930*, ed. Gregory L. Schneider (New York: New York University Press, 2003), 107. More recently still, Harvey Mansfield has declared, "But I understand conservatism as a reaction to liberalism. It isn't a position that one takes up from the beginning but only when one is threatened by people who want to take away or harm things that deserve to be conserved." *The Point* (Fall 2010), http://www.thepointmag.com/archive/an-interview-with-harvey-mansfield, accessed April 9, 2011.

52. Burke, *Regicide Peace*, 73.

53. Cited in John Ramsden, *An Appetite for Power: A History of the Conservative Party since 1830* (New York: Harper Collins, 1999), 5.

54. *The Faber Book of Conservatism*, ed. Keith Baker (London: Faber and Faber, 1993), 6; also see Hugh Cecil, *Conservatism* (London: Thornton Butterworth, 1912), 39–44, 241, 244.

55. Robert Peel, speech at Merchant Taylor Hall (May 13, 1838), in *British Conservatism: Conservative Thought from Burke to Thatcher*, ed. Frank O'Gorman (London: Longman, 1986), 125.

56. Nash, *Conservative Intellectual Movement*, xiv.

57. Michael Oakeshott, "Rationalism in Politics" and "On Being Conservative," in *Rationalism in Politics and Other Essays* (Indianapolis: Liberty Press, 1991), 31, 408, 435.

58. At one point in his essay, Oakeshott himself entertains this notion, only to dismiss it: "What would be the appropriateness of this disposition in

circumstances other than our own, whether to be conservative in respect of government would have the same relevance in the circumstances of an unadventurous, a slothful or a spiritless people, is a question we need not try to answer: we are concerned with ourselves as we are. I myself think that it would occupy an important place in any set of circumstances." Why that is so he does not say. Oakeshott, "On Being Conservative," 435.

59. Benjamin Disraeli, *The Vindication of the English Constitution*, in *Whigs and Whiggism: Political Writings by Benjamin Disraeli*, ed. William Hutcheon (New York: Macmillan, 1914), 126.

60. Karl Mannheim, "Conservative Thought," in *Essays on Sociology and Social Psychology*, ed. Paul Kesckemeti (London: Routledge & Kegan Paul, 1953), 95, 115; also see Freeden, *Ideologies and Political Theory*, 335ff. Evidence for this argument from the conservative tradition can be found in Frank Meyer, "Freedom, Tradition, Conservatism," in *In Defense of Freedom and Related Essays* (Indianapolis: Liberty Fund, 1996), 17–20; Mark C. Henrie, "Understanding Traditionalist Conservatism," in *Varieties of Conservatism in America*, 11; Nash, *Conservative Intellectual Movement*, 50; Scruton, *Meaning of Conservatism*, 11.

61. Thus, when Irving Kristol claims in his *Reflections of a Neoconservative* that neoconservatism "aims to infuse American bourgeois orthodoxy with a new self-conscious intellectual vigor," he is not departing from conservative norms; he is articulating them. As the conservative sociologist and theologian Peter Berger writes in *The Sacred Canopy*, "The facticity of the social world or of any part of it suffices for self-legitimation as long as there is no challenge. When a challenge appears, in whatever form, the facticity can no longer be taken for granted. The validity of the social order must then be explicated, both for the sake of the challengers and of those meeting the challenge. . . . The seriousness of the challenge will determine the degree of elaborateness of the answering legitimations." In *Conservatism: An Anthology of Social and Political Thought from David Hume to the Present*, ed. Jerry Muller (Princeton, N.J.: Princeton University Press, 1997), 4, 360.

62. Quintin Hogg, *The Case for Conservatism*, in *British Conservatism*, 76.

63. Boswell, *Life of Johnson*, 1018.

64. Edmund Burke, *An Appeal from the New to the Old Whigs*, in *Further Reflections on the Revolution in France*, ed. Daniel F. Ritchie (Indianapolis: Liberty Fund, 1992), 167.

65. Giuseppe di Lampedusa, *The Leopard* (New York: Pantheon, 2007), 28.

66. Mattson, *Rebels All!* 23, 35–36, 62.

67. Burke, *Regicide Peace*, 142.

68. Kirk, "The Conservative Mind," 109; Oakeshott, "On Being Conservative," 414–415.

69. Cited in Allitt, *Conservatives*, 242; also see Arthur Moeller van den Bruck, *Germany's Third Empire*, in *The Nazi Germany Sourcebook: An Anthology of*

Texts, ed. Roderick Stackelberg and Sally A. Winkle (New York: Routledge, 2002), 77–78.

70. Edmund Burke, *Letter to a Noble Lord*, in *On Empire, Liberty, and Reform: Speeches and Letters*, ed. David Bromwich (New Haven, Conn.: Yale University Press, 2000), 479.

71. Cecil is one of the few conservatives to acknowledge how difficult it is to distinguish between reform and revolution (Cecil, *Conservatism*, 221–222). For a useful critique, see Ted Honderich, *Conservatism: Burke, Nozick, Bush, Blair?* (London: Pluto, 2005), 6–31.

72. Peter Kolozi, *Conservatives Against Capitalism: From the Industrial Revolution to Globalization* (New York: Columbia University Press, 2017), 106–139; Clinton Rossiter, *Conservatism in America: The Thankless Persuasion* (New York: Vintage, 1955, 1962), 241–242; Sam Tanenhaus, *Whittaker Chambers: A Biography* (New York: Modern Library, 1997), 165, 466, 488.

73. Nash, *Conservative Intellectual Movement*, xiv.

74. Abraham Lincoln, address at Cooper Institute (February 27, 1860), in *The Portable Abraham Lincoln*, ed. Andrew Delbanco (New York: Penguin 1992), 178–179. The typical conservative vision of reform, notes one scholar, "can be part of other political ideologies on account of—at least on the surface—its sheer reasonableness. It is, by itself, purely relative or 'positional,'" and can thus be applied to or invoked by any ideology." Jan-Werner Müller, "Comprehending Conservatism: A New Framework for Analysis," *Journal of Political Ideologies* 11 (October 2006), 362.

75. Ramsden, *Appetite for Power*, 28.

76. Cited in C. B. Macpherson, *Burke* (New York Hill and Wang, 1980), 22; also see Burke, *Regicide Peace*, 381.

77. Ramsden, *Appetite for Power*, 46, 95. Carnarvon's was the minority position on the British right; under the leadership of Derby and Disraeli, the Conservatives presided over the Act's passage. But that should not be taken as evidence of a deep Burkean impulse on the right. Disraeli's North Star throughout the debate was simple opposition to Gladstone. If Gladstone was for it, Disraeli was against it. If there was any vision beyond that, it was partisan and tactical, involving decidedly non-Burkean tactics at that. Explaining his support for a series of measures more radical than anything initially countenanced by the Liberals, Disraeli said to Derby, "The bold line is the safer one." See Ramsden, *Appetite for Power*, 91–99. For a dissenting view, see Gertrude Himmelfarb, "Politics and Ideology: The Reform Act of 1867," in *Victorian Minds* (New York: Knopf, 1968), 333–392.

78. Allitt, *Conservatives*, 48. For other examples, see Allan Bloom, *The Closing of the American Mind* (New York: Simon and Schuster, 1987), 101; Calhoun, "Speech on the Oregon Bill," in *Union and Liberty*, 565; Adams, *Discourses on Davila*, in *Political Writings*, 190–192, 201; *Theodore Roosevelt: An American*

Mind, ed. Mario R. DiNunzio (New York: Penguin, 1994), 116, 119; Phillips-Fein, *Invisible Hands*, 82.

79. Michael J. Gerson, *Heroic Conservatism: Why Republicans Need to Embrace America's Ideals (And Why They Deserve to Fail If They Don't)* (New York: Harper Collins, 2007), 261, 264.

80. While Huntington is right to stress the "situational" or "positional" dimensions of conservatism—that it is called into being in response to systemic challenges to the established order—he is wrong to suggest that the conservative defends the established order simply because it is the established order. The conservative defends a particular type of order—the hierarchical institution of personal rule—because he sincerely believes that inequality is a necessary condition of excellence. At times, he is willing to contest the established order, if he believes it is too egalitarian; such was the case with the postwar conservative movement in America. Samuel Huntington, "Conservatism as an Ideology," *American Political Science Review* 51 (June 1957), 454–473.

81. With every passing month, the number of books about American conservatism seems to increase. Among the more notable of the last two decades are Rick Perlstein, *Before the Storm: Barry Goldwater and the Unmaking of the American Consensus* (New York: Hill & Wang, 2001); Lisa McGirr, *Suburban Warriors: The Origins of the New American Right* (Princeton, N.J.: Princeton University Press, 2001); Donald Critchlow, *Phyllis Schlafly and Grassroots Conservatism: A Woman's Crusade* (Princeton, N.J.: Princeton University Press, 2005); Kevin Kruse, *White Flight: Atlanta and the Making of Modern Conservatism* (Princeton, N.J.: Princeton University Press, 2005); Jason Sokol, *There Goes My Everything: White Southerners in the Age of Civil Rights, 1945–1975* (New York: Vintage, 2006); Matthew Lassiter, *The Silent Majority: Suburban Politics in the Sunbelt South* (Princeton, N.J.: Princeton University Press, 2006); Joseph Lowndes, *From the New Deal to the New Right: Race and the Southern Origins of Modern Conservatism* (New Haven, Conn.: Yale University Press, 2008); Allan J. Lichtman, *White Protestant Nation: The Rise of the American Conservative Movement* (New York: Grove Press, 2008); Mattson, *Rebels All!*; Steven Teles, *The Rise of the Conservative Legal Movement: The Battle for Control of the Law* (Princeton, N.J.: Princeton University Press, 2008); Bethany Moreton, *To Serve God and Wal-Mart: The Making of Christian Free Enterprise* (Cambridge, Mass.: Harvard University Press, 2009); Phillips-Fein, *Invisible Hands*. Also see Julian Zelizer, "Reflections: Rethinking the History of American Conservatism," *Reviews in American History* 38 (June 2010), 367–392; Kim Phillips-Fein, "Conservatism: A State of the Field," *Journal of American History* 98 (December 2011), 723–743.

82. T. S. Eliot, "The Literature of Politics," in *To Criticize the Critic and Other Writings* (Lincoln: University of Nebraska Press, 1965), 139.

83. "'Metaphysical pathos' is exemplified in any description of the nature of things, any characterization of the world to which one belongs, in terms which, like the words of a poem, awaken through their associations, and through a sort of empathy which they engender, a congenial mood or tone of feeling on the part of the philosopher or his readers." Arthur O. Lovejoy, *The Great Chain of Being: A Study of the History of an Idea* (New York: Harper & Brothers, 1936), 11. Cited in Joseph F. Femia, *Against the Masses: Varieties of Anti-Democratic Thought since the French Revolution* (New York: Oxford University Press, 2001), 13–14.

84. Cf. Bruce Frohnen, *Virtue and the Promise of Conservatism: The Legacy of Burke and Tocqueville* (Lawrence: University of Kansas Press, 1993); Nash, *Conservative Intellectual Movement*; Allitt, *Conservatives*; Scruton, *Meaning of Conservatism*; Berkowitz, *Varieties of Conservatism*. More useful treatments include Robert Nisbet, *Conservatism: Dream and Reality* (Minneapolis: University of Minnesota Press, 1986); Stephen Holmes, *The Anatomy of Antiliberalism* (Cambridge, Mass.: Harvard University Press, 1993); Albert O. Hirschman, *The Rhetoric of Reaction: Perversity, Futility, Jeopardy* (Cambridge, Mass.: Harvard University Press, 1991); Mannheim, "Conservative Thought"; Muller, *Conservatism*; Femia, *Against the Masses*; and Herzog, *Poisoning the Minds of the Lower Orders*.

85. Mattson, *Rebels All!*, 3, 11–12, 42, 79. Also see Sam Tanenhaus, *The Death of Conservatism* (New York: Random House, 2009), 16–19, 49–51.

86. Cara Camcastle, *The More Moderate Side of Joseph de Maistre: Views on Political Liberty and Political Economy* (Montreal and Kingston: McGill-Queen's University Press, 2005); Isaiah Berlin, "Joseph de Maistre on the Origins of Modern Fascism," in *The Crooked Timber of Humanity: Chapters in the History of Ideas*, ed. Henry Hardy (New York: Vintage, 1992), 91–174.

87. Nash, *Conservative Intellectual Movement*, 69–70.

88. Published in June 2008, Lichtman's *White Protestant Nation* appeared before the advent of the Tea Party—indeed, before the election of Barack Obama—but its analysis of the continuities between the conservatism that arose in the aftermath of World War I and the conservatism of George W. Bush can be extrapolated to today.

89. Mattson, *Rebels All!*, 7, 15; Farber, *Rise and Fall of Modern American Conservatism*, 78; Donald T. Critchlow, *The Conservative Ascendancy: How the GOP Right Made Political History* (Cambridge, Mass.: Harvard University Press, 2007), 6–13; Tanenhaus, *Death of Conservatism*, 29, 32, 104, 109, 111, 114.

90. "The right's political philosophy, organizing strategy, and grassroots appeal transcend its hostility to liberalism. Modern conservatism has a life, history, and logic of its own." Lichtman, *White Protestant Nation*, 2. For a different version of the antibacklash argument, see Lowndes, *New Deal to the New Right*, 3–5, 92–93, 160–162.

91. Noberto Bobbio, *Left & Right: The Significance of a Political Distinction* (Chicago: University of Chicago Press, 1996).

92. Müller, "Comprehending Conservatism," 359; Muller, *Conservatism*, 22–23; J. G. A. Pocock, introduction to Burke, *Reflections on the Revolution in France* (Indianapolis: Hackett, 1987), xlix.

93. Nash, *Conservative Intellectual Movement*, xiv–xv.

94. Zelizer, "Reflections: Rethinking the History of American Conservatism," 371–374.

95. Cited in Mattson, *Rebels All!*, 112.

96. *Händler und Helden. Patriotische Besinnungen*, in *Nazi Germany Sourcebook*, 36.

97. The defense of the free market "became stationary when it was most influential," while it "often progressed when on the defensive" from attacks on the left (Hayek, *Constitution of Liberty*, 7). "It is ironic, although not historically unprecedented, that such a burst of creative energy on the intellectual level [on the right] should occur simultaneously with a continuing spread of the influence of Liberalism in the practical political sphere" (Frank Meyer, "Freedom, Tradition, Conservatism," in *Defense of Freedom*, 15). "In times of crisis," observes Scruton, "conservatism does its best" (Scruton, *Meaning of Conservatism*, 11). On the "dialectical" relationship between left and right in recent American history, see Zelizer, "Reflections: Rethinking the History of American Conservatism," 388–389.

98. Matthew Arnold, *Culture and Anarchy*, in *Culture and Anarchy and Other Writings*, ed. Stefan Collini (New York: Cambridge University Press, 1993), 95.

99. Joseph Schumpeter, "Social Classes in an Ethnically Homogenous Environment," in *Conservatism: An Anthology*, 227.

100. Attaining and maintaining real economic power, Schumpeter adds, requires a continuous "departure from routine." Schumpeter, "Social Classes," 227. "We must make it clear to ourselves that there can be no standing still, no being satisfied for us, but only progress or retrogression, and that it is tantamount to retrogression when we are contented with our present place." Friedrich von Bernhardi, *Germany and the Next War*, trans. Allen Powles (London: Edward Arnold, 1912), 103.

101. Burke, *Reflections*, 207. Also see Justus Möser, "No Promotion According to Merit," in *Conservatism: An Anthology*, 74–77.

102. Burke, *Letter to a Noble Lord*, 484.

103. Fritz Lens, *Psychological Differences between the Leading Races of Mankind*, in *Nazi Germany Sourcebook*, 75.

104. Muller, *Conservatism*, 26–27, 210.

105. Sumner, *What the Social Classes Owe to Each Other*, 59–60, 66–67.

106. Sumner, "Liberty," in *On Liberty, Society, and Politics*, 246.

107. "All ownership derives from occupation and violence. . . . That all rights derive from violence, all ownership from appropriation or robbery, we may freely admit." Mises, *Socialism*, 32.

108. Sumner, "The Absurd Effort to Make the World Over," in *On Liberty, Society, and Politics*, 254.

109. Burke, *Letter to a Noble Lord*, 484.

Chapter 2

1. Michael Oakeshott, "On Being Conservative," in *Rationalism in Politics and Other Essays* (Indianapolis: Liberty Press, 1991), 408.

2. Russell Kirk, "Introduction," in *The Portable Conservative Reader*, ed. Russell Kirk (New York: Penguin, 1982), xi–xiv; Robert Nisbet, *Conservatism: Dream and Reality* (Minneapolis: University of Minnesota Press, 1986); Peter Viereck, *Conservatism: From John Adams to Churchill* (Princeton, N.J.: D. Van Nostrand, 1956), 10–17.

3. Joseph de Maistre, *Considerations on France*, trans. and ed. Richard A. Lebrun (New York: Cambridge University Press, 1974, 1994), 10. Also see Maistre's criticism of Europe's old regimes in Jean-Louis Darcel, "The Roads of Exile, 1792–1817," and Darcel, "Joseph de Maistre and the House of Savoy: Some Aspects of his Career," in *Joseph de Maistre's Life, Thought, and Influence: Selected Studies*, ed. Richard A. Lebrun (Montreal: McGill-Queen's University Press, 2001), 16, 19–20, 52.

4. Cf. Edmund Burke, *Letter to a Noble Lord*, in *On Empire, Liberty, and Reform: Speeches and Letters*, ed. David Bromwich (New Haven, Conn.: Yale University Press, 2000), 500–501; Burke, *Letters on a Regicide Peace* (Indianapolis: Liberty Fund, 1999), 69–70, 74–76, 106, 108–111, 158–160, 167, 184, 205, 218, 218, 222, 271, 304–305.

5. Edmund Burke, *Reflections on the Revolution in France*, ed. J. C. D. Clark (Stanford, Calif.: Stanford University Press, 2001), 239.

6. Edmund Burke, *A Philosophical Enquiry into the Origins of Our Ideas of the Sublime and the Beautiful*, ed. David Womersley (New York: Penguin, 1998), 177.

7. Burke, *Regicide Peace*, 75.

8. Though sometimes it is the old regime itself. Cf. Burke, *Regicide Peace*, 384–385.

9. Edmund Burke, "Speech on American Taxation" (April 19, 1774), in *Selected Works of Edmund Burke*, vol. 1 (Indianapolis: Liberty Fund, 1999), 186; also see Burke, *Regicide Peace*, 69–70, 154–155, 184–185, 304–306, 384–385. This critique runs counter to Burke's praise for the aristocrat as the man of the long view; in these texts, Burke claims that the long view blinds men to the problems they face. See Bromwich's brief introduction to Burke's *Letter to a Noble Lord*, in his *On Empire, Liberty, and Reform*, 466.

10. Thomas Roderick Dew, *Abolition of Negro Slavery*, and William Harper, *Memoir on Slavery*, in *The Ideology of Slavery: Proslavery Thought in the Antebellum South, 1830–1860*, ed. Drew Gilpin Faust (Baton Rouge: Louisiana

State Press, 1981), 25, 123. Also see John C. Calhoun, "Speech on the Force Bill," "Speech on the Reception of Abolitionist Petitions," and "Speech on the Oregon Bill," in *Union and Liberty: The Political Philosophy of John C. Calhoun*, ed. Ross M. Lence (Indianapolis: Liberty Fund, 1992), 426, 465, 475, 562; Manisha Sinha, *The Counterrevolution of Slavery: Politics and Ideology in Antebellum South Carolina* (Chapel Hill: University of North Carolina Press, 2000), 33–93.

11. Barry Goldwater, *The Conscience of a Conservative* (Princeton, N.J.: Princeton University Press, 1960, 2007), 1.

12. Calhoun, "Speech on the Reception of Abolitionist Petitions," 476.

13. Oakeshott, "On Being Conservative," 407–408.

14. Charles Loyseau, *A Treatise of Orders and Plain Dignities*, ed. Howell A. Lloyd (New York: Cambridge University Press, 1994), 75.

15. Cited in Anne Norton, *Leo Strauss and the Politics of American Empire* (New Haven, Conn.: Yale University Press, 2004), 49.

16. Joseph de Maistre, *St. Petersburg Dialogues or Conversations on the Temporal Government of Providence*, trans. and ed. Richard A. Lebrun (Montreal and Kingston: McGill-Queen's University Press, 1993), 216.

17. Maistre, *Considerations*, 16–17. Also see Jean-Louis Darcel, "The Apprentice Years of a Counter-Revolutionary: Joseph de Maistre in Lausanne, 1793–1797," in *Joseph de Maistre's Life, Thought, and Influence*, 43–44.

18. Burke, *Sublime and the Beautiful*, 86, 96, 121, 165.

19. Burke, *Reflections*, 207, 243, 275. Also see Burke, *Regicide Peace*, 66, 70, 107, 157, 207, 222.

20. Burke, *Regicide Peace*, 184.

21. Darrin M. McMahon, *Enemies of the Enlightenment: The French Counter-Enlightenment and the Making of Modernity* (New York: Oxford University Press, 2001), 27–28.

22. Cited in Robert Perkinson, *Texas Tough: The Rise of America's Prison Empire* (New York: Metropolitan, 2009), 297.

23. Cited in Alexander P. Lamis, "The Two-Party South: From the 1960s to the 1990s," in *Southern Politics in the 1990s*, ed. Alexander P. Lamis (Baton Rouge: Louisiana State University Press, 1990), 8.

24. David Horowitz, "The Campus Blacklist," *FrontPage* (April 18, 2003), http://www.studentsforacademicfreedom.org/essays/blacklist.html, accessed March 24, 2011.

25. Cited in Lamis, "Two-Party South," 8.

26. Phyllis Schlafly, *The Power of the Positive Woman* (New York: Harcourt Brace Jovanovich, 1977), 7–8.

27. "Interview with Phyllis Schlafly," *Washington Star* (January 18, 1976), in *The Rise of Conservatism in America, 1945–2000: A Brief History with Documents*, ed. Ronald Story and Bruce Laurie (Boston: Bedford/St. Martin's, 2008), 104.

28. Susan Faludi, *Backlash: The Undeclared War against American Women* (New York: Doubleday, 1991), 251.

29. Maistre, *Considerations*, 79.

30. "Why the South Must Prevail," *National Review* (August 24, 1957), in *Rise of Conservatism in America*, 53.

31. Gary Wills, *Reagan's America* (New York: Penguin, 1988), 355.

32. Cited in J. C. D. Clark, introduction to Burke, *Reflections*, 104.

33. Alexander Stephens, "The Cornerstone Speech," in *Defending Slavery: Proslavery Thought in the Old South*, ed. Paul Finkelman (Boston: Bedford/St. Martin's, 2003), 91.

34. Goldwater, *Conscience of a Conservative*, 70.

35. Maistre, *Considerations*, 89.

36. Ibid., 69, 74.

37. James Oakes, *The Ruling Race: A History of American Slaveholders* (New York: Vintage, 1982), 37, 42, 141–143, 230–232.

38. Calhoun, "Speech on the Oregon Bill," 564.

39. Cited in Peter Kolchin, *American Slavery 1619–1877* (New York: Hill and Wang, 1993, 2003), 195.

40. Dew, *Abolition of Negro Slavery*, 66–67.

41. Cited in Jacob Heilbrunn, *They Knew They Were Right: The Rise of the Neocons* (New York: Random House, 2008), 6.

42. Burke, *Reflections*, 229; William F. Buckley Jr., "Publisher's Statement on Founding National Review," *National Review* (November 19, 1955), in *Rise of Conservatism in America*, 50.

43. Andrew Sullivan, *The Conservative Soul: Fundamentalism, Freedom, and the Future of the Right* (New York: Harper Perennial, 2006), 9.

44. Burke, *Regicide Peace*, 138.

45. Maistre, *Considerations*, 77.

46. Corey Robin, "The Ex-Cons: Right-Wing Thinkers Go Left!" *Lingua Franca* (February 2001), 32.

Chapter 3

1. Jim Sidanius, Michael Mitchell, Hillary Haley, and Carlos David Navarrete, "Support for Harsh Criminal Sanctions and Social Dominance Beliefs," *Social Justice Research* 19 (December 2006), 440; Tom Pyszczynski, Abdolhossein Abdollahi, Sheldon Solomon, Jeff Greenberg, Florette Cohen, and David Weise, "Mortality Salience, Martyrdom, and Military Might: The Great Satan Versus the Axis of Evil," *Personality and Social Psychology Bulletin* 32 (April 2006), 525–537; Frank Newport, "Sixty-Nine Percent of Americans Support Death Penalty," http://www.gallup.com/poll/101863/Sixtynine-Percent-Americans-Support-Death-Penalty.aspx, accessed April 5, 2011; Pew Research Center, "The Torture Debate: A Closer Look," http://pewforum.org/

Politics-and-Elections/The-Torture-Debate-A-Closer-Look.aspx, accessed April 5, 2011; "McCain Amendment No. 1977," http://www.sourcewatch. org/index.php?title=McCain_Amendment_No._1977, accessed April 5, 2011; Sean Olson, "Senate Approves Abolishment of Death Penalty," *Albuquerque Journal* (March 13, 2009). I am grateful to Shang Ha for providing me with these citations.

2. Andrew Sullivan, *The Conservative Soul: Fundamentalism, Freedom, and the Future of the Right* (New York: Harper Perennial, 2006), 276–277.

3. Francis Fukuyama, *The End of History and the Last Man* (New York: Harper Collins, 1992), xxiii, 147, 150–151, 255–256, 318, 329.

4. This statement comes from MacArthur's 1962 address at West Point, and he attributes it to Plato. No scholar has ever found such a statement in Plato, but it (and the Plato attribution) does appear on a wall in London's Imperial War Museum and in Ridley Scott's 2001 film *Black Hawk Down*. The most likely source of the statement is George Santayana, in his *Soliloquies in England* (New York: Scribner's, 1924), 102. See Bernard Suzanne's excellent and thorough discussion at http://plato-dialogues.org/faq/faq008. htm#note1, accessed April 8, 2011.

5. *Selections from Treitschke's Lectures on Politics*, trans. Adam L. Gowans (New York: Frederick A. Stokes, 1914), 24–25.

6. Edmund Burke, *A Philosophical Enquiry into the Origin of Our Ideas of the Sublime and the Beautiful*, ed. David Womersley (New York: Penguin, 1998, 2004), 79.

7. Ibid., 82.

8. Ibid., 88.

9. Ibid., 96.

10. Ibid., 164.

11. Ibid., 177–178.

12. Michael Oakeshott, "On Being Conservative," in *Rationalism in Politics and Other Essays* (Indianapolis: Liberty Press, 1962), 408. Also see Walter Bagehot, "Intellectual Conservatism," in *The Works and Life of Walter Bagehot*, Vol. 9 (London: Longmans, Green, and Co., 1915), 254–258; Russell Kirk, "What Is Conservatism?" in *The Essential Russell Kirk*, ed. George A. Panichas (Wilmington, Del.: ISI Books, 2007), 7; Roger Scruton, *The Meaning of Conservatism* (London: Macmillan, 1980, 1984), 21–22, 40–43; Robert Nisbet, *Conservatism* (Minneapolis: University of Minnesota Press, 1986), 26–27.

13. Ronald Reagan, First Inaugural Address and address before a Joint Session of the Congress (April 28, 1981), in *Conservatism in America since 1930*, ed. Gregory L. Schneider (New York: New York University Press, 2003), 343, 344, 351, 352.

14. Barry Goldwater, acceptance speech at 1964 Republican National Convention (July 16, 1964), in *Conservatism in America*, 238–239.

15. Hugo Young, *One of Us* (London: Macmillan, 1989, 1991), 224.

16. William Manchester, *The Last Lion: Winston Spencer Churchill: Visions of Glory 1874–1932* (Boston: Little, Brown, 1982), 222–231.

17. Winston Churchill, *My Early Life: 1874–1904* (New York: Scribner, 1996), 77.

18. Burke, *Sublime and the Beautiful*, 177.

19. Ibid., 86.

20. Ibid., 101, 106, 108, 111.

21. Ibid., 96, 123.

22. Ibid., 121.

23. Jean-Jacques Rousseau, *Discourse on the Origin and Foundations of Inequality among Men*, in *Rousseau's Political Writings*, ed. Alan Ritter and Julia Conaway Bondanella (New York: Norton, 1988), 54.

24. John Adams, *Discourses on Davila*, in *The Political Writings of John Adams* (Indianapolis: Hackett, 2003), 176.

25. Ibid., 183–184.

26. Burke, *Sublime and the Beautiful*, 108.

27. Ibid., 109.

28. Ibid.

29. Joseph de Maistre, *Considerations on France*, trans. and ed. Richard A. Lebrun (New York: Cambridge University Press, 1974, 1994), 4, 9–10, 13–14, 16–18, 100.

30. Ibid., 17. For other examples, see Jean-Louis Darcel, "The Roads of Exile, 1792–1817," and Darcel, "Joseph de Maistre and the House of Savoy: Some Aspects of His Career," in *Joseph de Maistre's Life, Thought, and Influence: Selected Studies*, ed. Richard A. Lebrun (Montreal: McGill-Queen's University Press, 2001), 16, 19–20, 52.

31. Cf. David Bromwich, "Introduction," in Edmund Burke, *On Empire, Liberty, and Reform: Speeches and Letters*, ed. David Bromwich (New Haven, Conn.: Yale University Press, 2000), 10; Jan-Werner Müller, "Comprehending Conservatism: A New Framework for Analysis," *Journal of Political Ideologies* 11 (October 2006), 360.

32. Georges Sorel, *Reflections on Violence*, ed. Jeremy Jennings (New York: Cambridge University Press, 1999), 61–63, 72, 75–76.

33. Carl Schmitt, *The Concept of the Political*, trans. George Schwab (New Brunswick, N.J.: Rutgers University Press, 1976), 22, 48, 62–63, 65, 71–72, 74, 78.

34. Schmitt, *Concept of the Political*, 63.

35. Sorel, *Reflections on Violence*, 75.

36. Theodore Roosevelt, address to Naval War College (June, 2, 1897), in *Theodore Roosevelt: An American Mind. Selected Writings*, ed. Mario R. DiNunzio (New York: Penguin, 1994), 175–176, 179.

37. Roosevelt, address to Hamilton Club of Chicago (April 10, 1899), and *An Autobiography*, in *Theodore Roosevelt*, 186, 194.

38. Roosevelt, Naval War College address, 174.

39. John C. Calhoun, "Speech on the Reception of Abolitionist Petitions" (February 6, 1837), in *Union and Liberty: The Political Philosophy of John C. Calhoun*, ed. Ross M. Lence (Indianapolis: Liberty Fund, 1992), 476.

40. Barry Goldwater, *The Conscience of a Conservative* (Princeton, N.J.: Princeton University Press, 1960, 2007), 1.

41. Fukuyama, *End of History*, 315–318, 329; also see chapter 9.

42. John Milton, *Aeropagitica*, in *Complete Poems and Major Prose*, ed. Merritt Y. Hughes (New York: Macmillan, 1957), 728.

43. Burke, *Sublime and the Beautiful*, 145.

44. Maistre, *Considerations on France*, 77.

45. Sorel, *Reflections on Violence*, 63, 160–161.

46. Cited in William Pfaff, *The Bullet's Song: Romantic Violence and Utopia* (New York: Simon and Schuster, 2004), 97.

47. Sorel, *Reflections on Violence*, 76–78, 85.

48. What follows is an abridged account of my discussion in *Fear: The History of a Political Idea* (New York: Oxford University Press, 2004), 88–94. Sources for all quotations cited here can be found there.

49. Fukuyama, *End of History*, 148, 180, 304–305, 312, 314, 328–329.

50. E. M. Forster, *A Passage to India* (New York: Harcourt, 1924), 289.

51. Roosevelt, *The Rough Riders*, in *Theodore Roosevelt*, 30–32, 37. One might also point to Roosevelt's Naval War College address, where several thousand words in praise of manliness and military preparedness come to a climax in a call for the United States to build a modern navy that might well never be used. *Theodore Roosevelt*, 178.

52. Roosevelt, Hamilton Club address, *Theodore Roosevelt*, 185, 188.

53. Roosevelt, Lincoln Club address of February 1899, and Hamilton Club address, ibid., 182, 189.

54. R. J. B. Bosworth, *Mussolini* (New York: Oxford University Press, 2002), 167–169; Robert O. Paxton, *The Anatomy of Fascism* (New York: Knopf, 2004), 87–91.

55. Sam Tanenhaus, *The Death of Conservatism* (New York: Random House, 2009).

56. Seymour Hersh, *Chain of Command: The Road from 9/11 to Abu Ghraib* (New York: Harper Collins, 2004); Jane Mayer, *The Dark Side: The Inside Story of How the War on Terror Turned into a War on American Ideals* (New York: Doubleday, 2008).

57. Mayer, *Dark Side*, 69, 132, 241.

58. Ibid., 55, 120, 150, 167, 231, 301.

59. Ibid., 223.

60. Ibid.

61. Burke, *Sublime and the Beautiful*, 86, 92, 165.

62. Ibid., 104.

63. Ibid., 105.

64. Ibid., 106.

65. Burke, *Reflections*, 232, 239.

Chapter 4

1. Noel Malcolm, *Aspects of Hobbes* (New York: Oxford University Press, 2002), 15–16; Richard Tuck, *Hobbes* (New York: Oxford University Press, 1989), 24; Quentin Skinner, *Visions of Politics,* vol. 3, *Hobbes and Civil Sciences* (New York: Cambridge University Press, 2002), 8–9; A. P. Martinich, *Hobbes* (New York: Cambridge University Press, 1999), 161–162.

2. Skinner, *Visions,* 16.

3. Malcolm, *Aspects of Hobbes,* 20–21; Skinner, *Visions,* 22–23; Martinich, *Hobbes,* 209–210.

4. T. S. Eliot, "John Bramhall," in *Selected Essays 1917–1932* (New York: Harcourt Brace, 1932), 302.

5. Perry Anderson, "The Intransigent Right," in *Spectrum: From Right to Left in the World of Ideas* (New York: Verso, 2005), 3–28.

6. Michael Oakeshott, "On Being Conservative," in *Rationalism in Politics and Other Essays* (Indianapolis: Liberty Press, 1991), 435. Also see the useful remarks of Paul Franco in his foreword to Michael Oakeshott, *Hobbes on Civil Association* (Indianapolis: Liberty Fund, 2000), v–vii; Paul Franco, *Michael Oakeshott: An Introduction* (New Haven, Conn.: Yale University Press, 2004), 10, 103, 106.

7. Friedrich A. Hayek, *The Constitution of Liberty* (Chicago: University of Chicago Press, 1960), 56; Carl Schmitt, *The Leviathan in the State Theory of Thomas Hobbes: Meaning and Failure of a Political Symbol* (Chicago: University of Chicago Press, 2008), 42, 68–69; Leo Strauss, *Natural Right and History* (Chicago: University of Chicago Press, 1953), 165–202; Leo Strauss, "Comments on Carl Schmitt's *Der Begriff des Politischen,*" in Carl Schmitt, *The Concept of the Political* (New Brunswick, N.J.: Rutgers University Press, 1967), 89.

8. Hayek, *Constitution of Liberty,* 397–411.

9. Hobbes, *Behemoth,* ed. Ferdinand Tönnies (Chicago: University of Chicago Press, 1990), 204.

10. Benjamin Constant, *The Liberty of the Ancients Compared with That of the Moderns,* in *Political Writings,* ed. Biancamaria Fontana (New York: Cambridge University Press, 1988), 307–328; Karl Marx, *The Eighteenth Brumaire of Louis Bonaparte,* in *The Marx-Engels Reader,* ed. Robert C. Tucker (New York: Norton, 1978), 595.

11. Hobbes, *Behemoth,* 28.

12. Quentin Skinner, *Hobbes and Republican Liberty* (New York: Cambridge University Press, 2008).

13. Skinner, *Hobbes,* xiv.

14. David Wootton, *Divine Right and Democracy* (New York: Penguin, 1986), 28.

15. Ibid., 25–26.

16. Skinner, *Hobbes,* 57ff.

17. Ibid., 27.
18. Hobbes, *Leviathan*, ed. Richard Tuck (New York: Cambridge, 1996), 149.
19. Skinner, *Hobbes*, x–xi, 25–33, 68–72.
20. Ibid., xi, 215.
21. Ibid., 211–212.
22. Hobbes, *Leviathan*, 44.
23. Ibid., 145–146.
24. Cited in Skinner, *Hobbes*, 130.
25. Ibid., 116–123, 157, 162, 173.
26. Hobbes, *Leviathan*, 146.
27. Hobbes, *De Cive*, in *Man and Citizen*, ed. Bernard Gert (Indianapolis: Hackett, 1991), 216; Hobbes, *Leviathan*, 148.

Chapter 5

1. *The Autobiography of Arthur Young*, ed. M. Betham-Edwards (London: Smith, Elder, & Co., 1898), 256–261; F. P. Lock, *Edmund Burke, Volume II: 1784–1797* (New York: Oxford University Press, 2006), 513–514, 561; Donald Winch, *Riches and Poverty: An Intellectual History of Political Economy in Britain, 1750–1834* (New York: Cambridge University Press, 1996), 198–199.
2. C. B. Macpherson, *Burke* (New York: Hill and Wang, 1980), 51–70; Isaac Kramnick, *The Rage of Edmund Burke: The Conscience of an Ambivalent Conservative* (New York: Basic, 1977); Gertrude Himmelfarb, *The Idea of Poverty: England in the Early Industrial Age* (New York: Vintage, 1985), 66–73.
3. As J. G. A. Pocock and J. C. D. Clark have argued, Burke and other 18th-century writers were not concerned with the distinction between a landed aristocracy and commercial bourgeoisie. The Whig order was thought to be an aristocratic commercial regime, in which the values of market, money, and land commingled. At various points, Macpherson seems to acknowledge as much. J. G. A. Pocock, "The Political Economy of Burke's Analysis of the French Revolution," in *Virtue, Commerce, and History* (New York: Cambridge University Press, 1985), 194–195, 198, 200, 209–210; J. C. D. Clark, *English Society 1660–1832* (New York: Cambridge University Press, 2000); Macpherson, *Burke*, 63–69.
4. Edmund Burke, *Reflections on the Revolution in France*, ed. J. C. D. Clark (Stanford: Stanford University Press, 2001), 151, 358.
5. Edmund Burke, *Thoughts and Details on Scarcity*, in *Miscellaneous Writings* (Indianapolis: Liberty Fund, 1990), 70.
6. Burke, *Reflections*, 260–261, 344–346, 353; Burke, *Scarcity*, 66, 70; Himmelfarb, *Idea of Poverty*, 70.
7. Introduction to Burke, *Reflections*, 104; Edmund Burke, *Letters on Regicide Peace* (Indianapolis: Liberty Fund, 1999), 232–233.

8. Joseph Schumpeter, *The Theory of Economic Development* (New Brunswick: Transaction, 1983), 93.

9. Francis Canavan, *The Political Economy of Edmund Burke: The Role of Property in His Thought* (New York Fordham University Press, 1995), 129; Macpherson, *Burke*, 52; Himmelfarb, *Idea of Poverty*, 67, 69.

10. Karl Polanyi, *The Great Transformation: The Political and Economic Origins of Our Time* (Boston: Beacon, 1944), 102.

11. Fred Block and Margaret Somers, "In the Shadow of Speenhamland: Social Policy and the Old Poor Law," *Politics & Society* 31 (June 2003), 301–302; Polanyi, 78; Lynn Hollen Lees, *The Solidarities of Strangers: The English Poor Laws and the People, 1700–1948* (New York: Cambridge University Press, 1998), 94–95; Samuel Fleischacker, *A Short History of Distributive Justice* (Cambridge: Harvard University Press, 2004), 80–81.

12. Lock, *Burke: Volume II*, 513–514; Winch, *Riches and Poverty*, 200–201; Himmelfarb, *Idea of Poverty*, 73–75.

13. Marx, *Capital*, Volume I (New York: Vintage, 1977), 925.

14. Burke, *Regicide Peace*, 157, 167, 176, 184, 232–233.

15. Lock, *Burke: Volume II*, 561–565.

16. Burke, *Regicide Peace*, 256–270.

17. Lock, *Burke: Volume II*, 498, 502, 503–506.

18. Ibid., 339, 498, 500, 502–503, 522.

19. Ibid., 522, 529.

20. Burke, Speech on the Army Estimates (February 9, 1790), in *The Portable Edmund Burke*, ed. Isaac Kramnick (New York: Penguin, 1999), 413–414.

21. Friedrich Nietzsche, *Beyond Good and Evil* (New York: Vintage, 1989), 27, 149, 201.

22. Jonathan Israel, *A Revolution of the Mind: Radical Enlightenment and the Intellectual Origins of Modern Democracy* (Princeton: Princeton University Press, 2010), 114–123.

23. William Doyle, *The Oxford History of the French Revolution* (New York: Oxford University Press, 1989), 290.

24. Burke, *Regicide Peace*, 268.

25. Adam Smith, *An Inquiry into the Nature and Causes of the Wealth of Nations* (Indianapolis: Liberty Fund, 1981), 14–15, 20; Daniel Rodgers, *Age of Fracture* (Cambridge: Harvard University Press, 2011), 44.

26. Burke, *Scarcity*, 77.

27. Ibid., 66.

28. Burke, *Regicide Peace*, 257. Emphasis added.

29. Rodgers, *Age of Fracture*, 41.

30. Marx, *Capital*, Vol. I, 280.

31. Burke, *Regicide Peace*, 258.

32. Burke, *Scarcity*, 64.

33. Burke, *Regicide Peace*, 257.

34. Burke, *Scarcity*, 68–69.

35. Burke, *Regicide Peace*, 265.

36. Smith, *Wealth of Nations*, 73.

37. Given the ease with which Burke moves in these late writings between low wages, capital accumulation, and the state (*Regicide Peace*, 258, 260, 268–270; *Scarcity*, 64), Pocock's insistence that Burke was merely concerned with the "monied interest" of traditional Toryism rather than "a commercial or industrial bourgeoisie" needs to be qualified. Pocock, "Political Economy," 200–201.

38. On economic subjectivism and the Marginal Revolution, see Mark Blaug, *Economic Theory in Retrospect*, 5th edition (New York: Cambridge University Press, 1996), chs. 8–9; Maurice Dobb, *Theories of Value and Distribution since Adam Smith* (New York: Cambridge University Press, 1973), ch. 7; Phyllis Deane, *The Evolution of Economic Ideas* (New York: Cambridge University Press, 1978), chs. 7–8; Donald Winch, *Wealth and Life: Essays on the Intellectual History of Political Economy in Britain, 1848–1914* (New York: Cambridge University Press, 2009), chs. 6, 9–10; Philip Mirowski, *More Heat than Light: Economics as Social Physics, Physics as Nature's Economics* (New York: Cambridge University Press, 1989), 217–241, 254–265, 280–327.

39. On Burke and Smith, see F. P. Lock, *Edmund Burke, Volume I: 1730–1784* (New York: Oxford University Press, 1998), 186–187, 537–538; Lock, *Burke: Volume II*, 52–54; Winch, *Riches and Poverty*, ch. 8; Emma Rothschild, *Economic Sentiments: Adam Smith, Condorcet, and the Enlightenment* (Cambridge: Harvard University Press, 2001), ch. 2; Himmelfarb, *Idea of Poverty*, 66–67; Canavan, *Political Economy*, 116–117.

40. Smith, *Wealth of Nations*, 48, 54.

41. Ibid., 47.

42. Ibid., 50–51; Samuel Fleischacker, *On Adam Smith's* Wealth of Nations: *A Philosophical Companion* (Princeton: Princeton University Press, 2004), 127.

43. Deane, *Evolution of Economic Ideas*, 26; also see Dobb, *Theories of Value*, 45–56.

44. Smith, *Wealth of Nations*, 85–86; also see 98.

45. Ibid., 103.

46. Ibid., 96.

47. Ibid., 80, 159.

48. Ibid., 96. On Smith as an egalitarian and precursor to the modern theory of distributive justice, see Fleischacker, *A Short History*, 62–68; Elizabeth Anderson, "Adam Smith and Equality," in *The Princeton Guide to Adam Smith*, ed. Ryan Patrick Hanley (Princeton: Princeton University Press, 2016), 157–172.

49. Smith, *Wealth of Nations*, 83–85.

50. Ibid., 157–158.

51. Ibid., 85, 147.

52. Smith, *Lectures on Jurisprudence*, ed. R. L. Meek et al. (Indianapolis: Liberty Fund, 1982), 341. Emphasis added.

53. Burke, *Scarcity*, 72.

54. Burke, *Scarcity*, 79; also see 71, 81, 90–92.

55. Burke, *Regicide Peace*, 269.

56. Smith, *Wealth of Nations*, 48n.

57. Burke, *Regicide Peace*, 258; *Scarcity*, 69.

58. Burke, *Scarcity*, 70.

59. Ibid., 66–67.

60. Burke, *Regicide Peace*, 258, 269.

61. Burke, *Letter to a Noble Lord*, in *On Empire, Liberty, and Reform: Speeches and Letters of Edmund Burke*, ed. David Bromwich (New Haven: Yale University Press, 2000), 484.

62. Ibid., 484–485.

63. Ibid., 483, 485, 487.

64. Ibid., 473.

65. Ibid., 491.

66. Ibid., 473.

67. Ibid., 473.

68. Ibid., 492.

69. Ibid., 492.

70. Ibid., 493.

71. Burke, letter to the Earl of Hillsborough and Viscount Stormont, and speech on Fox's East India Bill, in *Empire, Liberty, and Reform*, 259–261, 282–283, 291, 295, 310–311, 317, 324, 326, 340.

72. Speech on Fox's East India Bill, in *On Empire, Liberty, and Reform*, 311.

73. Smith, *Lectures on Jurisprudence*, 341.

Chapter 6

1. Friedrich Nietzsche, *Ecce Homo* (New York: Vintage, 1967), "Why I Am a Destiny," §1, p. 326.

2. Thomas H. Brobjer, "Nietzsche's Knowledge, Reading, and Critique of Political Economy," *Journal of Nietzsche Studies* 18 (Fall 1999), 56–70; Thomas H. Brobjer, "Nietzsche's Knowledge of Marx and Marxism," *Nietzsche Studien* 31 (November 2003), 301–332.

3. When this chapter first appeared as an article in *The Nation*, it set off a storm of controversy across the political spectrum. Libertarians and leftists alike were troubled by my claims of an elective affinity between Nietzsche and the Austrians, my understanding of value, my argument regarding Hayek's elitism, and my view of the relationship between Hayek and Pinochet. I wrote two lengthy responses to my critics, which I have not included in this revised version of the essay, but readers may find those two responses

gathered as a single statement here: "Nietzsche, Hayek, and the Meaning of Conservatism," *Jacobin* (June 26, 2013), https://www.jacobinmag.com/2013/06/nietzsche-hayek-and-the-meaning-of-conservatism/.

4. Julian Young, *Friedrich Nietzsche: A Philosophical Biography* (New York: Cambridge University Press, 2010), 99, 101–102; Friedrich Nietzsche, *The Birth of Tragedy* (New York: Vintage, 1967), 32.

5. Young, *Nietzsche*, 139, 158–159.

6. Ibid., 135–138.

7. Rüdiger Safranski, *Nietzsche: A Philosophical Biography* (New York: Norton, 2002), 72.

8. *Political Writings of Friedrich Nietzsche*, ed. Frank Cameron and Don Dombowsky (London: Palgrave, 2008), 11.

9. *Pages from the Goncourt Journals* (New York: NYRB; 2007), 194.

10. Letter of November 10, 1887, cited in Friedrich Nietzsche, *Twilight of the Idols* (Penguin, 2003), 204.

11. Friedrich Nietzsche, "The Greek State," in *The Nietzsche Reader*, ed. Keith Ansell Pearson and Duncan Large (Oxford: Blackwell, 2006), 88–90.

12. Ibid., 88–89.

13. Brobjer, "Nietzsche's Knowledge of Marx and Marxism," 301–332; Safranski, 72; Nietzsche, *Birth of Tragedy*, 111; http://www.marxists.org/archive/marx/iwma/documents/1869/basle-report.htm; Nietzsche, *Twilight of the Idols*, 106.

14. Nietzsche, "Greek State," 90.

15. Ibid., 93–94.

16. Ibid., 92–93.

17. Friedrich Nietzsche, *The Will to Power*, trans. Walter Kaufmann (New York: Vintage, 1967), 77.

18. *Political Writings of Friedrich Nietzsche*, 6–9, 16–18.

19. Nietzsche, "Greek State," 90–91.

20. John Maynard Keynes, "William Stanley Jevons," in *Essays in Biography* (New York: Norton, 1963), 255–58, 263, 265, 274, 299.

21. Friedrich von Hayek, "Introduction," in Carl Menger, *Principles of Economics* (New York: New York University Press, 1976), 15–16, 21.

22. John Medearis, *Joseph A. Schumpeter* (New York: Continuum, 2009), 7–8.

23. Brobjer, "Nietzsche's Knowledge of Marx," 301, 304; Brobjer, "Nietzsche's Knowledge, Reading, and Critique of Political Economy," 57. On Marx's rejection of the labor theory of value, see William Clare Roberts, *Marx's Inferno: The Political Theory of Capital* (Princeton: Princeton University Press, 2016), 74–81; Moishe Postone, *Time, Labor, and Social Domination: A reinterpretation of Marx's critical theory* (New York: Cambridge University Press, 1993), 123–157.

24. Mark Blaug, *Economic Theory in Retrospect* (Cambridge: Cambridge University Press, 1996), 5th edition, 286.

25. William Stanley Jevons, "The Importance of Diffusing a Knowledge of Political Economy," in *Papers and Correspondence of William Stanley Jevons, Vol. VII: Papers on Political Economy* (London: MacMillan Press, 1981).

26. Menger, *Principles of Economics*, 174.

27. Bruce Caldwell, *Hayek's Challenge: An Intellectual Biography of F. A. Hayek* (Chicago: University of Chicago, 2004), 101; see also 338.

28. *The Wanderer and His Shadow*, cited in Brobje, "Nietzsche's Knowledge, Reading, and Critique of Political Economy," 63; Nietzsche, *Will to Power*, 8.

29. Friedrich Nietzsche, *Beyond Good and Evil*, trans. Walter Kaufmann (New York: Vintage, 1966), 27, 149.

30. Nietzsche, *Will to Power*, 9, 24.

31. Ibid., 126.

32. Ibid., 464.

33. Friedrich Nietzsche, *Thus Spake Zarathustra*, trans. Walter Kaufmann (New York: Viking, 1954), 59.

34. Nietzsche, *Beyond Good and Evil*, 205.

35. Ibid., 201.

36. Friedrich Nietzsche, *The Gay Science*, trans. Walter Kaufmann (New York: Vintage, 1974), 242.

37. Menger, *Principles of Economics*, 116.

38. Jeremy Bentham, *The Principles of Morals and Legislation* (New York: Hafner, 1948), 2; William Stanley Jevons, *The Theory of Political Economy* (London: Macmillan, 1871), 46.

39. Jevons, *Theory of Political Economy*, 46.

40. Ibid., 13–14.

41. Menger, *Principles of Economics*, 119.

42. Ibid., 116, 121.

43. Ludwig von Mises, *Socialism* (Indianapolis: Liberty Fund, 1981), preface to 2nd German edition, 9.

44. Ibid., 96, 107.

45. Friedrich von Hayek, *The Road to Serfdom*, in *The Collected Works of F. A. Hayek*, Vol. 2, ed. Bruce Caldwell (Chicago: University of Chicago Press, 2007), 125.

46. Mises, *Socialism*, 97–98.

47. Hayek, *Road to Serfdom*, 126.

48. Jevons, *Theory of Political Economy*, 21.

49. Hayek, *Road to Serfdom*, 127.

50. Ibid., 126.

51. Ibid., 217.

52. Menger, *Principles of Economics*, ch. 3.

53. Nietzsche, *Beyond Good and Evil*, 100.

54. Ibid., 100.

55. Ibid., 136.
56. Carl Schmitt, *Political Theology*, trans. George Schwab (Chicago: University of Chicago Press, 2005), 15, 66.
57. Hayek, *Road to Serfdom*, 125.
58. Joseph Schumpeter, *Capitalism, Socialism and Democracy* (New York: Harper Perennial, 1942), 137.
59. Joseph Schumpeter, "Social Classes in an Ethnically Homogenous Environment," in *Conservatism: An Anthology of Social and Political Thought from David Hume to the Present*, ed. Jerry Z. Muller (Princeton: Princeton University Press, 1997), 227–228.
60. Schumpeter, *Capitalism, Socialism, and Democracy*, 132–133.
61. Ibid., 138.
62. Ibid., 131.
63. Nietzsche, *Will to Power*, 170; Schumpeter, "Social Classes," 226, 227.
64. Schumpeter, *Capitalism, Socialism, and Democracy*, 83–85, 89, 131.
65. Joseph Schumpeter, *The Theory of Economic Development* (New Brunswick: Transaction, 1983), 93.
66. Schumpeter, *Capitalism, Socialism, and Democracy*, 132–134.
67. Ibid., 256–257.
68. Friedrich von Hayek, *The Constitution of Liberty*, ed. Ronald Hamowy (Chicago: University of Chicago Press, 2011), 84.
69. Ibid., 81, 83.
70. Ibid., 192. Also see 79–80, 83, 104, 176.
71. Ibid., 104.
72. Ibid., 186–189.
73. Ibid., 97–98.
74. Ibid., 78, 96–98, 191.
75. Ibid., 152–154, 190, 192–193.
76. Ibid., 193.
77. Perry Anderson, "The Intransigent Right," *Spectrum: From Right to Left in the World of Ideas* (London: Verso, 2005), 28.
78. Andrew Farrant, Edward McPhail, and Sebastian Berger, "Preventing the 'Abuses' of Democracy: Hayek, the 'Military Usurper' and Transitional Dictatorship in Chile?" *American Journal of Economics and Sociology* 71 (July 2012), 522.
79. Hayek, *Constitution of Liberty*, 220, 309.
80. Farrant et al., "Preventing the 'Abuses' of Democracy," 521.
81. Karin Fischer, "The Influence of Neoliberals in Chile before, during, and after Pinochet," in *The Road From Mont Pèlerin: The Making of the Neoliberal Thought Collective*, ed. Philip Mirowski and Dieter Plehwe (Cambridge: Harvard University Press, 2009), 327.

Chapter 7

1. Anne C. Heller, *Ayn Rand and the World She Made* (New York: Knopf, 2009), xii; http://www.randomhouse.com/modernlibrary/100bestnovels.html, accessed April 8, 2011.

2. Amy Wallace, "Farrah's Brainy Side," *The Daily Beast* (June 25, 2009), http://www.thedailybeast.com/blogs-and-stories/2009-06-25/farrahs-brainy-side, accessed April 8, 2011; Heller, *Ayn Rand,* 401.

3. Heller, *Ayn Rand,* 167.

4. Ayn Rand, "The Objectivist Ethics," in Rand, *The Virtue of Selfishness* (New York: Penguin, 1961, 1964), 39.

5. Elizabeth Gettelman, "I'm With the Rand," *Mother Jones* (July 20, 2009), http://motherjones.com/media/2009/07/im-rand, accessed April 8, 2011.

6. Ayn Rand, *The Fountainhead* (New York: Signet, 1996), 678.

7. Heller, *Ayn Rand,* 155, 275, 292; Rand, *Fountainhead,* 24–25; http://en.wikipedia.org/wiki/1957_in_literature, accessed April 8, 2011; http://atlasshrugged.com/book/history.html#publication, accessed May 1, 2010.

8. Heller, *Ayn Rand,* 88, 186, 278.

9. Rand, *Fountainhead,* 675; Ayn Rand, *Atlas Shrugged* (New York: Plume, 1957, 1992), 1022.

10. Heller, *Ayn Rand,* 1–3.

11. Ibid., 5.

12. Ibid., 29; Jennifer Burns, *Goddess of the Market: Ayn Rand and the American Right* (New York: Oxford University Press, 2009), 14–15.

13. Cited in Theodor Adorno, *Prisms* (Cambridge: MIT Press, 1967), 109.

14. Heller, *Ayn Rand,* 32, 35, 69, 159, 299, 395–396.

15. Ibid., 38–39, 44, 82–83, 114, 336, 371.

16. Ibid., 9, 11, 15.

17. Burns, *Goddess of the Market,* 3, 229, 285.

18. Ibid., 16–17, 21, 27.

19. Ayn Rand, *For the New Intellectual* (New York: Signet, 1961), 18.

20. Burns, *Goddess of the Market,* 307.

21. Julian Sanchez, "An Interview with Robert Nozick" (July 26, 2001), http://www.trinity.edu/rjensen/NozickInterview.htm, accessed April 8, 2011.

22. Sidney Hook, "Each Man for Himself," *New York Times,* April 9, 1961, BR3.

23. Rand, "The Cult of Moral Grayness," in *The Virtue of Selfishness,* 92.

24. Rand, "Objectivist Ethics," 16.

25. Tara Smith, *Ayn Rand's Normative Ethics: The Virtuous Egoist* (New York: Cambridge University Press, 2006), 28–29; Rand, "Objectivist Ethics," 25.

26. Rand, "Objectivist Ethics," 28.

27. *The Nazi Germany Sourcebook,* ed. Roderick Stackelberg and Sally Winkle (London: Routledge, 2002), 302–303.

28. Ibid., 105.

29. Rand, *Capitalism: The Unknown Ideal* (New York: Signet, 1967), 2, 6, 8, 11, 24.

30. *Nazi Germany Sourcebook*, 131.

31. Ibid., 130.

32. Rand, *Capitalism*, 18.

33. *Nazi Germany Sourcebook*, 105, 131.

34. Rand, *Atlas Shrugged*, 1065.

35. Rand, *Fountainhead*, 681.

36. Burns, *Goddess of the Market*, 16, 22, 25; Heller, *Ayn Rand*, 57.

37. Burns, *Goddess of the Market*, 28, 70.

38. Ibid., 42.

39. Ibid., 177.

40. Ibid., 43.

41. Joseph de Maistre, *St. Petersburg Dialogues*, trans. and ed. Richard Lebrun (Montreal: McGill-Queen's University Press, 1993), 335. Burke also traced the French Revolution back to the Reformation. See Conor Cruise O'Brien, *The Great Melody: A Thematic Biography and Commented Anthology of Edmund Burke* (Chicago: University of Chicago Press, 1992), 452–453.

42. Joseph de Maistre, *Considerations on France*, ed. Richard Lebrun (New York: Cambridge University Press, 1974, 1994), 27.

43. Friedrich Nietzsche, *On the Genealogy of Morals*, trans. Walter Kaufmann (New York: Random House, 1967), 24–56.

44. Friedrich Nietzsche, *The Will to Power*, trans. Walter Kaufmann and R. J. Hollingdale (New York: Random House, 1967), 401. Also see Nietzsche, *Genealogy*, 36, 54; Friedrich Nietzsche, *Beyond Good and Evil* (New York: Vintage, 1989), 116.

45. Burns, *Goddess of the Market*, 2, 4.

46. Matthew Yglesias, "Beck vs Social Justice" https://thinkprogress.org/beck-vs-social-justice-f720faddafc4, accessed April 8, 2011; Matthew Yglesias, "LDS Scholars Confirm Mormon Commitment to Social Justice" https://thinkprogress.org/lds-scholars-confirm-mormon-commitment-to-social-justice-50b707359fcf, accessed April 8, 2011.

47. Rand, *Fountainhead*, 606.

Chapter 8

1. George Will, foreword to Barry Goldwater, *The Conscience of a Conservative* (Princeton, N.J.: Princeton University Press, 2007, 1960), xi.

2. *The Rise of Conservatism in America, 1945–2000: A Brief History with Documents*, ed. Ronald Story and Bruce Laurie (Boston: Bedford/St. Martin's, 2008), 1.

3. William F. Buckley Jr., "Publisher's Statement on Founding *National Review*," *National Review* (November 19, 1955), in *Rise of Conservatism in America*, 51.

4. Joseph de Maistre, *Considerations on France*, trans. and ed. Richard A. Lebrun (New York: Cambridge University Press, 1974, 1994), 69, 74.

5. Judith N. Shklar, "Jean-Jacques Rousseau and Equality," in *Political Thought and Political Thinkers*, ed. Stanley Hoffmann (Chicago: University of Chicago Press, 1998), 290.

6. Edmund Burke, *Reflections on the Revolution in France*, ed. J. C. D. Clark (Stanford, Calif.: Stanford University Press, 2001), 232–233.

7. Hugo Young, *One of Us: A Biography of Margaret Thatcher* (London: Pan Books, 1989, 1991).

8. Goldwater, *Conscience of a Conservative*, 1.

9. Ibid., xxiii.

10. Edmund Burke, *Letters on a Regicide Peace* (Indianapolis: Liberty Fund, 1999), 69.

11. Young, *One of Us*, 406.

12. "Speech at the Meeting of the Citizens of Charleston," in *Union and Liberty: The Political Philosophy of John C. Calhoun*, ed. Ross M. Lence (Indianapolis: Liberty Fund, 1992), 536.

13. Goldwater, *Conscience of a Conservative*, 54.

14. Ibid., 2.

15. Ibid., 3–4.

16. Karl Mannheim, "Conservative Thought," in *Essays on Sociology and Social Psychology*, ed. Paul Kesckemeti (London: Routledge & Kegan Paul, 1953), 106.

17. Goldwater, *Conscience of a Conservative*, 3, 78–79, 119.

18. Mannheim, "Conservative Thought," 107.

19. Goldwater, *Conscience of a Conservative*, 17–18, 25.

20. "Introduction," in *Rightward Bound: Making America Conservative in the 1970s*, ed. Bruce J. Schulman and Julian E. Zelizer (Cambridge, Mass.: Harvard University Press, 2008), 4.

21. Matthew D. Lassiter, "Inventing Family Values," and Joseph Crespino, "Civil Rights and the Religious Right," in *Rightward Bound*, 14, 90–91, 93.

22. Crespino, "Civil Rights," 91, 92–93, 97, 102–103.

23. Marjorie J. Spruill, "Gender and America's Right Turn," in *Rightward Bound*, 77–79.

24. "Interview with Phyllis Schlafly," *Washington Star* (January 18, 1976), in *The Rise of Conservatism in America*, 104–105.

25. Lassiter, "Inventing Family Values," and Paul Boyer, "The Evangelical Resurgence in 1970s American Protestantism," in *Rightward Bound*, 19–20, 34, 37, 40–41.

26. Bethany E. Moreton, "Make Payroll, Not War," in *Rightward Bound*, 53, 55–57, 65, 69.

27. Thomas J. Sugrue and John D. Skrentny, "The White Ethnic Strategy," in *Rightward Bound*, 174–175, 189, 191.

28. Rick Perlstein, *Before the Storm: Barry Goldwater and the Unmaking of the American Consensus* (New York: Hill & Wang, 2001), 17.

Chapter 9

1. Corey Robin, "The Ex-Cons: Right-Wing Thinkers Go Left!" *Lingua Franca* (February 2001), 32–33; Irving Kristol, interview with author (Washington, D.C., August 31, 2000).
2. Frank Rich, "The Day before Tuesday," *New York Times*, September 15, 2001, A23; Maureen Dowd, "From Botox to Botulism," *New York Times*, September 26, 2001, A19; David Brooks, "The Age of Conflict: Politics and Culture after September 11," *Weekly Standard*, November 7, 2001.
3. Francis Fukuyama, "Francis Fukuyama Says Tuesday's Attack Marks the End of 'America's Exceptionalism,'" *Financial Times*, September 15, 2001, 1; Nicholas Lemann, "The Next World Order," *New Yorker*, April 1, 2002, 48; David Brooks, "Facing Up to Our Fears," *Newsweek*, October 22, 2001.
4. Andrew Sullivan, "High Impact: The Dumb Idea of September 11," *New York Times Magazine*, December 9, 2001; George Packer, "Recapturing the Flag," *New York Times Magazine*, September 30, 2001, 15–16; Brooks, "Facing Up to Our Fears"; Brooks, "The Age of Conflict."
5. Brooks, "Facing Up to Our Fears."
6. Ibid.
7. On 9/11, trust in government, and the welfare state, see Jacob Weisberg, "Feds Up," *New York Times Magazine*, October 21, 2001, 21–22; Michael Kelly, "The Left's Great Divide," *Washington Post*, November 7, 2001, A29; Robert Putnam, "Bowling Together," *American Prospect* (January 23, 2002); Bernard Weinraub, "The Moods They Are a'Changing in Films," *New York Times*, October 10, 2001, E1; Nina Bernstein, "On Pier 94, a Welfare State That Works, and Possible Models for the Future," *New York Times*, September 6, 2001, B8; Michael Kazin, "The Nation: After the Attacks, Which Side Is the Left On?" *New York Times*, October 7, 2001, section 4, 4; Katrina vanden Heuvel and Joel Rogers, "What's Left? A New Life for Progressivism," *Los Angeles Times*, November 25, 2001, M2; Michael Kelly, "A Renaissance of Liberalism," *Atlantic Monthly* (January 2002), 18–19. On 9/11 and the culture wars, see Richard Posner, "Strong Fiber after All," *Atlantic Monthly* (January 2002), 22–23; Rick Lyman, "At Least for the Moment, a Cooling of the Culture Wars," *New York Times*, November 13, 2001, E1; Maureen Dowd, "Hunks and Brutes," *New York Times*, November 28, 2001, A25; Richard Posner, "Reflections on an America Transformed," *New York Times*, September 8, 2002, Week in Review, 15. On 9/11, bipartisanship, and the new presidency, see "George Bush, G.O.P. Moderate," *New York Times*, September 29, 2001, A18; Maureen Dowd, "Autumn of Fears," *New York Times*, November 23, 2001, Week in Review, 17; Richard L. Berke, "Bush 'Is My Commander,' Gore Declares in Call for

Unity," *New York Times*, September 30, 2001, A29; Frank Bruni, "For President, a Mission and a Role in History," *New York Times*, September 21, 2001, A1; "Politics Is Adjourned," *New York Times*, September 20, 2001, A30; Adam Clymer, "Disaster Forges a Spirit of Cooperation in a Usually Contentious Congress," *New York Times*, September 20, 2001, B3. For a general statement of these various themes, see "In for the Long Haul," *New York Times*, September 16, 2001, Week in Review, 10.

8. Judy Keen, "Same President, Different Man in Oval Office," *USA Today*, October 29, 2001, 6A; Christopher Hitchens, "Images in a Rearview Mirror," *The Nation* (December 3, 2001), 9.

9. Lemann, "Next World Order," 44; Joseph S. Nye Jr., *The Paradox of American Power: Why the World's Only Superpower Can't Go It Alone* (New York: Oxford University Press, 2002), 168; Brooks, "The Age of Conflict."

10. George Steiner, *In Bluebeard's Castle: Some Notes toward the Redefinition of Culture* (New Haven, Conn.: Yale University Press, 1971), 11.

11. Cheney cited in Donald Kagan and Frederick W. Kagan, *While America Sleeps: Self-Delusion, Military Weakness, and the Threat to Peace Today* (New York: St. Martin's Press, 2000), 294; Condoleezza Rice, "Promoting the National Interest," *Foreign Affairs* (June 2000), 45; Nye, *Paradox of American Power*, 139.

12. *The Clinton Foreign Policy Reader: Presidential Speeches with Commentary*, ed. Alvin Z. Rubinstein, Albina Shayevich, and Boris Zlotnikov (Armonk, N.Y.: M. E. Sharpe, 2000), 9, 20, 22–23. It should be pointed out that after several years of reduced military spending, Clinton, in his second term, steadily began to increase military appropriations. Between 1998 and 2000, military expenditures went from $259 billion to $301 billion. This increase in spending coincided with a reconsideration of the dangers confronting the United States. In his last years in office, Clinton began to sound the alarm more forcefully against the threat of terrorism and rogue states. See *Clinton Foreign Policy Reader*, 36–42; Paul-Marie de la Gorce, "Offensive New Pentagon Defence Doctrine," *Le Monde Diplomatique*, March 2002.

13. David Halberstam, *War in a Time of Peace* (New York: Scribner, 2001), 22–23, 110–113, 152–153, 160–163, 193, 242.

14. Nye, *Paradox of American Power*, 8–11, 110. On occasion, Clinton even went so far as to suggest that pouring so much money into fighting the Cold War was, if not exactly a waste, then at least an unnecessary strain on the nation's vital resources. "The Cold War," he said at American University in 1993, "was a draining time. We devoted trillions of dollars to it, much more than many of our more visionary leaders thought we should have." *Clinton Foreign Policy Reader*, 9.

15. Brooks, "The Age of Conflict"; Robert D. Kaplan, *The Coming Anarchy: Shattering the Dreams of the Post Cold War* (New York: Vintage, 2000),

23–24, 89. Also see Francis Fukuyama, *The End of History and the Last Man* (New York: Harper Collins, 1992, 2002), 304–305, 311–312.

16. See Robert Putnam, *Bowling Alone: The Collapse and Revival of American Community* (New York: Simon & Schuster, 2000); Dinesh D'Souza, *The Virtue of Prosperity: Finding Values in an Age of Techno-Affluence* (New York: Simon & Schuster, 2000); John B. Judis, *The Paradox of American Democracy: Elites, Special Interests, and the Betrayal of the Public Trust* (New York: Pantheon, 2000); Kagan and Kagan, *While America Sleeps*.

17. Indeed, the Clinton administration's many pronouncements on the issue of multi- and unilateralism sound remarkably similar to those of the administration of George W. Bush. In an address to the United Nations in 1993, Clinton stated, "We will often work in partnership with others and through multilateral institutions such as the United Nations. It is in our national interests to do so. But we must not hesitate to act unilaterally when there is a threat to our core interests or to those of our allies." That same year, Anthony Lake declared, "We should act multilaterally where doing so advances our interest—and should act unilaterally when that will serve our purpose." In 1994, Clinton affirmed that he sought U.S. "influence over" multilateral decisions and operations. In 1995, he declared, "We will act with others when we can, but alone when we must." Joseph Nye, Clinton's assistant secretary of defense, has since declared, against the counsel and advice of classic balance-of-power realists, that the United States should maintain its monopoly of power as the surest path to peace. As for the debates between realists and humanitarians, internationalists and isolationists, the fact is that many of the neoconservative critics of the Clinton administration are as committed to humanitarian, internationalist intervention as the Clinton administration was. *Clinton Foreign Policy Reader*, 6, 16–17, 26, 28; Nye, *Paradox of American Power*, 15; Robert Kagan and William Kristol, "The Present Danger," *National Interest* (Spring 2000); "Paul Wolfowitz, Velociraptor," *The Economist* (February 9, 2002); Lemann, "Next World Order," 42; Robert Kagan, "Fightin' Democrats," *Washington Post*, March 10, 2002.

18. Kagan and Kagan, *While America Sleeps*, 1–2, 4; Kaplan, *Coming Anarchy*, 157, 172, 176.

19. Brooks, "Age of Conflict"; Steven Mufson, "The Way Bush Sees the World," *Washington Post*, February 17, 2002, B1.

20. Lemann, "Next World Order," 43, 47–48; Seymour M. Hersh, "The Iraq Hawks," *New Yorker* (December 24 and 31, 2001), 61; Kagan, "Fightin' Democrats"; Kagan and Kagan, *While America Sleeps*, 293, 295.

21. Emily Eakin, "All Roads Lead to D.C.," *New York Times*, March 31, 2002, Week in Review, 4; Lemann, "Next World Order," 44. Also see Alexander Stille, "What Is America's Place in the World Now?" *New York Times*, January 12, 2002, B7; Michael Ignatieff, "The American Empire (Get Used to It),"

New York Times Magazine, January 5, 2003, 22ff; Bill Keller, "The I-Can't-Believe-I'm-a-Hawk Club," New York Times, February 8, 2003, A17; Lawrence Kaplan, "Regime Change," New Republic (March 3, 2003).

22. Lemann, "Next World Order," 43–44; Hersh, "The Iraq Hawks," 61; George W. Bush, "State of the Union Address," New York Times, January 30, 2002, A22: Mufson, "Way Bush Sees the World," B1.

23. Eric Schmitt and Steve Lee Myers, "U.S. Steps Up Air Attack, While Defending Results of Campaign," New York Times, October 26, 2001, B1; Susan Sachs, "U.S. Appears to Be Losing Public Relations War So Far," New York Times, October 28, 2001, B8: Warren Hoge, "Public Apprehension Felt in Europe over the Goals of Afghanistan Bombings," New York Times, November 1, 2001, B2; Dana Canedy, "Vietnam-Era G.I.'s Watch New War Warily," New York Times, November 12, 2001, B9.

24. Robin Wright, "Urgent Calls for Peace in Mideast Ring Hollow as Prospects Dwindle," Los Angeles Times, March 31, 2002.

25. Ibid.

26. David E. Rosenbaum, "Senate Deletes Higher Mileage Standard in Energy Bill," New York Times, March 14, 2002, A28.

27. Diana B. Henriques and David Barstow, "Victim's Fund Likely to Pay Average of $1.6 Million Each," New York Times, December 21, 2001, A1. For an excellent critique, see Eve Weinbaum and Max Page, "Compensate All 9/11 Families Equally," Christian Science Monitor, January 4, 2002, 11.

28. Tim Jones, "Military Sees No Rush to Enlist," Chicago Tribune, March 24, 2002; David W. Chen, "Armed Forces Stress Careers, Not Current War," New York Times, October 20, 2001, B10.

29. Andrew Gumbel, "Pentagon Targets Latinos and Mexicans to Man the Front Lines in War on Terror," The Independent, September 10, 2003.

30. R. W. Apple Jr., "Nature of Foe Is Obstacle in Appealing for Sacrifice," New York Times, October 15, 2001, B2; Frank Rich, "War Is Heck," New York Times, November 10, 2001, A23; Alison Mitchell, "After Asking for Volunteers, Government Tries to Determine What They Will Do," New York Times, November 10, 2001, B7. Also see Michael Lipsky, "The War at Home: Wartime Used to Entail National Unity and Sacrifice," American Prospect (January 28, 2002), 15–16.

31. Elisabeth Bumiller, "Bush Asks Volunteers to Join Fight on Terrorism," New York Times, January 31, 2002, A20; Mitchell, "After Asking for Volunteers," B7. Also see David Brooks, "Love the Service Around Here," New York Times Magazine, November 25, 2001, 34.

Chapter 10

1. Joan Biskupic, American Original: The Life and Constitution of Supreme Court Justice Antonin Scalia (New York: Farrar, Straus and Giroux, 2009), 340.

2. *Nixon v. Missouri Municipal League*, 541 U.S. 125, 141–142 (2004) (Scalia, concurring).

3. *Hamdi v. Rumsfeld*, 542 U.S. 507, 576 (2004) (Scalia, dissenting).

4. Biskupic, *American Original*, 282.

5. Cited in Mark Tushnet, *A Court Divided* (New York: Norton, 2005), 149.

6. Biskupic, *American Original*, 7, 11, 14, 346.

7. Ibid., 17, 19, 21, 25.

8. Ibid., 23, 40–41, 73.

9. Ibid., 41.

10. Ibid., 66–67.

11. Antonin Scalia, *A Matter of Interpretation: Federal Courts and the Law* (Princeton, N.J.: Princeton University Press, 1997), 23, 145.

12. Ibid., 23.

13. Ibid., 46.

14. Remarks at Catholic University (October 18, 1996), http://www.joink.com/homes/users/ninoville/cua10-18-9.asp, accessed April 8, 2011; Scalia, *A Matter of Interpretation*, 47, 149.

15. Scalia, *A Matter of Interpretation*, 14.

16. Robert H. Bork, *The Tempting of America* (New York: Simon and Schuster, 1990), 133, 188.

17. Biskupic, *American Original*, 25, 209, 211.

18. *PGA TOUR, Inc. v. Casey Martin*, 532 U.S. 661 (2001) (Scalia, dissenting).

19. Alexis de Tocqueville, *Democracy in America* (New York: Harper, 1969), 150.

20. *Lawrence v. Texas*, 539 U.S. 568, 590 (2003) (Scalia, dissenting).

21. Biskupic, *American Original*, 189.

22. *Board of County Commissioners, Wabaunsee County, Kansas v. Umbehr*, 518 U.S. 668, 711 (1996) (Scalia, dissenting).

23. Maureen Dowd, "Nino's Opéra Bouffe," http://www.nytimes.com/2003/06/29/opinion/29DOWD.html, accessed April 8, 2011.

24. Biskupic, *American Original*, 362.

25. William J. Brennan, "Speech to the Text and Teaching Symposium," in *Originalism: A Quarter-Century of Debate*, ed. Steven Calabresi (Washington, D.C.: Regnery, 2007), 59, 61.

26. Scalia, *A Matter of Interpretation*, 67.

27. *Citizens United v. Federal Election Commission*, 558 U.S. 201, 209, 212 (2010) (Stevens, dissenting).

28. Biskupic, *American Original*, 9, 134, 196.

29. *Scalia Dissents: Writings of the Supreme Court's Wittiest, Most Outspoken Justice*, ed. Kevin A. Ring (Washington, D.C.: Regnery, 2004), 9.

30. http://www.law.yale.edu/news/5658.htm, accessed April 8, 2011.

31. Biskupic, *American Original*, 8.

32. Jeffrey Toobin, *The Nine: Inside the Secret World of the Supreme Court* (New York: Random House, 2008), 65.

33. Tara Trask and Ryan Malphurs, "'Don't Poke Scalia!' Lessons for Trial Lawyers from the Nation's Highest Court," *Jury Expert* 21 (November 2009), 46.

Chapter 11

1. Donald Trump with Tony Schwartz, *The Art of the Deal* (New York: Ballantine, 1987), 2, 7, 8, 21–22, 34, 52–53, 77, 91, 171–172, 187.
2. Michael Kruse and Noah Weiland, "Donald Trump's Greatest Self-Contradictions," *Politico* (May 5, 2016), http://www.politico.com/magazine/story/2016/05/donald-trump-2016-contradictions-213869; Inae Oh, "Watch Donald Trump Contradict Himself on Every Major Campaign Issue," *Mother Jones* (August 9, 2016), http://www.motherjones.com/politics/2016/08/donald-trump-contradicting-himself-hypocrisy-video; David Bier, "Four Ways Trump Contradicts Himself with His New Travel Ban," *Newsweek* (March 9, 2017), http://www.newsweek.com/four-ways-trump-contradicts-himself-his-new-travel-ban-564902.
3. The most important statement of this position on the right remains Michael Oakeshott, *Rationalism and Politics and Other Essays* (Indianapolis: Liberty Fund, 1991). I discuss Oakeshott's argument in chapter 1. On Oakeshott's reflections on inconsistency, see Dale Hall and Tariq Modood, "Oakeshott and the Impossibility of Philosophical Politics," *Political Studies* 30 (June 1982), 157–176.
4. Walter Bagehot, "Intellectual Conservatism," in *The Works and Life of Walter Bagehot*, Vol. 9 (London: Longmans, Green, and Co., 1915), 254.
5. Joseph de Maistre, *Considerations on France*, ed. Richard Lebrun (New York: Cambridge, 1974), 50; Edmund Burke, *A Philosophical Enquiry into the Origin of Our Ideas of the Sublime and the Beautiful*, ed. David Womersley (New York: Penguin, 1998, 2004), 106. Also see Edmund Burke, *Reflections on the Revolution in France* (Stanford: Stanford University Press, 2001), 209, 238, 345–347.
6. Kevin Mattson, *Rebels All! A Short History of the Conservative Mind in Postwar America* (New Brunswick: Rutgers University Press, 2008).
7. Trump, *Art of the Deal*, 1.
8. Andrew Prokop, "Trump backers hate 'political correctness.' That's why gaffes don't hurt him," *Vox* (February 29, 2016), http://www.vox.com/2016/2/29/11133796/donald-trump-political-correctness; Lauren Berlant, "Trump, or Political Emotions," *The New Inquiry* (August 5, 2016), https://thenewinquiry.com/features/trump-or-political-emotions/.
9. Fred Barnes, *Rebel in Chief: Inside the Bold and Controversial Presidency of George W. Bush* (New York: Crown, 2006). About this book, and the general reputation Bush sought to cultivate among his conservative base, historian Kevin Mattson writes, "Barnes does not see Bush as a statesman (or as

stately); rather, his idealized president looks like Marlon Brando mounting his motorcycle and raising hell in the iconic 1953 film *The Wild One*. For Barnes, Bush is 'defiant of the press, scornful of the conventional wisdom, and keen to reverse or at least substantially reform long-standing policies.' The president is 'edgy' and 'blunt'; he leads an 'army of insurgents.'" Mattson, 2.

10. Trump, *Art of the Deal*, 5.

11. Allan J. Lichtman, *White Protestant Nation: The Rise of the American Conservative Movement* (New York: Grove Press, 2008); Theda Skocpol and Vanessa Williamson, *The Tea Party and the Remaking of Republican Conservatism* (New York: Oxford University Press, 2013), 4, 11, 56–57, 68, 71–72, 76, 79, 81, 193–196.

12. Albert O. Hirschman, *The Passions and the Interests: Political Arguments for Capitalism before Its Triumph* (Princeton: Princeton University, 1977).

13. Kim Phillips-Fein, *Invisible Hands: The Businessman's Crusade Against the New Deal* (New York: Norton, 2009).

14. David Gordon, *Fat and Mean: The Corporate Squeeze of Working Americans and the Myth of Managerial Downsizing* (New York: Free Press, 1996).

15. Hannah Arendt, *The Origins of Totalitarianism* (New York: Schocken, 1951), 232.

16. Gary Orfield and Erica Frankenberg, with Jongyeon Ee and John Kuscera, "Brown at 60: Great Progress, a Long Retreat and an Uncertain Future" (The Civil Rights Project/Proyecto Derechos Civiles, May 15, 2014), 10–11; Thomas Shapiro, Tatjana Meschede, and Sam Osoro, "The Roots of the Widening Racial Wealth Gap: Explaining the Black-White Economic Divide" (Institute on Assets and Social Policy, February 2013).

17. The question of who is the modal Trump voter is controversial, and often conflated, wrongly, with the question of the white working class. In many discussions of Trump's victory, the assumption seems to be that the archetypal Trump voter was a white working class man, which is not the case. The most typical Trump voter was a Republican, skewing above the median household income level. That doesn't mean it was those voters who gave Trump the White House; those voters are simply the loyal Republican Party base, which is overwhelmingly white and voted for Romney and for McCain. In all likelihood, what tipped the election in Trump's favor were, first, those white working class swing voters in depressed areas of the Rust Belt, many of whom had cast their ballots twice for Obama, and, second, and even more important, the working class voters, white and of color, from that region who voted for Obama but stayed home in 2016. But these were not the typical Trump voter. As Matt Yglesias rightly argued after the election, there were three kinds of Trump voters. The first were his hardcore supporters within the Republican Party, who rallied to him early on in the primaries. The second were the vast remainder of the Republican Party

who voted for Trump because they vote Republican. The third was that small group of swing voters in the Rust Belt states. One of the best studies of Trump voters within the Republican Party found that Trump's earliest supporters in the primaries tended to live in more economically desperate areas than other Republican voters, in areas where income and well-being were less evenly distributed than in other Republican-leaning counties. Trump's later supporters in the Republican primaries lived in wealthier areas, and came around to support Trump when it seemed as if the energy he was generating at the base might put their party into the White House. Another eye-opening report looks at swing voters in the Rust Belt states who voted for Obama and then went for Trump. This report, based on ethnographic research, describes these voters as "exhausted." Matthew Yglesias, "The 3 different things we talk about when we talk about 'Trump voter,'" *Vox* (December 7, 2016), https://www.vox.com/policy-and-politics/2016/12/7/13854512/who-are-trump-supporters; Benjy Sarlin, "United States of Trump," *NBC News* (June 20, 2016), http://www.nbcnews.com/specials/donald-trump-republican-party; Justin Gest, "The Two Kinds of Trump Voters," *Politico* (February 8, 2017), http://www.politico.com/magazine/story/2017/02/trump-voters-white-working-class-214754; Nate Cohn, "A 2016 Review: Turnout Wasn't the Driver of Clinton's Defeat," *New York Times* (March 28, 2017), https://mobile.nytimes.com/2017/03/28/upshot/a-2016-review-turnout-wasnt-the-driver-of-clintons-defeat.html; Nicholas Carnes and Noam Lupu, "It's Time to Bust the Myth: Most Trump Voters Were Not Working Class," *Washington Post* (June 5, 2017), https://www.washingtonpost.com/news/monkey-cage/wp/2017/06/05/its-time-to-bust-the-myth-most-trump-voters-were-not-working-class/.

18. Nate Silver, "Donald Trump's Base Is Shrinking," *FiveThirtyEight* (May 24, 2017), https://fivethirtyeight.com/features/donald-trumps-base-is-shrinking/; Tim Marcin, "Donald Trump's Approval Rating in Swing Counties and Election Strongholds Show How Unpopular He Is," *Newsweek* (May 18, 2017), http://www.newsweek.com/donald-trumps-approval-rating-swing-counties-election-strongholds-show-611873; Tim Marcin, "How Popular Is Trump? Latest Approval Rating Plummets as White Supporters Flee," *Newsweek* (May 11, 2017), http://www.newsweek.com/how-popular-trump-latest-approval-rating-white-supporters-flee-president-607478; Greg Sargent, "This Brutal New Poll Shows that Fewer and Fewer People Believe Trump's Lies," *Washington Post* (April 17, 2017), https://www.washingtonpost.com/blogs/plum-line/wp/2017/04/17/this-brutal-new-poll-shows-that-fewer-and-fewer-people-believe-trumps-lies/?utm_term=.fee2fa1b9733; "Majority in US No Longer Thinks Trump Keeps His Promises," Gallup (April 17, 2017), http://www.gallup.com/poll/208640/majority-no-longer-thinks-trump-keeps-promises.aspx; Philip Bump, "Trump's Approval Hits a New Low of 36 percent—but That's Not the Bad

News," *Washington Post* (March 27, 2017), https://www.washingtonpost.com/news/politics/wp/2017/03/27/trumps-approval-hits-a-new-low-of-36-percent-but-thats-not-the-bad-news/; Vegas Tenold, "The Alt-Right and Donald Trump Get a Divorce," *The New Republic* (April 26, 2017), https://newrepublic.com/article/142276/alt-right-donald-trump-get-divorce.

19. Alan Brinkley, *Voices of Protest: Huey Long, Father Coughlin, and the Great Depression* (New York: Knopf, 1982), 143–168, 287–288; Michael Kazin, *The Populist Persuasion: An American History* (New York: Basic, 1995), 109–133, 221–242; Dan T. Carter, *The Politics of Rage: George Wallace, the Origins of the New Conservatism, and the Transformation of American Politics* (New York: Simon and Schuster, 1995), 352, 281–283; Joseph E. Lowndes, *From the New Deal to the New Right* (New Haven: Yale University Press, 2008), 85, 101–104; Peter Kolozi, *Conservatives Against Capitalism: From the Industrial Revolution to Globalization* (New York: Columbia University Press, 2017), 167–189.

20. In addition to the citations in note 17, see Jonathan Chait, "What's Less Popular Than Donald Trump? Pretty Much Everything Paul Ryan and Mitch McConnell Are Doing," *New York* (May 29, 2017), http://nymag.com/daily/intelligencer/2017/05/whats-less-popular-than-donald-trump-paul-ryan-and-mitch-mcconnell.html; Jeff Stein, "Paul Ryan's Agenda has been a much bigger liability for the GOP than Trump's Scandals," *Vox* (May 23, 2017), https://www.vox.com/policy-and-politics/2017/5/23/15674450/paul-ryan-special-election; Eric Levitz, "'Small Government' Conservatism Is Killing Republican Voters," *New York* (March 26, 2017), http://nymag.com/daily/intelligencer/2017/03/small-government-conservatism-is-killing-republican-voters.html

21. Donald Trump, *Time to Get Tough: Make America Great Again!*® (Washington, DC: Regnery, 2011, 2015), 4.

22. Roger Scruton, *The Meaning of Conservatism* (London: Macmillan, 1980, 1984), 11; Friedrich A. Hayek, *The Constitution of Liberty* (Chicago: University of Chicago Press, 1960), 7; Frank Meyer, "Freedom, Tradition, Conservatism," in *In Defense of Freedom and Related Essays* (Indianapolis: Liberty Fund, 1996), 15.

23. Jane Mayer, "Donald Trump's Ghostwriter Tells All," *The New Yorker* (July 25, 2016).

24. Andrew Prokop, "Steve Bannon's longtime suspicion of successful immigrants is the key to this weekend's chaos," *Vox* (January 29, 2017), http://www.vox.com/2017/1/29/14429984/trump-immigration-order-steve-bannon. On Bannon's uncertain fate in the Trump administration, see Greg Sargent, "Is Stephen Bannon Getting Pushed Out? The Latest Signs Point to Yes." *Washington Post* (April 12, 2017), https://www.washingtonpost.com/blogs/plum-line/wp/2017/04/12/is-stephen-bannon-getting-pushed-out-the-latest-signs-point-to-yes/; Domenico Montanaro, "Trump Signals Steve Bannon Could Be On His Way Out," *NPR* (April 12, 2017), http://www.npr.

org/2017/04/12/523569897/trump-signals-steve-bannon-could-be-on-his-way-out; Ryan Lizza, "How Climate Change Saved Steve Bannon's Job," *The New Yorker* (June 2, 2017), http://www.newyorker.com/news/ryan-lizza/how-climate-change-saved-steve-bannons-job.

25. We get a glimpse of this back and forth in a November 2015 interview that Bannon did with Trump. Bannon had been defending nativist immigration policies to Trump, who responded by claiming, against Bannon, that at a minimum, foreign-born economic elites should be allowed to remain in the United States: "We have to keep our talented people in this country." That is what provoked Bannon to reply, "A country's more than an economy. We're a civic society." The exchange between the two men captures both sides of Trump's thinking: in the one moment, a privileging of the economic over the political; in the next, a privileging of the political over the economic. Prokop, "Steve Bannon's longtime suspicion of successful immigrants is the key to this weekend's chaos."

26. Trump, *Art of the Deal*, 61, 273.

27. Ibid., 60–61.

28. Ibid., 192–193.

29. Ibid., 1, 47.

30. Ibid., 176–177. Also see 37–38.

31. Ibid., 189.

32. Trump, *Time to Get Tough*, 72–73.

33. Glenn Thrush and Maggie Haberman, "Trump and Staff Rethink Tactics After Stumbles," *New York Times* (February 6, 2017), A1.

34. Debora Silverman, *Selling Culture: Bloomingdale's, Diana Vreeland, and the New Aristocracy of Taste in Reagan's America* (New York: Pantheon, 1986).

35. Trump, *Art of the Deal*, 41.

36. Ibid., 79–80.

37. Friedrich Nietzsche, "Homer's Contest," in *The Nietzsche Reader*, ed. Keith Ansell Pearson and Duncan Large (Oxford: Blackwell, 2006), 95–100.

38. Burke, *Letter to a Noble Lord*, in *On Empire, Liberty, and Reform: Speeches and Letters of Edmund Burke*, ed. David Bromwich (New Haven: Yale University Press, 2000), 473, 484–485.

39. Trump, *Art of the Deal*, 226, 234, 237; Trump, *Time to Get Tough*, 60–62; David Cay Johnston, *The Making of Donald Trump* (Brooklyn: Melville House, 2016), 15.

40. Trump, *Art of the Deal*, 45–48, 63.

41. Despite Trump's rhetorical opposition to the Republican establishment, his vision is similar to the economic Darwinism that animates figures like Scalia, Paul Ryan, and conservative mega-donor and billionaire hedge funder Robert Mercer, who believes that "human beings have no inherent value other than how much money they make." Jane Mayer, "The Reclusive Hedge-Fund Tycoon Behind the Trump Presidency," *The*

New Yorker (March 27, 2017), http://www.newyorker.com/magazine/2017/03/27/the-reclusive-hedge-fund-tycoon-behind-the-trump-presidency.

42. Trump, *Art of the Deal*, 46–47.

43. Ibid., 63.

44. Johnston, *Making of Donald Trump*, 22.

45. Trump, *Art of the Deal*, 1.

46. Ibid., 2, 63.

47. Max Weber, *The Protestant Ethic and the Spirit of Capitalism* (New York: Routledge, 1992), 124.

48. Ronald Reagan, *Radio Address to the Nation on Taxes, the Tuition Tax Credit, and Interest Rates* (April 24, 1982), http://www.presidency.ucsb.edu/ws/index.php?pid=42445#axzz1SZbhcOIv.

49. We find the contrast between Reagan's vision of the economy and Trump's— and their corresponding visions of the role of the state and the presidency— repeated, even more starkly, in a comparison between the two presidents' First Inaugural Addresses. Corey Robin, "Trump's Inaugural Address versus Reagan's Inaugural Address" (January 20, 2017), http://coreyrobin.com/2017/01/20/trumps-inaugural-address-versus-reagans-inaugural-address/.

50. John Maynard Keynes, "Social Consequences of Changes in the Value of Money," in *Essays in Persuasion* (New York: Norton, 1963), 94–95.

51. Trump, *Art of the Deal*, 58. Also see 181: "We were selling fantasy."

52. Ibid., 57.

53. Ibid., 197, 261.

54. William Clare Roberts, *Marx's Inferno: The Political Theory of Capital* (Princeton: Princeton University Press, 2016), 1, 20–28.

55. Trump, *Time to Get Tough*, 2.

56. Ibid., 8, 24, 27, 29, 33, 36, 41, 48; David K. Johnson, *The Cold War Persecution of Gays and Lesbians in the Federal Government* (Chicago: University of Chicago Press, 2006), 70.

57. Trump, *Time to Get Tough*, 26.

58. Ibid., 33, 36; Robert O. Paxton, *The Anatomy of Fascism* (New York: Knopf, 2004), 41.

59. Trump, *Time to Get Tough*, 2, 45, 48.

60. Ibid., 46–47.

61. Ibid., 2, 38; Donald Trump, *Great Again: How to fix Our Crippled America* (New York: Simon & Schuster, 2015), 32.

62. Trump, *Time to Get Tough*, 9–13, 154.

63. Missy Ryan and Greg Jaffe, "Military's Clout at White House Could Shift U.S. Foreign Policy," *Washington Post* (May 28, 2017), https://www.washingtonpost.com/world/national-security/military-officers-seed-the-ranks-across-trumps-national-security-council/2017/05/28/5f10c8ca-421d-11e7-8c25-44d09ff5a4a8_story.html .

64. Trump, *Great Again*, 1, 32.

65. Trump, *Time to Get Tough*, 19, 21, 23.

66. Johnston, xvii, 23, 38, 48, 55–56.

67. Dara Lind, "Even the Trump administration doesn't seem to care about the travel ban anymore," *Vox* (May 31, 2017), https://www.vox.com/policy-and-politics/2017/5/31/15712294/trump-muslim-ban; Corey Robin, "Think Trump is an authoritarian? Look at his actions, not his words," *The Guardian* (May 2, 2017), https://www.theguardian.com/commentisfree/2017/may/02/donald-trump-authoritarian-look-actions-not-words.

68. Trump, *Time to Get Tough*, 4.

69. Wendy Brown, *Undoing the Demos: Neoliberalism's Stealth Revolution* (Brooklyn: Zone Books, 2015).

70. Quoted in Stephen Skowronek, *The Politics Presidents Make: Leadership from John Adams to Bill Clinton* (Cambridge: Harvard University Press, 1993, 1997), 379.

71. Isaac Chotiner, "Is Donald Trump a Fascist? Yes and no." *Slate* (February 10, 2016), http://www.slate.com/articles/news_and_politics/interrogation/2016/02/is_donald_trump_a_fascist_an_expert_on_fascism_weighs_in.html.

72. Victoria de Grazia, "Many call Trump a fascist. 100 days in, is he just a reactionary Republican?" *The Guardian* (April 30, 2017), https://www.theguardian.com/commentisfree/2017/apr/30/donald-trump-fascist-republican-100-days; Robert O. Paxton, "Is Donald Trump a fascist or a plutocrat?" *Harper's* (May 2017), 38–39; Timothy Snyder, *On Tyranny: Twenty Lessons from the Twentieth Century* (New York: Tim Duggan Books, 2017).

73. Paxton, "Is Donald Trump a fascist or a plutocrat?"

74. In addition to the sources listed in note 1 to the preface, see Ashley Parker, Phillip Rucker, and Sean Sullivan, "Trump Scrambles to Show Progress as the 100-day Mark Approaches," *Washington Post* (April 25, 2017), https://www.washingtonpost.com/politics/trump-scrambles-to-show-progress-as-the-100-day-mark-approaches/2017/04/25/9fc6803c-29d4-11e7-b605-33413c691853_story.html; David Lewis, "So Far Trump Is Struggling as a Chief Executive," *Washington Post* (April 27, 2017), https://www.washingtonpost.com/news/monkey-cage/wp/2017/04/27/so-far-trump-gets-a-failing-grade-at-managing-the-executive-branch/; Billy House, Erik Wasson, and Laura Litvan, "Trump Says He'll Sign Congress Spending Deal That Jettisons His Goals," *Bloomberg Politics* (April 30, 2017), https://www.bloomberg.com/politics/articles/2017-05-01/congress-strikes-tentative-deal-on-1-1-trillion-spending-bill; Aaron Blake, "President Trump Just Had His Bluff Called—Again," *Washington Post* (April 25, 2017), https://www.washingtonpost.com/news/the-fix/wp/2017/04/25/president-trump-just-had-his-bluff-called-again/; James Hohmann, "Trump Is Caving on Border Wall Funding after Showing His Base that He Tried," *Washington Post* (April 25, 2017), https://www.washingtonpost.com/news/powerpost/paloma/daily-202/2017/04/25/

daily-202-trump-is-caving-on-border-wall-funding-after-showing-his-base-
that-he-tried/58fea413e9b69b3a72331ec4/; Amber Phillips, "Trump Is About
to Be 0-4 on His Legislative Promises for His First 100 Days," *Washington
Post* (April 27, 2017), https://www.washingtonpost.com/news/the-fix/wp/
2017/04/27/trump-is-about-to-be-0-4-on-his-legislative-promises-for-his-
first-100-days/; Patrick Jenkins and Barney Jopson, "Wall Street's hopes
for deregulation switch from laws to watchdogs," *Financial Times* (May 7,
2017), https://www.ft.com/content/8d46739c-31ac-11e7-9555-23ef563ecf9a;
Ben White and Annie Karni, "America's CEOs fall out of love with
Trump," *Politico* (June 3, 2017), http://www.politico.com/story/2017/06/03/
donald-trump-ceos-corporate-relationship-239080.

75. See citations in note 17.

76. Leighton Akio Woodhouse, "Obama's Deportation Policy Was Even
Worse Than We Thought," *The Intercept* (May 15, 2017), https://theinter-
cept.com/2017/05/15/obamas-deportation-policy-was-even-worse-than-
we-thought/; Aviva Chomsky, "Making Sense of the Deportation Debate,"
TomDispatch.com (April 25, 2017), http://www.tomdispatch.com/blog/
176271/; Alan Aja and Alejandra Marchevsky, "How Immigrants Became
Criminals," *Boston Review* (March 17, 2017), http://bostonreview.net/poli-
tics/alan-j-aja-alejandra-marchevsky-how-immigrants-became-criminals.

77. Robin, "Trump's Inaugural Address versus Reagan's Inaugural Address."

78. Corey Robin, *Fear: The History of a Political Idea* (New York: Oxford University
Press, 2004), 199–205; Corey Robin, "American institutions won't keep
us safe from Donald Trump's excesses," *The Guardian* (February 2, 2017),
https://www.theguardian.com/commentisfree/2017/feb/02/american-
institutions-wont-keep-you-safe-trumps-excesses.

79. Skowronek, 310–313.

80. "Presidential Approval Ratings—Bill Clinton," http://www.gallup.com/
poll/116584/presidential-approval-ratings-bill-clinton.aspx; Rick Perlstein,
Nixonland (New York: Scribner, 2008), 202–203, 237–241, 363–365.

81. For the first two of his eight years in the White House, Bill Clinton enjoyed
a Democratic majority in Congress. After 1994, however, he faced a
Republican majority in both chambers.

82. Richard J. Evans, *The Coming of the Third Reich* (New York: Penguin, 2003),
206, 274.

83. On the parallels between Trump and Carter, see Corey Robin, "The Politics
Trump Makes," *n+1* (January 11, 2017), https://nplusonemag.com/online-
only/online-only/the-politics-trump-makes/.

84. Corey Robin, "The G.O.P.'s Existential Dilemma," *New York Times* (March
24, 2017), SR1, https://www.nytimes.com/2017/03/24/opinion/sunday/the-
gops-existential-crisis.html.

85. Data provided to me by Phil Klinkner and Seth Ackerman.

86. Gary Langer, "President Trump at 100 Days" (April 23, 2017), http://abc-news.go.com/Politics/president-trump-100-days-honeymoon-regrets-poll/story?id=46943338; "How Popular/Unpopular Is Donald Trump," https://projects.fivethirtyeight.com/trump-approval-ratings/#historical, accessed on Day 130 (May 29, 2017) of the Trump Presidency.

87. In addition to some of the works cited in note 94 of chapter 1, see Thomas Frank, *One Market Under God: Extreme Capitalism, Market Populism, and the End of Economic Democracy* (New York: Random House, 2000); Bethany Moreton, "Make Payroll, Not War," in *Rightward Bound: Making America Conservative in the 1970s*, ed. Bruce J. Schulman and Julian E. Zelizer (Cambridge: Harvard University Press, 2008), 52–70.

88. Alan Feuer and Jeremy W. Peters, "First Rule of Far-Right Clubs: Be White and Proud," *New York Times* (June 2, 2017), https://www.nytimes.com/2017/06/02/us/politics/white-nationalists-alt-knights-protests-colleges.html; Jamelle Bouie, "What We Have Unleashed," *Slate* (June 1, 2017), http://www.slate.com/articles/news_and_politics/politics/2017/06/this_year_s_string_of_brutal_hate_crimes_is_intrinsically_connected_to_the.html; Evan Malgrem, "Don't Feed the Trolls," *Dissent* (Spring 2017), https://www.dissentmagazine.org/article/dont-feed-the-trolls-alt-right-culture-4chan.

89. Marc Mulholland, *Bourgeois Liberty and the Politics of Fear: From Absolutism to Neo-Conservatism* (Oxford: Oxford University Press, 2012), 44–46; John Ramsden, *An Appetite for Power: A History of the Conservative Party Since 1830* (New York: Harper Collins, 1998), 42–46.

90. Rebecca Ballhaus, "Americans Back Immigration and Trade at Record Levels," *Wall Street Journal* (April 25, 2017), https://www.wsj.com/articles/americans-back-immigration-and-trade-at-record-levels-1493092861.

91. Edmund Burke, *Letters on a Regicide Peace* (Indianapolis: Liberty Fund, 1999), 142, 167; Nixon cited in David Remnick, "Is the Comey Memo the Beginning of the End for Trump?" *The New Yorker* (May 17, 2017), http://www.newyorker.com/news/daily-comment/is-the-comey-memo-the-beginning-of-the-end-for-trump?intcid=mod-latest; also see Perlstein, 419.

92. Ashley L. Watts et al., "The Double-Edged Sword of Grandiose Narcissism," *Psychological Science* 24 (2013), 2379–2389; Scott O. Lilienfeld and Ashley L. Watts, "The Narcissist in Chief," *New York Times* (September 6, 2015), SR10.

93. Donald J. Trump, tweet (May 18, 2017), https://twitter.com/realDonaldTrump/status/865173176854204416; Dan Merica, "Trump to graduates: 'No politician in history . . . has been treated worse,'" *CNN* (May 18, 2017), http://www.cnn.com/2017/05/17/politics/trump-coast-guard-speech/index.html.

94. Paxton, *Anatomy of Fascism*, 3; Claudia Koonz, *The Nazi Conscience* (Cambridge: Harvard University Press, 2003), 29.

95. Hannah Levintova, "Trump Just Held His First Campaign Rally for the 2020 Race," *Mother Jones* (February 18, 2017), http://www.motherjones.com/

politics/2017/02/trump-just-held-rally-his-2020-presidential-campaign; Isaac Chotiner, "Does Donald Trump Believe in Anything but Himself?" *Slate* (October 24, 2016), http://www.slate.com/articles/news_and_politics/interrogation/2016/10/donald_trump_s_fascism_is_rooted_in_his_own_self_interest.html.

96. David Graham, "Melania Trump's Secret Speechwriter: Michelle Obama?" *The Atlantic* (July 19, 2016), https://www.theatlantic.com/politics/archive/2016/07/melania-trump-plagiarism/491918/; Alex Caton and Grace Watkins, "Trump Pick Monica Crowley Plagiarized Parts of Her Ph.D. Dissertation," *Politico* (January 9, 2017), http://www.politico.com/magazine/story/2017/01/monica-crowley-plagiarism-phd-dissertation-columbia-214612; Josh Bresnahan and Burgess Everett, "Gorsuch's writings borrow from other authors," *Politico* (April 4, 2017), http://www.politico.com/story/2017/04/gorsuch-writings-supreme-court-236891; Andrew Kaczynski, Christopher Massie and Nathan McDermott, "Sheriff David Clarke plagiarized portions of his master's thesis on homeland security," *CNN* (May 21, 2017), http://www.cnn.com/interactive/2017/05/politics/sheriff-clarke-plagiarism/.

97. *Great Again*, 8.

98. Jeremy Diamond, "Trump: I could 'shoot somebody and I wouldn't lose voters,'" *CNN* (January 24, 2016), http://www.cnn.com/2016/01/23/politics/donald-trump-shoot-somebody-support/.

99. Steven Mufson, "Trump's Budget Owes a Huge Debt to This Right-Wing Washington Think Tank," *Washington Post* (March 27, 2017), https://www.washingtonpost.com/news/wonk/wp/2017/03/27/trumps-budget-owes-a-huge-debt-to-this-right-wing-washington-think-tank/; Abby Phillip and John Wagner, "Trump as 'Conventional Republican'? That's What Some in GOP Establishment Say They See," *Washington Post* (April 13, 2017), https://www.washingtonpost.com/politics/gop-establishment-sees-trumps-flip-flops-as-move-toward-a-conventional-republican/2017/04/13/f9ce03f6-205c-11e7-be2a-3a1fb24d4671_story.html; Julie Hirschfeld Davis and Kate Kelley, "Trump Plans to Shift Infrastructure Funding to Cities, States and Business," *New York Times* (June 4, 2017), A18.

ACKNOWLEDGMENTS

Much of this book originated in literary periodicals and magazines. Were it not for editors Alex Star, Paul Laity, Mary-Kay Wilmers, Paul Meyerscough, Adam Shatz, John Palattella, and Jackson Lears, I never would have written about the right. It's often assumed that academics who publish in nonacademic venues are trotting out their scholarly research for popular consumption, simplifying complex ideas first worked out in the laboratories of academe. For me, the process of writing this book has been the reverse: conservatism became a scholarly interest of mine through my nonacademic writing, and most of my ideas about the right were formulated in conversation with and writing for these editors, especially Alex and John.

Intellectually, this book owes its inspiration to Arno Mayer and Karen Orren. No two scholars have done more to advance my understanding of "the persistence of the old regime"—in Europe and the United States—than Karen and Arno. Against the conventional wisdom of the left and the right, which assumes that medievalism has been washed away by modernity, Karen and Arno opened my eyes to the "belated feudalism" of our post-feudal world. While they undoubtedly would disagree with my interpretation of conservatism, I could not have come to it without their enormously generative work.

In the course of writing and revising these essays, I have been sustained by a broad circle of readers: historians and political scientists, poets and essayists, theorists and philosophers, literary critics and sociologists, journalists and editors. For their contributions to one or more of these essays, I would like to thank Jed Abrahamian, Bruce Ackerman, Joel Allen, Gaston Alonso, Joyce Appleby, Moustafa Bayoumi, Seyla Benhabib, Marshall Berman, Sara Bershtel, Akeel Bilgrami, Norman Birnbaum, Steve Bronner, Dan Brook, Sebastian Budgen, Josh Cohen, Peter Cole, Paisley Currah, Lizzie Donahue, Jay Driskell, Tom Dumm, John Dunn, Sam Farber, Liza Featherstone, Jason Frank, Steve Fraser, Josh Freeman, Paul Frymer, Sam Goldman, Manu Goswami, Alex Gourevitch, Pete Hallward, Harry Harootunian, Chris Hayes, Doug Henwood, Dick Howard, David Hughes, Judy Hughes, Allen Hunter, Jack Jacobs, Ira Katznelson, Gordon Lafer, Jill Lepore, Penny Lewis, Joe Lowndes, Steven Lukes, Kieko Matteson, Kevin Mattson, John Medeiras, Kathy Newman, Molly

Nolan, Anne Norton, Jolie Olcott, Christian Parenti, Di Paton, Rick Perlstein, Ros Petchesky, Kim Phillips-Fein, Katha Pollitt, Aziz Rana, Andy Rich, Andrew Ross, Kristin Ross, Saskia Sassen, Ellen Schrecker, George Scialabba, Richard Seymour, Nikhil Singh, Quentin Skinner, Jim Sleeper, Rogers Smith, Katrina vanden Heuvel, John Wallach, Eve Weinbaum, Keith Whittington, Daniel Wilkinson, Wesley Yang, Brian Young, and Marilyn Young.

A good portion of this material has been presented in workshops and talks at universities across the country. I am grateful for the comments and suggestions I received on those occasions from Arash Abizadeh, Anthony Appiah, Banu Bargu, Seyla Benhabib, Akeel Bilgrami, Elizabeth Cohen, Josh Cohen, Julie Cooper, the late Jack Diggins, Matt Evans, Nancy Fraser, Mark Graber, Nan Keohane, Steve Macedo, Karuna Mantena, Andrew March, Tom Medvetz, Andrew Murphy, Andrew Norris, Anne Norton, Joshua Ober, Philip Pettit, Andy Polsky, Robert Reich, Austin Sarat, Peter Singer, Rogers Smith, Miranda Spieler, Zofia Stemplowska, Nadia Urbinati, and Leo Zaibert.

I would like to thank the following institutions for providing much needed release time from my teaching: the American Council of Learned Societies; the Princeton University Center for Human Values; the Office of the Provost at Brooklyn College; and the Professional Staff Congress of the City University of New York.

An extra special thanks goes to my kitchen cabinet of first readers: Greg Grandin, Adina Hoffman, Robert Perkinson, and Scott Saul; to Marco Roth, who came up with the book's title; to Charles Petersen, copy editor extraordinaire; to my students at Brooklyn College and the CUNY Graduate Center, who have worked with me through the texts and tomes of the right; to Alexandra Dauler and Marc Schneider at Oxford University Press (OUP); and to David McBride, my editor at OUP, an unfailing source of excellent advice who believed in this project from its inception and shepherded it through with what seems to be effortless wisdom, patience, and grace.

My greatest thanks go to Laura Brahm, who listened to these ideas when they were half-sentences and read them when they were half-baked. She has brought to these essays an eye for what matters and an unerring sense of taste. She is always and inevitably the only reader I want to please.

Acknowledgments for the Second Edition

My first thanks go to my editor David McBride, who in the immediate aftermath of the November 2016 election saw the need for a new edition of this book, and to Niko Pfund, president of Oxford USA, who championed this book and its second edition from the beginning. Additional thanks to Seth Ackerman and Adina Hoffman for much needed help with titles; to Andrew Seal for a last-minute copy edit and work on the index; to Ellen Tremper for talking me through some of the thornier problems in the book's re-conception and offering shrewd criticism of the Trump chapter and preface; and to Jed Purdy, Tim Barker, and Rob Mickey for initial reads and comments on the Trump chapter. Alex Gourevitch has been a constant prod and provocation, pushing me to think harder and better about Trump and the current political moment as well as the economic arguments in chapters five and six; it was also Alex who envisioned the new structure of the second edition. Not only was John Palattella the original editor on four of the book's chapters but he also did a heroic close read of the entire manuscript of the revised edition. More than anyone, John has given this book its final sense and shape; I owe him an incalculable debt. This book has had a life I never anticipated; that it took the form it did is due in large part to Laura Brahm. She turned a collection of essays into an event, seeing in every moment of its adversity an opportunity for its advocacy. She has never hesitated to tell me a piece of writing, no matter how small, isn't quite what it needs to be. She demands that a sentence be a statement: in writing and in life. That we share that life seems a miracle.

"On Counterrevolution" first appeared as "Conservatism and Counterrevolution" in *Raritan* (Summer 2010), 1–17. "The Soul of Violence" first appeared as "Easy To Be Hard: Violence and Conservatism" in *Performances of Violence*, ed. Austin Sarat, Carleen Basler, and Thomas L. Dumm (Amherst: University of Massachusetts Press, 2011), 18–42. "The First Counterrevolutionary" first appeared in *The Nation* (October 19, 2009), 25–32. "Burke's Market Value" first appeared as "Edmund Burke and the Problem of Value" in *Raritan* (Summer 2016), 82–106. "In Nietzsche's Margins" first appeared as "Nietzsche's Marginal Children" in *The Nation* (May 27, 2013), 27–36. "Metaphysics and Chewing Gum" first appeared as "Garbage and Gravitas" in *The Nation* (June 7, 2010), 21–27. "The Prince As Pariah" first appeared as "Out of Place" in *The Nation* (June 23, 2008), 25–33. "Remembrance of Empires Past" first appeared in *Cold War Triumphalism: The Misuse of History after the Fall of Communism*, ed. Ellen Schrecker (New York: New Press, 2004), 274–297. "Affirmative Action Baby" first appeared as "Get Over It!" in the *London Review of Books* (June 10, 2010), 29–31.

INDEX

abolition, 3, 6, 9, 28, 30, 43, 44, 53–54, 162, 193. *See also* emancipation, freedom, race, slavery

Acheson, Dean, 259

Adams, Abigail, 14

Adams, John, 14–15, 29, 33, 67–69

Addington, David, 84

affirmative action, 199, 235, 238

Afghanistan War, 215, 216

African Americans, xii, 6, 10–11, 13–14, 30, 45, 48, 53–54, 55, 138, 199, 241, 243, 245

agency, 6, 7–8, 10, 13, 50–51, 66, 114, 244. *See also* democracy, emancipation, freedom, power, reform, suffrage

Al Qaeda, 85, 205

Allende, Salvador, 164

Antoinette, Marie, 41, 55, 87, 190

American Revolution, 15, 27–28

Americans with Disabilities Act (ADA), 230–231, 233

Anderson, Perry, 92, 163

anticommunism, xi, 242; and the end of the Cold War xii, 201, 204, 208, 215; and persecution of homosexuals, 259. *See also* Cold War, Communism, CIA, McCarthyism, national security, Soviet Union

Apple, R. W., Jr., 219

Arendt, Hannah, 32, 169

aristocracy, xv, xvi, 13, 16–18, 30–31, 35, 37, 41, 46, 53–54, 71–72, 106–108, 112, 129–134, 136, 139, 144, 145, 154, 157, 191, 242, 251–252, 284n9, 291n3. *See also* capitalism, elites, master class, Old Regime, old regime, ruling class

Aristotle, 67, 169, 174–178, 185, 186

Arnold, Matthew, 33

Atwater, Lee, 48–49

Austrian school of economics, xv, xvii, 108, 119, 132, 134, 141, 143, 149, 152, 153, 294n3. *See also* Böhm-Bawerk, Hayek, Marginal Revolution, Menger, Mises, Schumpeter, Wieser

Austro-Hungarian Empire, 134

authority, *see* hierarchy

Axelrod, David, 250

Bagehot, Walter, xvii, 240

Baldwin, James, 10–11

Bannon, Steve, 187, 247, 258, 310n25

battle, *see* struggle

Beck, Glenn, 185, 187

Bedford, Francis Russell, 5th Duke, 112, 128–131, 253

Beethoven, Ludwig van, 153, 172

Bell, Daniel, 214–215

Bentham, Jeremy, 147

Bernstein, Eduard, 26

Bickel, Alexander, 229

Biddle, Nicholas, 28

bin Laden, Osama, 205

Black Hawk Down, 287n4

Black Lives Matter, 245

Bloom, Allan, 55

Bloomingdale, Betsy, 251

Böhm-Bawerk, Eugen, 141

Bolshevik Revolution, xvi, 30, 39, 92, 172. *See also* Communism, Soviet Union

Bonald, Louis de, 15, 31

bourgeoisie, 72–73, 76–80, 134, 140, 156–157, 163, 210–212, 242, 247, 252, 279n61, 291n3, 293n37. *See also* decadence, ennui, ruling class

Boykin, Jerry, 84

Brazil, 139

Brennan, William, 235–236

fear, 20, 46, 65, 79, 101, 103, 205–206, 207. *See also* counterrevolution, power

federalism, 32, 195. *See also* Constitution, Goldwater

feminism,xii, xiii, 9, 30, 39, 49–50, 196–197, 244. *See also* Equal Rights Amendment, household, marriage, rape, reproductive freedom, women's liberation

feudalism, 15, 34, 41, 54, 67, 194, 195, 232, 252–253; and capitalism, 108; democratic feudalism, 30, 54, 191. *See also* aristocracy, hierarchy, inequality, master class, old regime, populism, ruling class, workplace

First International (International Workingmen's Association), 138

force, *see* violence

Force Bill, 6

Fox, Charles, 109

Franco-Prussian War, 135–136, 139

Frankfurt School, 32

free market, 16, 32, 124, 175, 199, 201–202, 210, 216; and Austrian school of economics, xv, 26, 140, 283n97. *See also* Burke, capitalism, globalization, Hayek, Jevons, labor, libertarianism, marginalism, Menger, Mises, neoconservatism, Schumpeter

freedom, 8, 9, 69–70, 94, 97, 100–103, 151–152, 159–160, 187, 193–197; and security, 203; of speech, 236; *See also* emancipation, reform, rights

French Revolution, xi, xvi, 4, 8, 13–14, 19–20, 25, 30, 39, 40, 41, 45–47, 76, 78, 93, 94, 105–115, 129, 183–184, 189, 195, 244; and Jacobins, 46–47. *See also* Burke, counterrevolution, Desmoulins, Directory, Maistre, Old Regime, Robespierre, Thermidor

Freud, Sigmund, 134, 152, 157

Friedman, Milton, 199

Fukuyama, Francis, 29, 79–80, 86, 205; and "end of history," 80

gender, xvi, 29; and equality, 228; and homosexuality, 39, 55, 230, 235; and masculinity, 129, 231, 289; and sexuality, 5, 12, 50; and traditional roles, 4–5, 50, 200. *See also* equality, feminism, homosexuality, marriage, morality, reproductive freedom, rights, women's liberation

Geneva Conventions, 84–85, 238. *See also* rule of law, terror, torture, war

Germany, 31, 139, 140, 164, 179; and Franco-Prussian War, 135–136

Gerson, Michael, 28

Gingrich, Newt, 33

Gladstone, William, 141, 280n77

globalization, 208, 210–211. *See also* capitalism, Clinton, free market, imperialism

God, 32, 50, 65, 95–96, 115, 232, 247. *See also* Catholicism, Christianity, morality

Goebbels, Joseph, 179

Goethe, Johann Wolfgang von, 153

Golden, Harry, 200

Goldwater, Barry, xiii, xvi, 31, 40, 43, 52, 64, 74, 189, 192–195, 200

Goncourt, Edmond, 136

Gorsuch, Neil, 235, 271

Graham, Billy, 197

Great Man, 36, 246–247, 254

Great Society, 33, 39, 275n5

Great Upheaval, 7

Greece, ancient, 231, 254; and democracy, 98; and work, 137–139

Guatemala, 6

Gulf War, 209

habeas corpus, 222–223

Hailsham, Douglass Hogg, 1st Viscount, 24

Haitian Revolution, 14, 138

Hale, Matthew, 5

Hamilton, Alexander, 55

Hapsburg Monarchy, *see* Austro-Hungarian Empire

Harper, William, 11, 43

Hart, H.L.A., 236

Hayden, Michael, 84

Hayek, Friedrich, xv, xvi, xvii, 26, 29, 32, 92, 133, 157–164, 242; and aristocracy, 154, 157, 242; and Austrian School of economics, 119, 141; and Austro-Hungarian Empire, 134; and conservatism, 33, 92, 93, 163; and the free market, 133, 150–151, 153, 245; and the "idle rich," 157–162; and knowledge, 158; and morality, 149; and neoliberalism, 133; and Pinochet, 164, 294n3; and Salazar, 164; and subjectivism, 150–151, 153; and value theory, 150–151

Hawaii, 82

Hearnshaw, F.J.C., 17

Hegel, Georg Wilhelm Friedrich, 73, 138

libertarianism, 16, 17, 175, 182, 193. *See also* freedom, Hayek, Menger, Mises, private sphere, Rand
liberty, *see* freedom
Lincoln, Abraham, 26–27
Lindsey, Hal, 198
Lingua Franca, 286n46, 301n1
Locke, John, 190
Long, Huey, 191
loss, 8, 21–23, 44, 56–57, 150, 189–190. *See also* Burke, conservatism, inheritance, Maistre, traditionalism
Loyseau, Charles, 44–45, 51
Luftwaffe, 164

MacArthur, Douglas, 60, 287n4
Macdonald, Dwight, 25
Macpherson, C. B. 291n3
Machiavelli, Niccolò, 84, 98, 155, 156
Maistre, Joseph de, 31, 33, 40, 55, 77, 79, 83, 86, 183, 190, 240; and counterrevolution, 51–53, 57, 76; and the French Revolution, 45, 71, 79, 189, 195; and the Old Regime, 41, 45, 71, 72, 75–76
Mamet, David, 186
Mann, Thomas, 154, 172
Mannheim, Karl, 23, 194
Mansfield, Harvey, 278n51
Marat, Jean-Paul, 28
Marginal Revolution, 134, 140–143, 293n38. *See also* Austrian School of economics
marginalism, 141; and socialism, 142–143; and value theory, 153–154
marriage, 4–5, 11–12, 49–50, 197, 198, 224, 274n2. *See also* feudalism, gender, hierarchy, household, private sphere
Marshall, Alfred, 143
Martin, Casey, 230–231
Marx, Karl, 22, 94, 110, 117, 137, 142, 143, 236, 257
Marxism, 9, 72, 73. *See also* Cold War, Communism, Soviet Union
mass culture, 29, 161–162, 172. *See also* capitalism, Clinton
masses, xi, 30, 40, 50, 52, 54, 134, 145, 158, 169–171, 183, 242–243, 244, 265, 268–269. *See also* hierarchy, labor movement, reform, workplace
master class, 13, 74; and slavery, 12–13, 43, 53–54; Nietzsche on, 182, 184–185. *See also* aristocracy, elites, hierarchy, order, power, ruling class

Mattson, Kevin, 18–19, 30, 306n9
Mayer, Jane, 84–85, 310n41
McCain, John, 217, 307n17
McCarthy, Joseph, 224
McCarthyism, 266; and persecution of homosexuals, 259. *See also* anticommunism, Communism
Mead, Lawrence, 9
media, 47, 174
Melville, Herman, 186
Menger, Carl, 119, 140, 141–142, 143, 146–148, 152
Mercer, Robert, 310n41
Mexicans and Mexican-Americans, xii, 218–219, 241
Meyer, Frank, 245, 279n60, 283n97
Middle East, 204, 216. *See also* Afghanistan War, Iraq War, Israel, Palestine
Mill, John Stuart, 56, 141, 192, 244
Mises, Ludwig von, 32, 119, 141, 148–150, 183
moderation, 39–40, 64, 77–79
modernism, 92, 134, 232
modernity, 137, 149, 184–185, 232
monarchy, 22, 41, 51, 52–53, 71, 93–99, 102–103, 108, 190, 191, 252; absolute monarchy, 91, 94, 102; despotism, 97, 98, 99; divine right, 95–97; and royalism, 91, 92, 97, 98, 99, 102. *See also* hierarchy, Hobbes, order
morality, 144, 146, 148–149, 151–152, 176–177, 184–185. *See also* Christianity, neoconservatism
Musil, Robert, 154
Muslims, 241

Napoleon, 78, 153
Nash, George, 21, 26
National Review, 25, 51, 190
national security, 203, 214. *See also* CIA, foreign policy, freedom, inequality, neoconservatism, war
National Security Agency (NSA), 84
National Socialist (Nazi) Party, 24, 182. *See also* Goebbels, Hitler
nationalism, 32, 195, 259, 268. *See also* imperialism, neoconservatism, war
nativism, 241, 243, 269, 310n25
neoconservatism, xvi, 30, 31, 45, 55, 86, 163, 192, 258; and capitalism, 211, 279n61; and foreign policy, 83, 211–213, 303n17; and imperialism, 83, 204, 213, 215–217; and old regime, 55; and rule of law, 86. *See also* Buckley, conservatism, Kristol

presidential election of 2016, xi, xii, xiii,
xv, 246, 259, 264, 267, 270, 271; and
composition of Trump vote, 307n17

private sphere, xvi, 10, 13–16; and political
life, 203, 217. *See also* household,
workplace, power

privilege, xi, xvi, 16, 17, 36, 40, 53–54, 56,
191–192, 232, 268. *See also* aristocracy,
elites, inheritance, master class, old
regime, ruling class

protest, *see* reform

Protestantism, 183–184

psychoanalysis, 134

race, 31, 35–36, 48–49, 51, 52, 243, 265; and
hierarchy, 51, 54, 243; and segregation,
35–36; and segregation, 11, 275n18. *See
also* abolition, civil rights movement,
emancipation, master class, slavery,
violence

Raleigh, Walter, 97

Rand, Ayn, xv, xvi, 29, 167–187, 249, 257;
and Aristotle, 169, 174–178, 185, 186; and
capitalism, 180, 186; and individualism,
181–182; and fascism, 171, 178–179; and
heroism, 169, 170, 177, 179, 181–182;
and Hollywood, 168, 173–174, 176; and
naturalism, 178; and Nietzsche,
182–185, 186; and religion, 183–186; and
Trump, 249, 257

rape, 5, 274n2. *See also* feminism, gender,
hierarchy, violence, women's liberation

Rawls, John, 169, 227, 236

rationalism, 22, 97, 157, 239, 257n57. *See also*
Enlightenment

reaction, *see* conservatism

Reagan, Ronald, xiii, 29, 33, 40, 51, 63–64, 187,
216, 218, 229, 244, 251, 255, 267, 268

Reaganomics, 244

realism, 77, 163, 211, 212, 214, 303n17. *See also*
foreign policy

reason, *see* rationalism

reform, 5–6, 14, 16, 21, 23, 26–28, 50, 57, 162,
191, 244–245. *See also* left, sixties, violence

reproductive freedom, 28, 228, 230, 235. *See
also* women's liberation

Republican Party, xi, xii–xiv, xvi, 13, 18, 43,
48–49, 55, 63–64, 74, 75, 185, 192, 197, 199,
202, 203, 211, 213, 217, 229, 264–267, 271–272,
274n1, 307n17, 310n41. *See also* conservatism

revanchism, *see* conservatism

revolution, *see* reform

Ricardo, David, 116

Rice, Condoleezza, 207, 208

Rich, Frank, 204, 219

rights, 3, 7, 9, 10, 39, 83, 137, 184–185, 191; and
homosexuality, 39, 230, 235; and national
security, 222. *See also* civil rights, equality,
homosexuality, labor movement, left, rule
of law, women's liberation, sixties

Robespierre, Maximillien, 28, 112, 113

Rockingham, Charles Watson-Wentworth,
Marquess, 111

Rodgers, Daniel, 116

romanticism, 77, 152, 168, 181. *See also*
neoconservatism, struggle

Rome, Ancient, 93, 98

Roosevelt, Franklin Delano, 193, 250, 266. *See
also* New Deal

Roosevelt, Theodore, 29, 31, 73–74, 86, 258;
and imperialism, 74, 82; and Spanish-
American War, 81–82; and struggle,
73–74, 81

Rorty, Richard, 234

Rossiter, Clinton, 26

Rousseau, Jean-Jacques, 47, 67, 102, 112, 190

Rumsfeld, Donald, 222

rule of law, 59, 78, 83, 86, 97, 164, 223, 263; and
capital punishment, 222; and international
law, 84; in private sphere, 5; and
torture, 84–85; and war on terror, 84–85.
See also civil society, equality, inequality,
rights, Supreme Court

ruling class, 18, 31, 53–54, 74, 76–77, 79, 82, 132,
134, 162, 190, 229, 253. *See also* aristocracy,
elites, hierarchy, master class

Ryan, Paul, 310n41

Salazar, António, 164

Salisbury, Robert Gascoyne-Cecil, 3rd
Marquess, 20, 21

Sanders, Bernie, 245

Sasse, Ben, xiii–xiv

Scalia, Antonin, xvi, 29, 55, 221–238,
241, 254, 270; and 24, 221, 223, 238; and
Americans with Disabilities Act (ADA),
230–233; and golf, 230–233; and inequality,
231–232, 234; and liberalism, 229, 235–
236, 238; and originalism, 224, 226–229,
235–237; and postmodernism, 229, 232;
and rule of law, 223; and traditionalism,
223–225, 233

Schlafly, Phyllis, 29, 49–50, 196–197. *See also*
Equal Rights Amendment (ERA)

Schmitt, Carl, 29, 72–73, 86, 92, 153, 155–156,
   163–164
Schumpeter, Joseph, 34, 108, 141,
   154–157, 242
Schwartz, Tony, 246. *See also* Trump
Scott, George C., 259
Scott, Ridley, 287n4
Scruton, Roger, 244
Sedgwick, Theodore, 13
"segregation academies," 196
Seinfeld, 210, 258
selfhood, 42, 46, 61–63, 65, 66, 67–68, 69, 121,
   151, 152, 153, 176, 254. *See also* Burke, Rand,
   struggle
September 11, 83–84, 86, 87, 203–208, 213,
   214, 217–218, 219, 222, 301n7. *See also*
   Afghanistan War, Bush, foreign policy,
   Iraq War, terrorism, torture, war
Serfdom, 11, 138–139. *See also* slavery
Silverman, Debora, 251
sixties, 40, 47, 173, 198, 225. *See also* Civil
   Rights Movement, labor movement,
   reform, university, women's liberation
Shelley, Mary, 137
Skinner, Quentin, 94, 97, 98
slavery, xii, 4, 6, 11–13, 16, 27, 39, 43, 52, 53–54,
   97, 98, 99–100, 138–139, 145–146, 184. *See also*
   abolition, Force Bill, Jim Crow, master
   class, Nullification Crisis, plantation, race,
   Tariff of Abominations
Smith, Adam, 116, 118, 119–124, 125
Social Darwinism, xvi, 229, 232, 257, 310n41.
   See also inequality, struggle
socialism, 3, 26, 80, 134, 138, 140, 142–143, 144,
   148–149, 184–185, 199
Sombart, Werner, 31
Sorel, Georges, 72–73, 76–77, 79, 80, 86
Soviet Union, xii, 57, 173, 192, 207, 208, 211.
   See also Bolshevik Revolution, Cold War,
   Communism, Joseph Stalin
Spanish-American War, 64, 74, 81–82
Speenhamland system, *see* Poor Laws
Spock, Benjamin, 197
Stalin, Joseph, 80
Stanton, Elizabeth Cady, 10
States' Rights Democratic (Dixiecrat)
   Party, 275n18
Stephens, Alexander, 52
Strauss, Leo, 32, 92, 163
struggle, 14, 24, 35, 64, 77, 136, 178–180,
   232, 237, 242, 253, 257. *See also* Burke,
   conservatism, inequality, violence, war

student movement, 25, 45, 173, 198. *See also*
   New Left, sixties, university
suffrage, 15, 30, 143, 228, 269. *See also*
   citizenship, women's liberation, rights
Sullivan, Andrew, 56, 59, 205
Sullivan, James, 15
Sumner, William Graham, 36, 55, 257, 277n40
Supreme Court, 7, 16, 196, 211, 221–238, 263,
   266, 267, 269, 270; and Burger Court, 228;
   and *Bush v. Gore*, 211, 237, 267; and Warren
   Court, 5, 83, 228. *See also* Constitution,
   rule of law, O'Connor, Scalia, Thomas

Taliban, 215. *See also* Afghanistan war
Tanenhaus, Sam, 83
Tariff of Abominations, 6
taxes, xiii, 48, 53, 88, 118, 193, 196, 217,
   253, 265. *See also* Republican Party,
   welfare state
Tea Party, xii, 32–33, 52, 241
Tenet, George, 84, 85
terrorism, 203; and war on terror, 83–84, 86,
   88, 207, 221–223. *See also* national security,
   neoconservatism, rule of law, September
   11, torture, war
Thatcher, Margaret, 29, 64, 191; and
   ideology, 192
Thermidor, 110, 114. *See also* French
   Revolution
Thomas, Clarence, 211, 221, 224, 230
Thurmond, Strom, 196, 275n18
Tocqueville, Alexis de, 29, 31, 77–79, 86, 173,
   234, 237
Tories, 17, 108. *See also* Conservative Party
   (Britain)
torture, 59, 84–85. *See also* rule of law,
   terrorism
traditionalism, 17, 23, 31, 34, 40, 69, 252–253,
   279n60. *See also* conservatism
Trilling, Lionel, 17, 192
Trump, Donald J., xi–xvii, 29, 40, 215,
   239–272, 307n17, 310n25; and ambition,
   239, 246, 248–249; and anti-elitism,
   241, 244; as businessman, 242, 246–252;
   and capitalism, 244, 247, 252–258; Jimmy
   Carter, comparison with, 264, 267, 313n83;
   and China, 259, 260–261; as conventional
   Republican, xi–xiv, 40, 52; and fascism,
   259–260, 264–265, 271; and immigration,
   265, 269; and inconsistency, 239; and the
   Iraq War, 261; and litigation, 263; and the
   market, 244, 246, 253–257; and Mexico, 241;